D0998506

Toulon in war
and revolution

War, Armed Forces and Society

General Editor: Ian F. W. Beckett

Editorial Board

Ian F. W. Beckett	Royal Military Academy, Sandhurst
John Childs	University of Leeds
Clive Emsley	The Open University
John Gooch	University of Lancaster
John B. Hattendorf	Naval War College, Newport, Rhode Island
Jacob W. Kipp	Soviet Army Studies Office, Fort Leavenworth
John A. Lynn	University of Illinois, Urbana-Champaign
Allan R. Millett	The Ohio State University
Klaus-Jürgen Müller	Universität der Bundeswehr Hamburg
Douglas Porch	The Citadel Military College of South Carolina
Geoffrey Till	Royal Naval College, Greenwich

Malcolm Crook

Toulon in war and revolution

From the *ancien régime*
to the Restoration, 1750–1820

Manchester University Press
Manchester and New York
Distributed exclusively in the USA and Canada by St. Martin's Press

Copyright © Malcolm Crook 1991

Published by Manchester University Press
Oxford Road, Manchester M13 9PL, UK
and Room 400, 175 Fifth Avenue,
New York, NY 10010, USA

*Distributed exclusively in the USA and Canada
by* St. Martin's Press, Inc.,
175 Fifth Avenue, New York, NY 10010, USA

A catalogue record for this book is available from the British Library

Library of Congress cataloging in publication data
Crook, Malcolm, 1948–
    Toulon in war and revolution : from the ancien régime to the
Restoration, 1750–1820 / Malcolm Crook.
    p.   cm. — (War, armed forces, and society)
    Includes bibliographical references and index.
    ISBN 0-7190-3567-8
    1. Toulon (France)—History. 2. France—History—Revolution,
1789–1790—Influence. 3. France—History, Naval. 4. Toulon
(France)—History—Siege, 1793. I. Title. II. Series.
DC195.T65C76   1991
944'.93—dc20
                                                                91-4172

ISBN 0 7190 3567 8 *hardback*

*Photoset in Linotron Sabon
by Northern Phototypesetting Co., Ltd, Bolton*

*Printed in Great Britain
by Billings Limited, Worcester*

Contents

Maps and tables

Acknowledgements

During the lengthy preparation of this book I have incurred a good many debts. Only a few of them can be recognised here and I must apologise to anyone who feels left out, though it is a pleasure to mention those who have helped me most. My commitment to the study of the past was fostered when I was an undergraduate at University College Swansea, especially by the late Alun Davies and Ralph Griffiths. Douglas Johnson proceeded to pilot me through postgraduate research at London University, where his seminar in French History was a great source of support and several lasting friendships. Much of my time, then as now, was spent in France, precisely as I had intended. I am particularly grateful to past and present personnel at archives and libraries in Toulon, for they exceeded the bounds of duty to assist and advise a callow researcher. In recent years the conversion of doctorate into monograph has been encouraged by my colleagues at Keele; I could wish for no better place to teach. Fellow historians of France, now grouped into the Society for the Study of French History, have been equally unfailing in their encouragement, above all Bill Doyle, who read the manuscript and offered invaluable criticism. Needless to say, what has emerged from the re-drafting is entirely my own responsibility. Both the British Academy and the Research Fund at Keele have assisted financially, while Agnes Fairclough and Jacqueline Ryles have proved patient typists. Andrew Lawrence, cartographer in the Geography Department at Keele, was responsible for the maps. Most of all, I must thank my wife, Josephine; without her unfailing love and encouragement this task would never have been completed. The Bicentenary of the Revolution in 1989 enabled me to develop aspects of my work on Toulon which could not be accommodated here. Interested readers should consult the Bibliography for references to a short study of 'revolutionary events', which includes many documentary extracts, and several specialised papers. My studies at Toulon began in a period of unrest and some optimism; they have been completed at a moment of uncertainty, amidst the collapse of the old order in Eastern Europe and the threat of conflict in the Middle East. I hope this book on War and Revolution will, in some respects, illuminate these 'interesting times' in which we are condemned to live.

Malcolm Crook
Keele, January 1991

Abbreviations

Actes Con. Nat.	*Actes du Congrès national des Sociétés savantes*
AD	Archives départementales du Var
ADBR	Archives départementales des Bouches-du-Rhône
AHR	*American Historical Review*
AHRF	*Annales historiques de la Révolution française*
AM	Archives municipales de Toulon
AN	Archives nationales
Annales ESC	*Annales: Economies, Sociétés, Civilisations*
Ann. Midi	*Annales du Midi*
AP	Archives du Port de Toulon
BM	British Museum
BMT	Bibliothèque municipale de Toulon
BP	Bibliothèque du Port de Toulon
Bull. Drag.	*Bulletin de la Société des Etudes scientifiques et archéologiques de Draguignan*
Bull. hist.	*Bulletin du Comité national des Travaux historiques*
Bull. T.	*Bulletin de la Société des Amis du vieux Toulon*
Bull. Var	*Bulletin de l'Académie du Var*
CHESRF	*Commission d'Histoire économique et sociale de la Révolution française*
FHS	*French Historical Studies*

HJ	*The Historical Journal*
JMH	*Journal of Modern History*
PRO	Public Record Office
Prov. hist.	*Provence historique*
RH	*Revue historique*
RHES	*Revue d'Histoire économique et sociale*
RHMC	*Revue d'Histoire moderne et contemporaine*
VHG	*Var historique et géographique*

To my mother and father

1

Introduction:
A naval town in upheaval

'The town of Toulon played an active part in all the events of the Revolution.'

In recent years a great deal has been written on the history of French towns in the eighteenth and nineteenth centuries.[1] This book represents a further contribution to the expanding corpus of literature. It focuses on revolutionary Toulon, an important city which has not received a full, modern treatment of the years examined here, from 1750 to 1820.[2] Between the Estates General of 1789 and the Hundred Days of 1815, Toulon experienced a degree of upheaval which has few parallels elsewhere. The exploration of this series of events contributes a good deal to an understanding of the Revolution as a whole. Disorder and dissent were partly a product of the naval role that Toulon exercised in a period of almost continuous warfare. This book thus also illuminates the badly neglected naval history of revolutionary France. However, this study of Toulon is not only unusual in terms of its subject matter, it is also ambitious in scope. A time-span of seventy years, from *ancien régime* to Restoration, allows conclusions to be drawn regarding the longer, as well as the short-term impact of war and revolution upon the town.

The rebellion of Toulon in 1793 lies at the heart of what follows. This ill-fated uprising was the longest lasting and the most serious of the so-called 'federalist' revolts, which swept through France during the summer months of that momentous year.[3] Like urban rebels elsewhere the Toulonnais rejected the authority of the central government in Paris, but they were alone in embracing royalism and declaring allegiance to Louis XVII. In a vain effort to avoid defeat they made common cause with the British enemy, who occupied the Mediterranean naval base for four months. It was only as 1793 drew to a close that Republican forces, inspired by a youthful Bonaparte, recaptured the town. Toulon, renamed Port-la-Montagne, suffered huge losses through executions and emigration. For the French navy this dreadful episode constituted a disaster worse than Trafalgar.

The great act of betrayal, on the part of a town which had earned a reputation for 'the most ardent patriotism', perplexed contemporaries as much as it has historians. Both have resorted to conspiracy theories and explained the Toulonnais's *volte-face* as a product of counter-revolutionary machinations. Yet, of late, more careful analysis has revealed the complexity of resistance to the Revolution.[4] The Counter-Revolution assumed many forms and encompassed diverse social groups; it was not simply aimed at a restoration of the old order, or led by nobles and priests, as this study amply confirms. In the case of Toulon, as in other towns, rebellion sprang from deep-rooted social and political divisions, some of which can be traced back into the *ancien régime* and need setting in their full revolutionary context.

A recent study of Lyon suggests that 'survival in revolutions is a matter of keeping in step or keeping out of sight'.[5] Toulon did neither. Throughout the period the city was at odds with a central government that could hardly ignore unrest in its Mediterranean naval port. The Toulonnais Jacobins' early accession to authority proved a disappointment to their supporters. An equally precocious ejection from local office followed in 1793, just after like-minded Montagnards had seized power in Paris. It was the latter whose threats of retribution pushed the anti-Jacobin 'federalists' of Toulon into the arms of the British and their allies. Rebellion became full-blown Counter-Revolution, with dire results for those involved. Yet the consequent absence of conservative elements from Toulon, during the later years of the Revolution, helped entrench republicanism and distinguish the town from much of France, as well as the region. The Bonapartist regime was accepted with reluctance, while the eventual return of the Bourbons encountered great hostility. Toulon experienced a final spasm of turmoil in 1815, before stability was finally re-established under the Restoration.

The naval dimension was crucial to all these momentous events. Few cities have been so closely associated with a particular role as Toulon with the French navy. After the foundation of a dockyard, or Arsenal, at the turn of the seventeenth century, the local community became a prisoner of the government's maritime strategy. The interaction between town and naval base thus constitutes another guiding thread for this survey, underlying the ebb and flow of urban development. The construction of a Mediterranean fleet and periodic mobilisation for war stimulated demographic and economic growth, while the return of peace reduced activity and brought recession. The uncertainties of this dependence of town upon dockyards was a source of deep concern to the urban bourgeoisie, whose ascendancy was threatened both by the arrival of a military aristocracy and the formation of a huge labour force at the Arsenal.

The naval presence accordingly shaped social relationships at Toulon and intruded into municipal politics. There was continual friction between town and dockyards, yet their respective destinies were inextricably intertwined. If urban developments can usually be explained by reference to what was happening at the Arsenal then, conversely, the situation at the shipyards was profoundly affected by events in the town. Vincent Brun reluctantly acknowledged this reciprocal influence as he continued his history of the port of Toulon into the revolutionary decade: 'I would like to have restricted myself to an account of naval affairs, leaving to one side many events which are so painful to recall, but the history of what happened in the town cannot be detached from what occurred at the naval base.'[6]

The intimate connection between naval and civilian history is one which historians have all too frequently ignored. They have readily blamed the Revolution for the demise of the French navy, whilst forgetting the fragility of victory in the recent American War. As a splendid new survey suggests, the failure of the revolutionaries' campaigns at sea, which contrast strongly with their success on land, can only be properly understood when set in the wider political and social context.[7] The reforms that were undertaken, the tactics which were adopted and the problems of supply that arose, all played a part in determining the unsatisfactory outcome. Events in Toulon and the other dockyard towns, not to mention the country as a whole, determined how much or how little could be achieved. In fact, as this study of the Mediterranean port demonstrates, rather more was done than has usually been supposed, in spite of extremely adverse circumstances. The base at Toulon revealed a remarkable capacity for recovery in the wake of three great disasters: the revolt of 1793; the collapse of the Egyptian expedition in 1798; and the defeat at Trafalgar in 1805.

As a consequence of uninterrupted naval mobilisation, over a period of more than twenty years, Toulon virtually became a 'colony' of the dockyards; never had the domination of the Arsenal been so pronounced. Yet the town itself remained deeply integrated into the surrounding region. Although Toulon may bear some resemblance to Brest, its Atlantic counterpart as a naval base, the visitor to both will instantly recognise that the former is a town of Provence, just as the latter patently belongs to Brittany. This characteristic was especially marked in the eighteenth century, when peacetime recruitment to the shipyards remained localised. Even in the following century, native Toulonnais refused to regard the increasing numbers of immigrants who hailed from outside Provence as their compatriots; on the contrary they were accustomed to call them 'Frenchies'.[8]

The conflicting loyalties of region and nation added a further dimension to the complex political and social struggle that occurred at Toulon. Not only geography and climate, but also culture and politics locate the city firmly in an area where 'the political dynamism of the urban communities . . . animated the entire course of the Revolution'.[9] Contemporaries were amazed by the passionate and impetuous nature of those who inhabited the Midi. When Thibaudeau was made Prefect of the Bouches-du-Rhône in 1803, Lazare Carnot warned him: 'You have no idea what it's like down there; it's a region unlike any other. Everyone is either a terrorist or a royalist. There is absolutely no middle ground. At Dijon or Poitiers they will reason and argue; at Marseille they immediately resort to the dagger.'[10]

The recent Bicentenary of the French Revolution has witnessed the triumph of political and ideological interpretations over socio-economic ones, but this study emphasises the importance of social divisions as well as political conflict.[11] At Toulon, as in much of the Midi, the revolutionary struggle generated a momentum which endured well into the nineteenth century.[12] A powerful Jacobin movement provoked the 'federalist' revolt, just as the ruthless crushing of 'federalism' produced a conservative backlash, not to mention a general recrudescence of violence in 1815, as the Hundred Days reopened old wounds. Yet, on account of its role as a naval port, Toulon had often experienced severe dislocation. The coming of war, with its attendant mobilisation of thousands of dockyard workers and sailors, produced a good deal of turmoil, especially from the mid-eighteenth century onwards when the French navy was accorded unprecedented strategic priority. Thus, the devastating upheaval of the revolutionary decade can only be fully grasped against the background of spectacular old-regime growth and development.

The years 1750 to 1820 straddle the Revolution and provide an excellent context for the investigation of its origins and outcome at Toulon. The final object of this study is, therefore, to combine the history of events in town and naval port with a wide-ranging, structural analysis of urban history. Concern with *la longue durée*, the broad chronological sweep, is generally associated with French historians of the Annales School, but it was Albert Soboul who suggested that 'It is necessary to insert the history of the French Revolution into a solid survey of the *ancien régime* . . . and it is equally essential to press the study of its repercussions well into the the Restoration.'[13] For the historian who seeks to understand demography in addition to democratic politics and social structure as well as political culture, this aspiration presents a daunting task, even when pursued in microcosm at a local level.[14] Toulon was a large community by eighteenth-century standards, yet it has proved possible to explore 'the totality of the town as a social complex' in some detail, before, during and after the Revolution.[15] In spite of the exceptional violence of the intervening years, the basic structures of Toulon were not altered as profoundly nor as permanently as might have been expected. A good many changes, not to mention the brave hopes of the revolutionary era, proved to be ephemeral. When peace returned after 1815, in the town as on the seas, many pre-revolutionary features reasserted themselves. On the surface aspects of the old order obstinately survived, to persist until the industrialisation of the dockyards in the mid-nineteenth century finally removed them. Yet the Arsenal had emerged more dominant than ever, church and nobility did not recover and the city was integrated into a modern nation-state. The *ancien régime* was not entirely destroyed, but it had been fatally weakened; such was the essential legacy of this age of war and revolution at Toulon.

Notes

1 D. Roche, 'Urban history in France: achievements, tendencies and objectives', *Urban History Yearbook*, 1980.

2 The local historians, Coulet, Parès and Poupé, have contributed a

great deal, as the Bibliography shows, but none of them produced a general history of the town. Maurice Agulhon has also studied Toulon and the Var at the end of the eighteenth century, but his book, *Une ville ouvrière au temps du socialisme utopique. Toulon de 1815 à 1851*, Paris, 1970, is concerned with the post-revolutionary period.

3   W. Edmonds, ' "Federalism" and urban revolt in France in 1793', *JMH*, 55, 1983.

4   F. Lebrun and R. Dupuy (eds.), *Les résistances à la Révolution*, Paris, 1987, renews the standard survey by J. Godechot, *La Contre-révolution: doctrine et action, 1789–1804*, Paris, 1961.

5   W. Edmonds, *Jacobinism and the Revolt of Lyon, 1789–1793*, Oxford, 1990 and see also P. R. Hanson, *Provincial politics in the French Revolution. Caen and Limoges, 1789–1794*, Baton Rouge, 1989.

6   V. F. Brun, *Les guerres maritimes de la France. Port de Toulon, ses armements, son administration depuis son origine jusqu'à nos jours*, 2 vols., Paris, 1861, t. 2, p. 138.

7   M. Acerra and J. Meyer, *Marines et Révolution*, Rennes, 1988.

8   H. Vienne, *Esquisses historiques. Promenades dans Toulon ancien et moderne*, Toulon, 1841, p. 48.

9   M. Vovelle, 'Etudes d'histoire révolutionnaire à la Faculté des Lettres d'Aix-en-Provence', *AHRF*, 1970, p. 685.

10   A. C. Thibaudeau, *Mémoires sur la Convention et le Directoire*, 2 vols., Paris, 1824, t. 2, p. 143.

11   O. Bétourné and A. I. Hartig, *Penser l'histoire de la Révolution. Deux siècles de passion française*, Paris, 1989.

12   H. C. Johnson, *The Midi in Revolution. A study of regional political diversity, 1789–1793*, Princeton, 1986, but see the far more incisive article by C. Lucas, 'The problem of the Midi in the French Revolution', *Transactions of the Royal Historical Society*, 28, 1978.

13   A. Soboul, 'Problèmes théoriques de l'histoire de la Révolution française', *La Nouvelle Critique*, 1971, p. 30.

14   P. Burke, *The French Historical Revolution. The Annales School, 1929–1989*, Cambridge, 1990.

15   Roche, 'Urban history in France', p. 12.

1

City and dockyards

'When the Arsenal is in motion, so is everything else at Toulon.'

The establishment of naval dockyards in the seventeenth century was the making of Toulon, a city which stands on the Mediterranean coast some forty miles to the east of Marseille. Like its great neighbour Toulon is endowed with a fine, natural harbour; a small roadstead, *la petite rade*, communicates with its larger but equally well-protected companion, *la grande rade*, by the slenderest of passages. Traders, however, were deterred from utilising these superb facilities to any great extent by the difficulty of intercourse with the interior of Provence, especially in a westward direction. The looming presence of the Faron massif behind the city, which prompted the revolutionary appellation of Port-la-Montagne, together with the plunging Ollioules gorges, prevented Toulon from becoming an important commercial centre. But inland barriers could serve as defensive outworks and the potential offered by the site at Toulon was eventually fulfilled with the creation of a naval base.

A settlement of sorts had existed since Roman times, but when Henry IV decided to adopt Toulon as his Mediterranean *port de guerre*, in preference to Marseille, the Toulonnais population was little more than 5,000 strong.[1] The small urban community was sustained by coastal trading, fishing and manufacturing, activities which were to persist well into the nineteenth century. Their survival was to fuel a good deal of nostalgia, a yearning for the independence and self-sufficiency of old, but traditional enterprises at Toulon were rapidly eclipsed once dockyard foundations had been laid. The dockyards, or Arsenal, that came to dominate the local economy were set on the western side of the town, which was itself fortified and considerably enlarged, both at the beginning and again towards the end of the seventeenth century. The population simultaneously increased by leaps and bounds: during a protracted period of maritime conflict, immediately succeeding the second aggrandisement, the temporary influx of seamen and dockyard workers pushed the number of residents well beyond the 20,000 mark.

Within the course of a century Toulon, like its Atlantic sisters, the naval ports of Brest and Rochefort, had been dramatically transformed. It had mushroomed to become one of the great cities of France, ranking towards the lower end of the thirty biggest towns in the kingdom. This development occurred not as a consequence of indigenous economic growth, but as the result of a governmental decision which effectively converted Toulon into an appendage of the mighty Arsenal. The environment that emerged, and was to endure until the middle of the nineteenth century, was inexorably shaped by the dictates of military security. 'Because Toulon is a fortified town the artistry of its inhabitants, though inclined towards decoration, has been inhibited. Indeed, it has been necessary to put solidity at a premium in all public works.'[2]

Since the Mediterranean naval base lay less than a hundred miles from the French fontier with the Duchy of Nice it was badly exposed to invasion and it was besieged by the Austrians on two occasions, in 1707 and 1747. Toulon was forced to erect defensive ramparts that quickly became a straitjacket.[3] Jules Michelet described 'a town strangled by its fortifications', as he set the scene for his account of obscurantism unleashed in the early eighteenth century by Jesuit–Jansenist rivalry, in the Girard–La Cadière affair.[4] Today's visitor to the old town, or *basse ville*, can still savour something of the claustrophobic atmosphere of *vieux Toulon* and it is not difficult to imagine the additional discomforts of a teeming population, an array of artisan activities and the lack of sanitation. The town supported one of the highest demographic concentrations in *ancien-régime* France.[5] Lacking the space for lateral expansion, buildings were driven upwards and in many cases housed in excess of forty persons.

The problem of overcrowding was especially acute in the eastern quarters of Saint-Jean, Saint-Lazare and Saint-Vincent, which were all products of the earlier seventeenth-century aggrandisement. According to an excellent census, taken in 1765, 40 per cent of Toulon's dockyard workers and 60 per cent of its seamen resided in

Toulon at the end of the eighteenth century

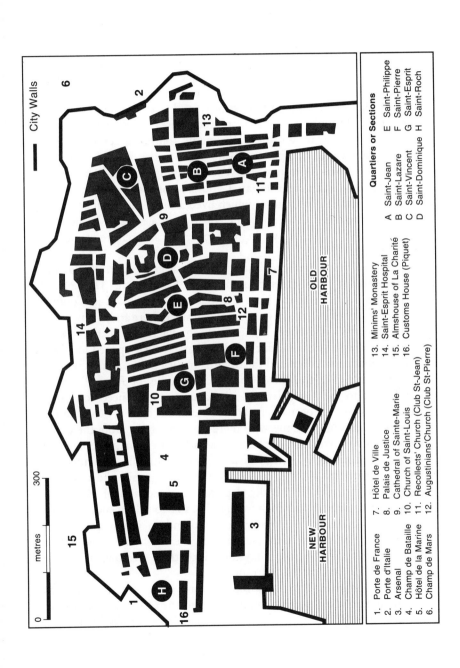

── City Walls

6

2

13

B

A

C

11

9

D

7

E

8

14

12

F

OLD
HARBOUR

G

10

4

5

3

NEW
HARBOUR

15

H

1

16

metres

0   300

Quartiers or Sections

A Saint-Jean   E Saint-Philippe
B Saint-Lazare   F Saint-Pierre
C Saint-Vincent   G Saint-Esprit
D Saint-Dominique   H Saint-Roch

1. Porte de France
2. Porte d'Italie
3. Arsenal
4. Champ de Bataille
5. Hôtel de la Marine
6. Champ de Mars
7. Hôtel de Ville
8. Palais de Justice
9. Cathedral of Sainte-Marie
10. Church of Saint-Louis
11. Recollects' Church (Club St-Jean)
12. Augustinians'Church (Club St-Pierre)
13. Minims' Monastery
14. Saint-Esprit Hospital
15. Almshouse of La Charité
16. Customs House (Piquet)

this part of the town, which housed few notables or military officers.[6] It is often alleged that in pre-industrial cities social stratification was horizontally rather than vertically structured, in other words segregation ran by storeys rather than by neigh-bourhood.[7] At Toulon, despite the occasional presence of aristocrats and unskilled labourers on the lower and upper floors of the same dwelling, this was not generally the case. In the revolutionary period, when they acquired an administrative and electoral significance as *sections*, the popular quarters played a great part in the town's political upheaval. Writing early in the following century Henri Lauvergne called this part of Toulon a 'Turkish souk', where the residents spoke: 'A form of Provençal, employing the idioms of the littoral alongside vulgar Italian, Genoese, Corsican – a bit of every-thing in fact. All the nations which lived around the Mediterranean were represented there and they constituted a mixture of peoples that, in our childhood, we held in contempt and referred to as the "Saint-Jean plebs".'[8]

At the other extreme, culturally as well as geographically, lay the more recently constructed *quartier* of Saint-Roch. This plush, western district was the least crowded neighbourhood in Toulon. Almost half of the military aristocracy resided there and, on average, its property values were higher than anywhere else in the town.[9] Facilities were good and included a theatre which opened in 1760. Saint-Roch also contained the town's solitary public square worthy of the title. The tree-lined Champ de Bataille, or Place d'Armes, adjacent to the Arsenal owed its existence to the need for troop exercises but had been opened to the better-off citizenry early in the eighteenth century. Otherwise there was little relief from the dense network of narrow, fetid streets. Local administrators, in reply to an enquiry from the Provençal *savant*, the *abbé* Expilly, described the town centre as 'a series of sordid alleyways', while the historian Fernand Braudel has vividly depicted 'a succession of extremely narrow passageways, which frequently came to a dead end, ideal for cut-throats, and everywhere open sewers and evil odours . . .'.[10] For most inhabitants the only escape from the crush and squalor was afforded by *le port*, the quayside which then, as now, permitted promenades and offered refreshments.

The commercial and institutional hub of the community was situated amidst the rambling passages of the old medieval *cité*. In 1765 over 80 per cent of the city's merchants, professional men, major retailers and hoteliers resided at business premises in the heart of town.[11] The economic centre of gravity had shifted to the Arsenal, but the Toulonnais bourgeoisie maintained a stronghold in the inner *quartiers* of Saint-Dominique, Saint-Philippe and Saint-Pierre. These central areas also housed the major public buildings, all of which had been constructed or refurbished in the course of the seventeenth century when the town grew in stature. As early as 1620, for example, a new *hôtel de ville* had been erected overlooking the sea, its portals embellished with caryatids by the local baroque sculptor Pierre Puget.[12] A *palais de justice* was situated in close proximity, as Toulon acquired a *sénéchaussée* court, the territorial counterpart of the coastal jurisdiction already exercised by the *amirauté*. Finally, on higher ground nearby, stood the cathedral church of Sainte-Marie. It had also been renovated when a fine, new façade was added in 1696.[13]

Like so many dioceses in the Midi that of Toulon was diminutive and poor, controlling a mere twenty-five parishes in the immediate hinterland. The bishop, who enjoyed a modest income of only 13,600 *livres* in the mid-eighteenth century, was a figure of relatively minor authority in the town. When Michelet, denouncing clerical oppression in eighteenth-century Toulon, asserted that 'the clergy occupied everything, the people practically nothing', he was referring to the numerous properties in the hands of regular rather than secular ecclesiastics: 'A string of large convents leaned against the ramparts, belonging to Minims, Oratorians, Jesuits, Capuchins, Augustinians, Recollects, Ursulines, Vistandines, Bernardines and the Ladies of the Good Shepherd while, in the centre of town, stood the enormous Dominican monastery.'[14] Only the Dominicans survived from the distant past, but the urban aggrandisements of the seventeenth century had coincided with the full flowering of the Catholic Reformation and the new orders had obtained prime intramural sites for their convents. The value of monastic real estate that was surrendered to the state as *biens nationaux* in 1790 might represent only 6 per cent of all Toulonnais property but, since this calculation includes the *terroir*, or surrounding countryside belonging to the town, clerical possessions did bulk large inside the city walls.[15] In the eighteenth century, as the convent population declined and the climate of opinion grew more utilitarian, envy of monastic holdings on the part of lay authorities and wealthy individuals increased. Despite the involvement of some regular clergy in educational and charitable work, the town's Saint-Esprit hospital and the almshouse of La Charité, erected outside the walls at the turn of the eighteenth century, had both passed into municipal hands. The implantation of the Arsenal had provided the opportunity for a big programme of public works at Toulon. By contrast, retrenchment at the naval base, during the decades of peace which followed 1713, was reflected in a period of urban decay. A visitation of plague in 1720 deepened the malaise and by the mid-eighteenth century the cathedral, *hôtel de ville* and *palais de justice* were all badly in need of repair. It took another, unprecedented phase of naval expansion to provide the stimulus for further urban renewal. During the late 1760s, when the dockyards were once again a hive of activity, the *palais* was renovated, while the *hôtel de ville* and cathedral were refurbished. Ten years later a *hôtel de marine* was built, offering a sumptuous residence for the naval command, close to the Arsenal and overlooking the Champ de Bataille. The bishop's palace, which now houses the municipal archives, was also given a new façade. At the very end of the *ancien régime*, the culmination of this redevelopment was marked by the completion of the *église* Saint-Louis as a second parish church for the town. Its cool, neo-classical façade, which was to make it an ideal Temple of Reason during the Revolution, symbolised 'an era of town-planning that was inspired by the outlook of the Enlightenment'.[16]

The buoyancy of the pre-revolutionary decades was also responsible for a series of measures to improve the urban environment. Better provision was made for cleaning, lighting and paving the city streets. Additional public fountains were built and a fire service was established. A *chasse-mendiant* was employed to remove unwanted beggars and a campaign was waged to stamp out prostitution, though to little effect. Yet all these ameliorative efforts were conducted within the same oppressive urban limits, which remained unchanged despite a concerted campaign for a further aggrandisement of the town during the final decade of the *ancien régime*.[17] The military authorities who decided such matters were unyielding and the Toulonnais were left bemoaning their cramped, confined circumstances.

Despite the recent improvements, few visitors found much to praise in the town; it was the Arsenal which attracted them. Whilst he admired the general setting, 'a striking *coup d'oeil*' formed by mountain and bay, Arthur Young reckoned that the dockyard was 'the great and only thing that is worth seeing at Toulon'.[18] He was bitterly disappointed when denied access on account of his English passport. The warships riding at anchor in the roadstead, or under construction in the yards, presented a splendid sight. To pass through the fine eighteenth-century gateway to the Arsenal was to enter a realm that both fascinated and astonished. Even before iron and steam began to supplant wood and sail, in the mid-nineteenth century, war was far more technically advanced at sea than on land. The sophisticated technology, as well as the size of the undertaking conducted at the royal dockyards, left an indelible impression upon contemporaries, who were not used to such gigantic enterprises.

Visiting at the turn of the nineteenth century, when the Arsenal was at full stretch, Millin, a distinguished archaeologist, described what he saw as a veritable 'work of the devil'.[19] His guided tour began with the slipways, where ships' keels were laid down to begin the process of construction. Frames were built next to receive the planking that was caulked with pitch and, in some cases, sheathed in copper so as to retard corrosion and increase speed. At this stage the hull was launched, so that raising the masts and fitting out could proceed afloat. The later stages of construction and repairs relied upon a series of specialised workshops, many of them organ-ised on a primitive production-line basis. These included carpentry, coopering, wood-carving, cannon-founding, metal-working, rope-weaving and sail-making. Millin was especially impressed to see a dry-dock in operation. Designed by the Toulonnais engineer Groignard, after many abortive attempts, its completion in 1778 was a considerable feat because it had to function without tidal assistance. Millin's imagination was also fired by the deployment of vast stocks of materials. He saw the hangars where timber was kept, oily ponds where masts were submerged to retain their flexibility and the huge sheds for general stores, munitions and victuals.

All this warehousing space was a reflection of the enormous resources required to build and maintain an eighteenth-century navy. It has been estimated that one of the largest battleships, a *vaisseau*, or ship of the line carrying 110 guns, consumed 120,000 cubic feet of oak in the course of construction.[20] This represents a total of 4,000 mature trees and does not include the other varieties of wood, such as fir or elm, that were employed for masts and planking. Cannons, chains, anchors and other metal fitments amounted to at least 100 tons of metal, while infinite quantities of hemp were necessary for sails, ropes and rigging. At prices prevailing in 1789 such a vessel would cost over 1,000,000 *livres* to commission, while essential maintenance and refitting during a lifespan of at best thirty years multiplied the initial outlay several times. Warships were not lightly lost; they took a year or more to replace.

A tour of the Arsenal culminated in an inspection of the fleet assembled in the roadstead. At the quayside, however, Millin's humanitarianism was aroused by the sorry sight of the prison hulks. These had been established at Toulon, as at Brest and Rochefort, by the conversion of redundant Mediterranean galleys into floating gaols.[21] Inmates were condemned to hard labour in chain gangs at the dockyards, though supervision was slack and they frequently escaped. The hulks, which survived until the Second Republic, inspired a good deal of fear in the locality (to this day wayward Toulonnais youngsters are threatened with *le bagne*), but their real purpose was to permit the naval administration to economise upon manpower.

The census of 1765 put the convict population in the dockyard at 730 individuals, a figure which later rose to around 1,000.[22] Nonetheless, the size of the free labour force at the eighteenth-century Arsenal was quite astounding, rivalling that of the very largest industrial concerns of the day. Millin's visit coincided with a moment of exceptional activity during the First Empire but, even after 1783 in the wake of the American War, over 2,000 workers had remained directly employed on shipbuilding and repairs.[23] Some two-thirds of them were specialised craftsmen, while the rest were unskilled labourers, or sailors engaged on harbour duties. Women and children, usually members of a craftsman's family, were also present in small numbers, assisting in tasks like caulking and hemp-dressing.

The great majority of these workers were residents of Toulon, but some travelled daily from the neighbouring communities of La Seyne, Ollioules or La Valette. For the duration of the American War the regular dockyard contingent had been doubled to a total in excess of 4,000, by summoning craftsmen in the 'reserved' shipbuilding trades who were registered along the Mediterranean littoral in the *Système des Classes*.[24] Created by Colbert, as an alternative to the press gang, this draft system was never as effective in practice as on paper, but it was easier to operate for sedentary workers than for sailors, whose movements were harder to monitor.[25] Despite its shortcomings, upwards of 8,000 experienced mariners were mobilised at Toulon between 1778 and 1783.

The dockyard labour force also included a host of military, administrative and ancillary staff. Although expeditions were rare in peacetime, when most ships were mothballed, some 400 naval officers were stationed at Toulon at the end of the *ancien régime*, together with a dozen port officers, a similar number of engineers and a company of naval gunners.[26] The administration of the Arsenal and the draft system was supervised by over 100 personnel, ranging from clerk to naval *intendant*. This civilian arm of the service was responsible for the prison hulks and general security, which accounted for 100 police, goalers and gate-keepers. There was also a dockyard tribunal, to deal with offences committed inside the Arsenal. Finally some thirty doctors and surgeons served on board ship or worked at the naval hospital, which was opened in 1785 and offered medical care to all dockyard employees.[27]

Even during periods of peace the maintenance of the naval base utterly dominated Toulon, rendering it a forerunner of the celebrated 'company towns' of the industrial era. The Anzin mining concern, the largest private firm in France, had only 4,000 employees on its books at the time.[28] Yet at Toulon approximately 3,000 persons, or over half of the adult male working population, were directly employed by the naval authorities on a regular basis. Those Toulonnais who were not engaged at the dockyards were no less reliant upon the level of activity there. The Arsenal indirectly determined their livelihoods too because the fate of most independent manufacturing, commerce and retailing was decided by naval commissions and, above all, by the spending power of the vast dockyard labour force.

The fortunes of Toulon thus came to rest upon a 'war industry', borne along by the titanic struggle for maritime hegemony that was waged by Britain and France between 1689 and 1815. This so-called 'Second Hundred Years War' brought a tremendous escalation in the size and sophistication of the rival fleets, though the French could ill afford the resultant 'arms race'.[29] After the naval build-up of the late seventeenth century the French navy had stagnated. During the first half of the eighteenth century it was deprived of strategic importance and starved of funds. With few orders for new vessels and little repair work the base at Toulon, and consequently the town as a whole, experienced a prolonged depression. Following the disastrous naval

defeats of the Seven Years War however, Choiseul, Minister for War
and the Navy, resolved to concentrate anew on the quest for naval
supremacy and to invest greater resources in the military marine.
After 1763, as the historian Paul Bamford suggests, 'the French navy
for the first and only time in modern history displaced the French
army as the first service of the realm'.[30]

It was generally accepted that French battleships enjoyed technical
superiority over the British, yet there were fewer of them and they
were frequently outmanoeuvred due to less experienced seamanship
and poorer material resources. The rectification of these defects
involved massive expenditure at the dockyards. An unprecedented
programme of naval expansion was launched in the mid-1760s and
by the end of the following decade the French navy, now under
Sartine, was in a good position to exploit the rebellion in Britain's
North American colonies. This time France remained free of continental entanglements, the enemy was isolated and *revanche* was
finally achieved. The Toulon fleet, commanded by d'Estaing, played
a vital role in the successful maritime campaigns, while in economic
terms the town benefited hugely from the billion *livres* allocated to
the navy between 1776 and 1783. Expenditure at the Mediterranean
Arsenal on shipbuilding alone, which had already risen from an
annual average of 1,500,000 *livres* in the first half of the century to
over 3,000,000 after 1760, shot up to 10,000,000 *per annum* for the
duration of the American War.[31]

An extremely high level of activity was sustained at Toulon
throughout the closing decades of the *ancien régime*. Even the considerable exertions of the late seventeenth century were surpassed.
Yet this upward trend was interrupted by some short-term fluctuations which had serious repercussions upon the town. Maritime
rivalry periodically culminated in conflict, but its resolution meant
demobilisation and severe retrenchment, always exacerbated by the
exhaustion of Treasury funds. The resulting pattern of boom and
slump produced a conjuncture at Toulon that was the exact reverse
of the commercial seaports. At neighbouring Marseille the outbreak
of hostilities was detrimental to trade, but the cessation of conflict
brought an immediate resumption of business. For the dockyard
town, by contrast, war provided jobs while peace spelled recession.
In 1760, for instance, though the Seven Years War was not settled for
another three years, naval operations ground to a halt. The consequences at Toulon were summed up in a gloomy municipal report:

The curtailment of construction work at the Arsenal; the dismissal of hundreds of workers which has accompanied it; the suspension of debt repayment by the navy and its failure to continue remunerating its employees; the drop in municipal income caused by the exodus of inhabitants: all these factors have inflicted such misery upon Toulon that the community is in dire straits and the town council may be obliged to provide sustenance for those unfortunate citizens who are unable to go elsewhere in search of a livelihood.[32]

There was little exaggeration in this grim assessment of post- war difficulties. The dockyard labour force was owed arrears of twelve months and those who continued in (unpaid) employment were working part-time.[33]

These familiar problems reappeared in a less draconian fashion after 1783, in the aftermath of the American campaigns. The Duc de Castries, another able, reforming naval minister, was certainly anxious to build upon recent victories and to maintain the pressure on Britain. His great Code of 1786, which assigned Toulon two of the nine squadrons (*escadres*) of standardised warships that were to comprise the French fleet, was directed to this end.[34] It was intended to allocate each squadron nine ships of the line (carrying seventy-four, eighty or 118 guns); nine frigates (thirty-four and forty-four guns); and a number of smaller craft. Such was the penury of the government that this ambitious programme had to be scaled down. Totals were lowered from eighty-one to sixty-three ships of the line and similarly reduced for frigates. In other words only seven vessels of each type would be allocated to each squadron, though it was hoped to hold sufficient materials in reserve to construct additional ships when the need arose.[35]

Castries resigned in protest, but a recent survey suggests his disappointment, like the verdict of many historians, was ill-founded. In 1789 the French navy possessed seventy-three ships of the line and sixty-three frigates. This represented a substantial increase over the number of vessels available in 1783 and the fleet was stronger in terms of quality as well as quantity. Work did diminish at Toulon once the American War had ended. In 1787 only one ship of the line and two frigates were on the stocks but, compared to previous post-war cutbacks, these orders reflected the priority still being accorded to naval rearmament.[36] The threat of fresh hostilities with Britain, later in the year, brought an upward revision of construction targets, though satisfaction in the port was as brief as the duration of

the 'war scare'. Just one ship of the line and one frigate were laid
down the following year, while in 1789 repairs and refitting were
reduced too. Yet even before the outbreak of war in 1792 the French
navy continued to expand at a rate which alarmed the British
command.

Post-war reductions after 1783 may not have been as drastic as
their predecessors, but they were automatically translated into a
wider urban recession at Toulon, not least among merchants
engaged in the lucrative and expanding task of supplying materials
to the Arsenal. During the eighteenth century the French navy ceased
to provision itself and came to rely upon local traders instead. Many
of the Toulonnais merchants, who worked hand in glove with senior
partners from Marseille, depended heavily upon naval contracts for
an income; the profits, though frequently delayed, were worth the
wait.[37] Data emanating from a later period reveals the dominant role
of dockyard supplies in the commerce of Toulon. In 1810, for
instance, between one-third and half of all cargoes entering the
harbour were wholly or partly related to shipbuilding.[38]

Remaining native resources in wood and naval stores were close to
exhaustion. Provence itself had been completely denuded and even
reserved timber from the forests of Dauphiné and Franche-Comté,
which was brought down the Rhône and floated along the coast on
specially designed rafts, was rapidly disappearing.[39] Stiff inter-
national competition for this vital commodity exacerbated the problem. After 1750, in order to satisfy the voracious appetite of the
Mediterranean Arsenal, recourse for timber was increasingly made
to Corsica (purchased partly for this reason), the Italian peninsula,
Albania and as far afield as the Black Sea.[40] Such long-distance traffic
often originated at Marseille, but the commercial port of Toulon,
'principally as a result of its Arsenal, maintained direct contacts with
Holland and the Baltic' that were much more significant than occasional links with the Levant.[41] Northern Europe had long served as
the main source for masts, planking, pitch and iron, with Dutch
intermediaries taking wine, brandy and soap in return. The
regularity of this particular trade at Toulon is reflected in the
membership of sea captains from Holland at one of the town's
masonic lodges, the *Saint-Jean de Jérusalem*, where local merchants
met.[42]

A transatlantic addition to these Baltic and Mediterranean circuits
was short-lived; like a later attempt to establish trade with India, it

lacked connections with the French navy. In 1759 a royal permit was obtained for direct commerce with the West Indies and many benefits for Toulonnais manufacturing interests were anticipated.[43] In the event only twenty-one departures were recorded in twenty-five years before the privilege was revoked.[44] By the end of the old regime, as the need for naval supplies diminished, little more than a western Mediterranean trading network survived. Between 1791 and 1792, for instance, sailings in and out of Toulon averaged some fifty a month.[45] Vessels emanated from, or were proceeding to ports on the Mediterranean shores of France, Italy and occasionally Spain. The ships plying these coastal routes were small, generally crewed by no more than half a dozen sailors. Only once a month was there a departure for, or arrival from northern Europe, although the importance of this traffic increased during 1792 after the outbreak of war.

Independent commerce, together with trade tied to the Arsenal, offered a livelihood to numerous seamen who constituted roughly 6 per cent of the male heads of household at Toulon in 1765.[46] Along with coastal fishing, seaborne commerce also helped to sustain some private shipbuilding. In a general review of the industry, for the years from 1762 to 1787, the *amirauté* of Toulon was credited with the completion of almost 500 vessels.[47] This total represented some 5 per cent of the tonnage constructed in France during the period. However, only small boats were built at Toulon and, within the *amirauté*, a much larger contribution was made by neighbouring La Seyne than by Toulon itself. In 1791, for example, there were four ships on the stocks across the bay at La Seyne, but only two at Toulon.[48]

Nevertheless, Toulon constituted a major inlet and outlet, not only for its own requirements, but also for those of the zone defined by local geographer Jean Gaignebet as *la région toulonnaise*: the hinterland bounded by Le Beausset to the west, Méounes to the north and the plain of Cuers to the east.[49] Toulon acted as a marketplace for surrounding communities and, while naval stores bulked large in the lists of incoming cargoes, foodstuffs always predominated. During 1810, when wartime mobilisation had swollen the population of the town, half the ships entering Toulon were laden with grain.[50] In 1766, a time of peace, the city fathers had calculated the proportion destined for the hinterland: 'According to the analysis we have made in recent years we reckon that at least 80,000 charges (roughly 10,000 tons) of grain arrive by sea each

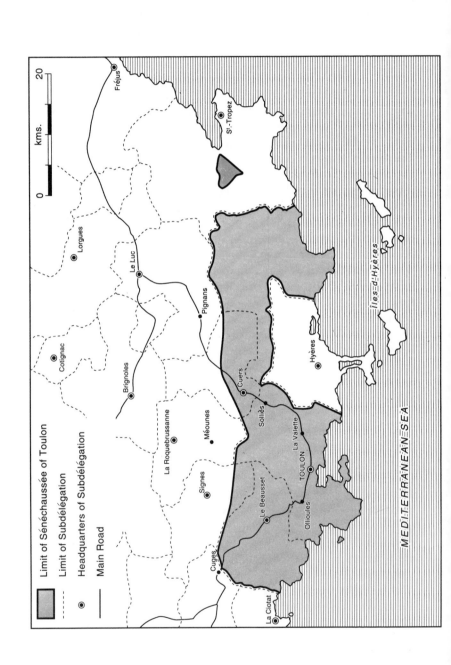

Limit of Sénéchaussée of Toulon
Limit of Subdélégation
Headquarters of Subdélégation
Main Road

0   kms.   20

Fréjus
St-Tropez
Lorgues
Le Luc
Cotignac
Brignoles
Pignans
La Roquebrussanne
Méounes
Cuers
Signes
Hyères
Solliès
La Valette
Le Beausset
TOULON
Ollioules
Cuges
La Ciotat

Îles-d'Hyères

MEDITERRANEAN SEA

year, while our own consumption barely exceeds 30,000 ...'[51] When supplies from Languedoc or Burgundy were exhausted, easy access to the Mediterranean granaries of Italy, and occasionally North Africa, protected Toulon from the worst ravages of dearth.[52]

It was an exaggeration to state that the soil of Toulon 'was impossible to cultivate', for some 5 per cent of the heads of household who lived *intra-muros* were rural workers, besides large numbers residing *extra-muros*.[53] Yet, situated in an area which received little rainfall, the land around the town was certainly 'dry, arid, stony and unyielding'.[54] It could produce only 200 tons of grain a year, less than 5 per cent of the annual peacetime consumption in the town, while the hinterland furnished stocks for only a few months.[55] Fruit and vegetables were more plentiful. Market gardening was well developed, producing peas, haricots, melons, figs, plums, peaches and honey for immediate sale by stallkeepers in the town. The crop was not sufficient to satisfy local demand, so additional supplies were obtained from the Italian peninsula, equally a source of rice and pasta. Meat was likewise imported because, apart from a few pigs, goats and hens, the terrain of Lower Provence was unsuitable for livestock.[56] Cattle and sheep, driven overland from the Auvergne and Dauphiné, cost a good deal as beef and mutton in the butchers' shops, but the Toulonnais turned to the sea to supplement their diets with fish, which were also dispatched inland.

This dependence upon external sources for foodstuffs, as well as naval supplies, ensured that Toulon ran up a huge trade deficit. Statistics culled from the First Empire show that over half the ships were leaving the port unladen though, on account of the adverse impact of war and revolution, the proportion may have been lower a couple of decades earlier.[57] Local produce and manufacturing did little to make ends meet, but it would be wrong to discount them altogether. The Toulonnais region, which the port served as a minor *entrepôt*, was poor in cereals but rich in vines. To rely upon later, imperial data once again, it appears that the *terroir* of Toulon alone yielded 60,000 gallons of wine a year.[58] With the exception of the La Malgue vintage most of it was of mediocre quality. Still, the hinterland produced more than could be consumed at home and much was exported direct to northern Europe, or to the West Indies via Marseille. During the pre-revolutionary decades no less than

Toulon and its region

one-third of the cargoes sent to Marseille from Toulon were loaded with wine.[59] As markets became glutted and viniculture declined in profitability, an attempt was made to divert more of the surplus into the distillation of brandy. Toulon itself housed three distilleries which exported most of their production.[60] Some 200,000 gallons were being processed annually in the 1780s, but this outlet too fell foul of the surpluses that were plaguing the parent wine trade.

Prospects for the olive crop, equally well-suited to the inhospitable terrain, were also diminishing at the end of the *ancien régime*. When ground into oil locally-grown olives yielded approximately 2,000 gallons a year in Toulon, while another 30,000 were produced by mills in the hinterland.[61] This was far in excess of immediate requirements for lighting and cooking but, aside from a small export trade, olive oil had traditionally served as the basis for the manufacture of candles and soap. Soap-boiling was a dominant enterprise everywhere in *la région toulonnaise* and the fortunes of olive growers relied heavily upon it. Hence their dismay as the manufacturing of soap entered a pronounced decline, largely due to competition from Marseille. Twenty establishments had been operating in the late seventeenth century, but only half a dozen remained in 1789. The survivors were all working short-time and output was reduced from 4,500 to 1,500 tons *per annum*.[62]

Soap-boiling was the most extensive form of independent manufacturing at Toulon. Other enterprises existed besides, though most of them were also in decline at the end of the *ancien régime*.[63] In 1789 there were six assorted textile manufactories producing cloth, silk and cotton that was woven into bonnets, stockings and other types of garment, compared to eighteen similar establishments a century earlier. A pair of tanneries was listed on the eve of the Revolution, but Toulon had supported as many as fifteen in the past. Closely associated with these undertakings was dyeing, which utilised crushed insects as colourants; only three dyeworks survived in the late 1780s. Brewing, glass-blowing and gunpowder manufacture were all represented by a single enterprise in the town. A forge and two paper mills, both dependent upon the demand for nails and stationery from the Arsenal, were situated in the *terroir*. On the eve of the Revolution, conscious of the need to create new businesses, the municipal administration subsidised the foundation of starch-making, a lead oxide works and a sugar refinery.[64]

A report to the Inspector-General in 1785 stated that manufacturing at Toulon occupied 500 heads of household.[65] To judge by other statistics collected then, and by the more exacting imperial bureaucracy later, this seems to have been a gross exaggeration. On the eve of the Revolution the pair of paper mills had ten persons on the books and the brace of tanneries a similar number.[66] Private industry at Toulon was dwarfed by the scale and extent of the 'service sector', which grew hand in hand with expansion at the naval dockyards. The provision of food and drink, housing and lodgings, domestic utensils and clothing all developed rapidly in response to the rising urban population. Such activities were unspectacular, but they represented the essence of the urban economy. Those craftsmen who, with the assistance of a few employees, made and sold their goods direct to the consumer, constituted a quarter of the Toulonnais heads of household in 1765.[67]

Despite the rise of these petty retailers and artisans, the demise of external trade and independent manufacturing was deeply regretted by the city fathers of Toulon. It especially irked them that neighbouring Marseille was prospering in those areas where they were experiencing contraction. Business was being attracted to the rival town, it was alleged, as a result of unfair competition: 'Before the edict of 1669, which made Marseille a free port, Toulon was a flourishing industrial centre.'[68] The former had received royal favours to the great detriment of the latter. The corollary of this contention was that the removal of Marseillais privileges would facilitate a commercial resurgence at Toulon. In their *cahier de doléances* of 1789, the Toulonnais naturally seized the opportunity to demand 'abolition of the privilege (a powerful terms of abuse at that moment) accorded to the town of Marseille, which allows it to operate as both a foreign and a national port'.[69]

Recent research suggests that such franchises consecrated, rather than created Marseille's economic domination of Western Provence. Its dynamism stemmed from long-accumulated capital resources, considerable expertise and a favourable location.[70] Toulonnais attempts to compete in the colonial trade, or sustain manufactures like soap-boiling and sugar-refining which were multiplying at Marseille, were bound to end in failure. However, the Marseillais provided a convenient scapegoat, because the Toulonnais were loath to admit that the decline, or rather the distortion of their traditional economic activities, was essentially due to the establishment of the Arsenal. Naval priorities inhibited the growth of independent trade and manufacturing, which migrated to neighbouring La Seyne instead. The Toulonnais did make strenuous attempts to overcome this constraint, but the difficulties which beset them are perfectly illustrated by a fruitless attempt to initiate a link with India in 1791: the naval administration was unwilling to assist in the provision of warehousing and flatly refused to surrender any space in the harbour.[71]

The naval *intendant* was more sympathetic to the project, first mooted in 1779, for excavating a new commercial harbour just to the east of the town at Le Mourillon.[72] With regard to private shipbuilding the authorities at the Arsenal were positively helpful, for they were anxious to prevent the emigration of skilled dockyard workers, made redundant as a result of post-war economy measures and a new system of employment at the Arsenal. The *intendant* was also prepared to assist a revival of soap manufacturing in the town because the effluents which drained into the harbour killed the bacteria that corroded ships' hulls.[73] Only rarely did urban and naval interests coincide so closely. In the competition for scarce resources of capital, as well as accommodation, it was the latter that usually triumphed.

The Toulonnais notables were therefore right to resent the royal dockyards. The Arsenal was an alien imposition grafted on to, rather than absorbed into the urban community. It remained a realm apart, its isolation symbolised by high surrounding walls and a separate harbour. The dockyard was beyond local control, dependent upon the vagaries of a distant central government. It was feared as an imperialistic intruder which threatened to turn the town into little more than a naval 'colony'. The economic balance of power at Toulon, which began to turn with the great burst of maritime activity at the end of the seventeenth century, shifted decisively in the pre-revolutionary decades. The Toulonnais themselves understandably recoiled from increasing reliance upon the Arsenal as a source of income. Local leaders were apt to argue that 'If Toulon was neither a fortified town, nor a naval base, it would be much less distinguished but a great deal wealthier; for commerce and merchant shipping would be able to flourish.'[74]

In fact, as other reports frankly admitted, 'commerce and manu-facturing have never really prospered at Toulon.'[75] The geographical barriers which restricted inland trade could not be overcome; com-munication with the interior remained too difficult, depite the upgrading of the local road network after 1760.[76] The best route out of Toulon lay in a north-easterly direction, away from Aix and Paris, towards Italy. Yet, when he wished to travel to Nice by road, Arthur Young was surprised by the paucity of traffic and decided to take a boat instead.[77] The acquisition of a military role was thus the making rather than the breaking of Toulon. From the mid-eighteenth century onwards, though the subordination of town to Arsenal grew inexorably greater, naval expenditure brought unprecedented wealth and opportunities. The Toulonnais realised the disadvantages of depending so heavily upon a single industry, resisted their fate as a 'company town', but there was little alternative. The domination of the dockyards was accordingly evident in all aspects of late eighteenth-century Toulon, not only in environment and economy but equally in demography and social structure.

Notes

1   Agulhon (ed.), *Histoire de Toulon*, Toulouse, 1980, is the best introduction to the town's history, though rather more detail is to be found in G. Lambert, *Histoire de Toulon*, 4 vols., Toulon, 1886–92, which ends at the Revolution.

2   AM BB29, Réponses aux demandes de M. l'abbé d'Expilly, c. 1770.

3   AM BB29, Mémoire pour l'histoire de Toulon, c. 1770; G. Parker, 'The urban geography of Toulon', M.A. thesis, University of Wales, Aberystwyth, 1960 and O. Teissier, *Histoire des divers agrandissements et des fortifications de la ville de Toulon*, Toulon, 1873.

4   J. Michelet, *La sorcière*, ed. L. Refort, 2 vols., Paris 1952–56, t. 2, p. 118.

5   F. de Dainville, 'Grandeur et population des villes aux XVIIIᵉ siècle, *Population*, 13, 1958, p. 471.

6   AM CC77, Dénombrement des habitants, 1765.

7   For example, J. Kaplow, *The names of kings: the Parisian laboring poor in the eighteenth century*, New York, 1972, pp. 67–8.

8   H. Lauvergne, *Le choléra-morbus en Provence*, Toulon, 1836, p. 18.

9   AM CC77, Dénombrement and L202, Contribution foncière, 1791.

10   AM BB29, Réponses aux demandes de M. l'abbé and F. Braudel, *L'identité de la France; espace et histoire*, Paris, 1986, pp. 317–18.

11   AM CC77, Dénombrement.

12   AM BB29, Mémoire pour l'histoire and *ibid.*, Réponses aux demandes de M. l'abbé.

13   M. Tortel, *Notice historique sur l'église Sainte-Marie de Toulon*, Toulon, 1898.

14   Michelet, *La sorcière*, t. 2, p. 121.

15   AM L202, Contribution foncière.

16   Agulhon (ed.), *Histoire de Toulon*, p. 152 and V. Pillon-Caillol, 'Un foyer négligé de néo-classicisme en Provence: Toulon dans les années 1780', *Prov. hist.*, XXXV, 1985, pp. 179–93.

17   AM BB89–96, Délibérations du conseil municipal, 1750–88.

18   A. Young, *Travels in France and Italy during the years 1787, 1788 and 1789*, ed. C. Maxwell, Cambridge, 1929, pp. 233–6.

19   A. L. Millin, *Voyage dans les départements du Midi de la France*, 4 vols., Paris, 1807–11, t. 2, pp. 389–421.

20   P. W. Bamford, *Forests and French seapower, 1660–1789*, Toronto, 1956, p. 11 and M. Acerra and J. Meyer, *La grande époque de la marine à voiles*, Rennes, 1987.

21   P. W. Bamford, *Fighting ships and prisons: the Mediterranean galleys in France in the age of Louis XIV*, Minneapolis, 1973, pp. 281–97.

22   AM CC77, Dénombrement.

23   AN B3 751, Etat des ouvriers, 5 July 1783 and AP IAI 238, Intendant de la marine à la cour, 18 May 1786.

24   Brun, *Port de Toulon*, t. 2, p. 62, and J. Dull, *The French navy and American independence. A study of arms and diplomacy, 1774–1787*, Princeton, 1975, p. 256, footnote.

25   M. Loir, *La marine royale en 1789*, Paris, 1892, pp. 28–41.

26   AP 2E4 71, Revues et soldes, 1789.

27   J. C. White, 'Un exemple des réformes humanitaires dans la marine française: l'hôpital maritime de Toulon, 1782–1787', *Ann. Midi*, LXXXIII, 1971.

28   R. Price, *An economic history of modern France*, 2nd. ed., London, 1981, p. 123.

29   J. Meyer and J. Bromley, 'The Second Hundred Years' War (1689–1815)', in D. Johnson, F. Bédarida and F. Crouzet (eds.), *Britain and France. Ten centuries*, Folkestone, 1980, pp. 139–72.

30   Bamford, *Forests and French seapower*, p. 9.

31   AP 1L325–408, Recettes et dépenses de la marine de Toulon, 1722–82.

32   AM BB29, Mémoire sur la misère qui régne à Toulon, 1760.

33   Brun, *Port de Toulon*, t. 1, p. 419.

34   BP Ordonnance du Roi portant division de la flotte, 1786.

35   Loir, *La marine royale*, p. 1; N. Hampson, *La marine de l'an II*, Paris, 1959, pp. 23–6 and, for a recent revision, Acerra and Meyer, *Marines et Révolution*, pp. 56–8.

36   Brun, *Port de Toulon*, t. 2, pp. 123–30 and 161.

37   AP 5E180–200, Marchés, entreprises, 1769–89.

38   AM L185 bis, Etat des mouvements du port, 1810.

39   Bamford, *Forests and French seapower*, pp. 60–1.

40   AP 1A1 227, Intendant, 4 Jan. 1775 and Brun, *Port de Toulon*, t. 1, p. 489.

41   AM L140, Observations de la communauté de Toulon sur le commerce, 7 May 1790.

42   BN FM2 441, *Saint-Jean de Jérusalem*, tableaux, 1784–85.

43   AM BB29, Divers mémoires sur le commerce des isles, 1757–59.

44   AM HH17, Commerce avec les colonies, 1759–84.

45   AM L159, Marine marchande, patentes expédiées, Aug. 1791–July 1792.

46   AM CC77, Dénombrement.

47   T. J. A. Le Goff and J. Meyer, 'Les constructions navales en France pendant la seconde moitié du XVIIIᵉ siècle', *Annales ESC*, 26, 1971, p. 178.

48   BM F1179(2), F. P. Delattre, Rapport sur la navigation française, 1791 and L. Baudoin, *Histoire général de La Seyne-sur-mer et de son port*, La Seyne, 1965, p. 265.

49   J. Gaignebet, 'Les limites historiques de la région toulonnaise: étude de géographie historique et politique', *Bull. T.*, 1935.

50   AM L185 bis, Etat des mouvements.

51   ADBR C1322, Consuls de Toulon à l'intendant, 24 Dec. 1766.

52   C. Morin, 'Le probèlme des subsistances à Toulon, seconde moitié du XVIIIᵉ siécle', mémoire pour la maîtrise, University of Nice, 1973.

53   AM II15, Mémoire pour la communauté de Toulon, 1760, and CC77, Dénombrement.

54   AM BB29, Réponses aux demandes de M. l'abbé.

55   AM L161, Produit des récoltes, 1790 and AD 1L392, Etat du produit des récoltes, District de Toulon, 1790.

56   AM BB30, Instruction sur la forme de notre boucherie, 1784.

57   AM L185 bis, Etat des mouvements.

58   AM L161, Tableau des produits en vin, 1812–13.

59   G. Rambert, 'Toulon et l'exportation des vins provençaux par Marseille au XVIIIᵉ siècle', *Prov. hist.*, XII, 1962, pp. 29–30.

60   AM L142, Manufactures et fabrications existantes avant 1789 et en l'an IX and C. Carrière, 'Le commerce des eaux de vie à Toulon au XVIIIᵉ siècle', *Prov. hist.*, XII, 1962, pp. 34–8.

61   AM L161, Produit des récoltes and AD 1L392, Etat du produit.

62   AM BB29, Mémoire sur la fabrication du savon, 1753 and HH18, Questionnaire sur les manufactures, 1780.

63   AM BB30, Demandes faites par l'Inspecteur-général des manufactures, 1785; HH18, Questionnaire and L142, Manufactures.

64   AM BB93–6, Délibérations, 1763–88.

65   AM BB30, Demandes faites par l'Inspecteur-général and AD 16M1–1 and 2, Statistique industrielle et manufacturière, 1811–12.

66   AM HH18, Questionnaire.

67   AM CC77, Dénombrement.

68   AM BB29, Réponses aux demandes de M. l'abbé.

69   AM L39, Cahier de doléances de la ville de Toulon, Mar. 1789.

70   C. Carrière, *Négociants marseillais au XVIIIᵉ siécle. Contribution à l'étude des économies maritimes*, 2 vols., Marseille, 1973, t. 1, pp. 316–19 and E. Baratier (ed.), *Histoire de Marseille*, Toulouse, 1973, pp. 202–16.

71   AM L139, Commerce avec l'Inde and Brun, *Port de Toulon*, t.2, p. 176.

72   AM BB96, Délibérations, June 1786.

73   AP 1A1 238, Intendant, 18 June and 7 Dec. 1786.

74   AM II15, Mémoire.

75　AM L140, Observations.

76　Agulhon (ed.), *Histoire de Toulon*, p. 150 and G. Arbellot, B. Lepetit and J. Bertrand, *Atlas de la Révolution française*. I, Routes et communications, Paris, 1987, *passim*.

77　Young, *Travels*, pp. 235–6.

2

People and society

'Whoever comes to Toulon, comes for the Arsenal.'

Fluctuations in the population of Toulon closely mirrored the rise and fall of activity at the Arsenal. Any increase in the scale of construction work at the royal dockyards was automatically translated into urban demographic growth and, conversely, any reduction into decline. Mobilisation for war, which drew in thousands of sailors and craftsmen, produced an especially dramatic, if essentially transient effect. Toulon was thus a particularly 'open' community with a constant turnover of inhabitants, though an accurate assessment of the shifting population is not easily obtained. This is not simply because full censuses were rare in the eighteenth century, or that data emanating from this pre-statistical era are often dubious. A clear distinction must also be drawn between 'fixed' and 'floating' residents, as well as between those living within and without the city walls. At Toulon the inclusion or omission of garrison and prison hulks, the conflation or separation of extra- and intramural inhabitants, and the selection of a year of peace rather than one of war, may all seriously distort the figures, rendering comparisons dangerous.[1]

The available materials usually give totals without further qualification. Fortunately one outstanding point of reference has been preserved for Toulon: the relevant volume of a superb census, 'detailed, precise and complete', that was undertaken in 1765.[2] This document formed part of a survey that was simultaneously conducted all over Provence, ostensibly to serve as the basis for a new system of taxation. It was the product of a carefully organised and meticulously recorded door-to-door head count, inspired by the locally-born demographer the *abbé* Expilly, who was a close friend of the provincial *intendant*. Expilly wished to exploit the findings, in order to formulate a reliable coefficient for use in his demographic calculations based upon the annual movement of population. Ultimately he hoped to refute the widespread assumption that the population of France was falling.[3] He published figures derived from this source in his unfinished *Dictionnaire ... de la France* (1762–70), but only a few of the original dossiers he consulted remain in existence.

As far as Toulon is concerned it is possible to follow in the footsteps of the census-takers. The town was first divided into 136 *isles*, blocks of houses rather than individual streets, and information was then collected from the inhabitants of these units according to a set questionnaire. Those who were temporarily absent, businessmen and sailors in the main, were recorded as if resident, while visitors were deliberately omitted. Intra- and extramural population was carefully distinguished, just as garrison soldiers and convicts held at the Arsenal were counted separately. The accumulated data were then transcribed on to printed sheets bearing thirteen columns, so that the populace of Toulon can be accurately analysed, not only by dwelling and *quartier*, but also according to family, sex and occupation. The attempt that was made to tabulate the geographical origins of non-natives does not appear to be satisfactory in the light of other available information, but the census is deficient in only one other respect: its addition. A slight adjustment must be made in the official total of 26,264 persons, which included 3,542 soldiers and 730 convicts. The global number of inhabitants for 1765, a year of no great activity at the dockyards, was in fact 26,109. The 'fixed' intramural population stood at 20,535 persons and goes up to 21,837 when civilian residents of the *terroir* are counted as well.[4]

At first sight Toulon did not appear to support Expilly's contention, disputed at the time but since accepted, that the French population was actually expanding in the late eighteenth century. To judge by the *abbé*'s own calculations, the populace of the naval port had fallen by at least a third over the preceding half century. However, as he explained: 'The drop in population at Toulon is due to the visitation of plague in 1721 and, still more so, to the reduction of naval activity in the *port de guerre*.'[5] Expilly was correct to point to the royal dockyards as the animator of demographic trends in the town. According to his extrapolations, on the basis of births recorded in the parish registers, naval mobilisation at the end of the seventeenth century had momentarily lifted the number of inhabitants towards the 40,000 mark, a level occasionally regained, but never permanently surpassed until the 1830s.[6] The 'floating' population accounted for a good deal of this total which was subsequently eroded by the Austrians' siege in 1707, the cruel winter of 1709 and, above all, the eventual cessation of the war at sea.

A final visitation of bubonic plague in Provence was nonetheless responsible for a catastophic loss of population in 1721. An attested census taken in August 1720, on the eve of the outbreak, recorded 26,276 residents in town and *terroir*, 'without taking into account the troops at garrison and dockyard'.[7] When the disease abated a year later, another count was conducted; only 10,493 inhabitants remained. When allowance is made for refugees from the stricken city, yet to return, it would appear that roughly half the population had succumbed.[8] Such losses were in line with those suffered by other towns in the region but, whereas Marseille quickly retrieved the deficit, the Toulonnais recovery was a protracted process.[9] The explanation for this contrast lies in the fact that commerce rapidly revived at Marseille and brought a high incidence of immigration. At Toulon, by contrast, the dockyards stagnated and few new recruits were attracted to the town. Only in the 1740s, with the first large-scale naval mobilisation for more than thirty years, did the population begin to rise above a plateau of 15,000 persons. The Seven Years War, which began in 1756, brought another large influx and pushed the total well beyond 20,000. Then, after this sharp upturn, the situation settled at the 22,000 'fixed', intra- and extra-mural inhabitants delineated in the great census of 1765.[10]

The determining influence of the Arsenal over the level of population was equally evident during the final decades of the *ancien régime*. Activity stimulated by the American War quickly raised the number of urban residents to roughly 28,000 and even during the economic crisis of the late 1780s the total did not fall far below a threshold of 26,000.[11] This last calculation is substantiated by another census collected in 1791. It is vastly inferior to Expilly's effort and two out of eight *quartiers* are missing from the surviving dossier, but the gaps can be filled to render its findings serviceable.[12] These indicate an intramural population of precisely 23,135 persons, to which some 2,400 inhabitants of the *terroir* should be added. If 'floating' elements from garrison and prison hulks are included, then a global figure approaching 30,000 is obtained, at a moment when dockyard activity was at a particularly low ebb.

Net demographic growth at Toulon between 1765 and 1791 thus amounted to some 3,500 persons, or 16 per cent. This was a small increase compared to the period of recovery from plague losses, during the 1740s and 1750s, and it was modest by the standards of surrounding communities like La Seyne or Six Fours, which rose by between 30 and 40 per cent during the same pre-revolutionary decades.[13] The pull of seaborne commerce was greater than the inconsistent attraction exerted by the Mediterranean Arsenal, for both neighbouring Marseille and more distant Bordeaux were also expanding faster.[14] Nonetheless, Toulon had become the third largest town in Provence, outpacing Arles through still just short of Aix in terms of 'fixed' civilian population.[15]

The growing towns of eighteenth-century France relied heavily upon immigration to boost or, in some cases, merely to maintain their numbers of inhabitants.[16] Toulon was no exception to this general rule, though a close analysis of the parish registers for the year from 1765 to 1791 reveals a surprisingly large, 'natural' surplus of births over deaths. Even when fatalities at hospital and almshouse are taken into account, births exceeded deaths by over 2,000.[17] As at Lyon and elsewhere, however, infant mortality was almost certainly 'under-recorded', because so many small children were sent from Toulon into the countryside for wet-nursing and were buried there in the event of death.[18] Moreover, those adult Toulonnais who died in the naval and military hospitals, where they were entitled to free treatment as employees of the armed services, are also missing from the parish registers.

The rise in population thus owed a great deal to the arrival of newcomers. In 1727, for example, even before the naval renaissance of the later eighteenth century was under way, less than half of the marriages celebrated at Toulon brought together native partners. Only 55 per cent of bridegrooms and 76 per cent of brides were of Toulonnais extraction, though most of the remainder were Provençaux; a mere 6 and 3 per cent respectively hailed from beyond the provincial boundaries. Further inroads by non-natives proceeded hand in hand with the programme of naval aggrandisement. In 1750, following mobilisation for the War of Austrian Succession, fewer than 50 per cent of the men and only 61 per cent of the women joined in matrimony were Toulonnais by birth. By 1786, in the wake of the American War, these figures had fallen to 44 and 55 per cent. At the latter date less than a quarter of these marriages were contracted between brides and grooms who both originated from Toulon. The bulk of the non-Toulonnais were still drawn from Lower Provence and the hinterland of Toulon, but 26 per cent of male partners and 14 per cent of the females had been born outside the region.

The frequent appearance of French coastal zones, especially those bordering the Mediterranean, as places of bith for bridegrooms and brides, underlines the fact that service at the Arsenal was the major source of attraction to Toulon. Of course, the parish registers do not reveal the stages by which these and other immigrants arrived in the town. There were many immigrants among 'civilian' artisans, who traditionally undertook the *tour de France*.[19] In the case of one tradesman, J. J. Esmieu, some fascinating autobiographical evidence of professional mobility is available. After leaving his native village in Upper Provence Esmieu practised a variety of crafts in Aix and Marseille, before he became a travelling salesman, briefly based at Toulon.[20]

Like Esmieu many immigrants settled in the town for only a short period before moving on again. It is evident that post-war redundancies and demobilisation produced a significant exodus from the port. In 1786, for instance, the naval *intendant* bemoaned the fact that so many unemployed craftsmen were demanding visas because they wished to travel along the Ligurian littoral, from Nice to Genoa, in search of work.[21] The status of Toulon as a *ville passagère*, especially for the least-favoured strata in society, is also reflected in the register of burials kept at the Saint-Esprit hospital. In 1789, for example, only 20 per cent of deceased adults were native-born, while 35.5 per cent had originated outside Provence.[22]

These 'moving pictures' provide valuable insights into the ebb and flow of population at Toulon, but they tend to exaggerate the proportion of immigrants who became long-term residents. For this reason it is salutary to examine the 'snapshot' provided by the register for National Guard service which was compiled early in the Revolution, in 1791, just prior to the outbreak of war.[23] Inscription was mandatory for all adult males above the age of twenty-five who possessed French nationality and had been domiciled in the town for at least twelve months. Foreigners, like dozens of fishermen who hailed from the Ligurian riviera, were *ipso facto* excluded, as well as recent arrivals and, no doubt, more marginal elements. Those exercising a military profession, who mostly emanated from outside the region, were ruled out too, by the nature of the document. The percentage of non-natives revealed by this survey must be considered a little low as a consequence. Nevertheless the great majority of male heads of household within the fixed population, some 5,000 *in toto*, is represented in Table 1.

Table 1 *Geographical origins of the adult male population of Toulon in 1791*

Category	Toulon	Var	Provence	Elsewhere	Total
	%	%	%	%	
Leading administrators	42.6	13.1	13.1	31.1	61
Retired officers & officials	57.8	11.1	8.9	22.2	45
Rentiers	73.5	13.5	5.8	7.1	155
Legal professions	67.0	14.3	4.4	14.3	91
Medical professions	57.1	24.2	13.2	5.5	91
Merchants	81.0	14.3	2.4	2.4	84
Retailers	70.7	8.6	9.5	11.2	348
Clerks	71.6	8.2	6.0	14.2	232
Artisans & shopkeepers	46.8	15.1	12.9	25.2	1,400
Dockyard workers	76.6	8.2	5.8	9.4	1,286
Fishermen	83.2	4.7	5.4	6.7	149
Rural professions	33.9	24.9	30.7	10.6	189
Unskilled workers	44.1	19.2	20.0	16.7	681
Priests	40.8	20.4	22.4	16.3	49
No profession indicated	46.2	18.8	11.2	23.8	80
Total	59.6	13.3	11.4	15.7	4,941

Source: AM L392, Inscription pour le service de la garde nationale, 1791.

A careful analysis shows that six out of every ten guardsmen had been born at Toulon. The newcomers were distributed in roughly equal proportions between those who originated within the bounds of the recently-created department of the Var, especially from the Toulonnais hinterland; those who hailed from elsewhere in Provence; and, thirdly, those attracted from still further afield. These findings help to put the geographical recruitment of the stable, adult, male populace into a firmer perspective (younger men and females in general, excluded from the register, were more rather than less likely to be Toulonnais by birth). Evidently the higher incidence of immigration suggested by the parish registers was a product of short-term residence on the part of many individuals. Outside periods of intensive mobilisation, when Toulon did become something of a naval colony, those who decided to settle were fewer than might have been expected. The extent of their absorption into Toulonnais society is indicated by the fact that in 1786, for instance, over half the marriages celebrated in the town united non-native with native spouses. The only group which displayed a pronounced tendency to resist assimilation in this manner was the Genoese fishing community.

The register established for National Guard duty also offers a good means of gauging the social profile of immigration into Toulon. Like their military counterparts, leading administrative personnel at dockyard and garrison were often drawn from outside the region by the dictates of their careers. Naval surgeons were also overwhelmingly non-Toulonnais, mostly of Provençal extraction. Conversely, doctor, lawyers, rentiers (*bourgeois*), merchants (*négociants*) and large retailers (*marchands*) were usually indigenous. Over 75 per cent of these notables, who ran the municipality, gave their place of birth as Toulon. In both absolute and relative terms, therefore, the great bulk of civilian immigrants were members of the popular classes. Mobility was the rule for journeymen artisans and small shopkeepers, though master craftsmen were more likely to be natives. Distant geographical origins were still more marked among the large numbers of rural labourers who lived in and around Toulon, as among the unskilled in general.

Most of these conclusions might have been anticipated, but what the register unexpectedly reveals is the indigenous, or local provenance of seamen and skilled dockyard workers. This finding flatly contradicts the basic contention of D. M. J. Henry, a leading and often-quoted nineteenth-century historian of the Revolution. He asserted that, in 1789, there were two sorts of Toulonnais inhabitant:

One local, with roots in the town, composed of rentiers and merchants, artisans and tradesmen. The latter, formed into guilds, were generally peaceable individuals, industrious and hardworking, who hoped eventually to acquire a plot of land as a result of their savings . . . The other sort of inhabitant comprised the dockyard workers, an ignorant, turbulent and vulgar class of men, easily incited to violence, who took part in every disorder. They were drawn from many different regions but chiefly from the rural areas; they were usually the sons of peasants, who had come to the Arsenal seeking a less arduous existence.[24]

As Maurice Agulhon has shown, Henry's neat division rests upon the anachronistic assumption that the widespread geographical recruitment of craftsmen in the nineteenth-century 'age of steam' was equally true of the late eighteenth-century 'age of sail'.[25] In fact, in 1791, 76 per cent of the artisans exercising traditional ship-building trades as carpenters, caulkers, coopers, drillers, pulley-makers, sailmakers, ropers and sawyers (the 'reserved occupations' which rendered a worker liable for call-up in the event of war, or labour shortage) had been born at Toulon. Other sources indicate that most of them were following in their fathers' professional footsteps, having been apprenticed in their early years.[26] Henry was right about their involvement in radical politics during the Revolution. Yet many urban artisans, less likely to be indigenous than he claimed, were also members of the town's Jacobin club.

The study of demography at Toulon provides no easy answers where political behaviour is concerned, but it does pave the way for an analysis of the town's social structure. The recent debate on social stratification in pre-industrial cities suggests that, ideally, urban society should be passed through a variety of filters and analysed according to several criteria, rather than relying on a single one. The distinctions of order, or *qualité*, employed by contemporaries, the hierarchy of wealth and the distribution of economic functions, are just a few of the relevant perspectives, not to mention age, family circumstances and geographical origins.[27] In the case of Toulon no individual tax records remain for the pre-revolutionary period because earlier in the eighteenth century the municipality had adopted the *abonnement*, or lump-sum payment, for *capitation* and *taille*, the major impositions. As a consequence, 'the manner in which contemporaries viewed current patterns of social stratification' has weighed heavily in the classification of occupational data recorded for 5,000 male heads of household in the great census of 1765.[28] (See Appendix, p. 244 and Table 2, The occupational structure of Toulon in 1765 and in 1791, pp. 52–3.) The twenty socio-professional categories employed in the table represent the main constituents of three basic groups, or classes, of Toulonnais society: the service aristocracy, comprising officers and leading administrators attracted by a career at Arsenal or garrison; the urban bourgeoisie, or notables, an elite who owned much of the wealth and wielded authority within the municipality; and thirdly the vast, heterogeneous mass of the popular classes, composed of artisan employers as well as employees, dockyard workers, sailors and unskilled labourers, in short all those who possessed relatively little or no property, power and status. Though this terminology may be slightly at variance with his, such divisions are similar to the ones described by another nineteenth-century historian of the revolutionary period at Toulon, Henri Lauvergne. Writing in 1839 and drawing upon memories of his youth, Lauvergne separated out a nobility, a middle class and the *menu peuple*.[29]

The omission of the clergy from this scheme reflects their small numbers and declining importance as much as their specific juridical situation. Ecclesiastics, male and female, furnished only 1 per cent of the total population at Toulon. Secular clergy were especially thin on the ground: in 1765 their ranks included the bishop, a chapter of twelve canons and sixteen auxiliary priests at the cathedral, plus three *curés* and eight *vicaires* serving the two urban parishes. This complement of only forty individuals represented a proportion of less than two priests for every 1,000 inhabitants. It was a remarkably low ratio, even by Provençal standards.[30] Regular clergy were rather more numerous: in 1765 there were fifteen religious communities in the town with 200 members, but this monastic population dwindled to 150 by 1789.[31] During the pre-revolutionary decades the women's orders remained stable, while their male counterparts experienced a sharp fall. Only the pair of masculine teaching orders, the Oratorians and Christian Brothers, who were responsible for secondary education and free primary instruction, resisted the downward trend and extended rather than reduced their activities.

The order of the nobility was much better represented at Toulon. In 1765 almost 9 per cent of Toulonnais heads of household were noblemen. This finding should be compared with contemporary estimates of less than 1 per cent at Marseille and just over 3 per cent at Aix, the regional capital.[32] In the naval town nearly all of these nobles were actively engaged in the armed forces. Few of them were indigenous. As one memorandum put it, 'at Toulon there are scarcely eight or ten noble households and none of them are illustrious'.[33] The handful of well-established local houses, like the Missiessy or Antrechaux, strove to place their siblings in navy or army, while nine out of ten Toulonnais ennoblements in the eighteenth century were awarded for military or administrative prowess in the services.[34] Such nobles, old and new, native and non-native, formed the backbone of a military elite at Toulon which also included a sprinkling of non-noble officers and administrators. Those enlisted in the navy, however, increasingly outnumbered their peers in the army, as the growth of the French fleet carried the total of seagoing officers past the 400 mark during the 1780s.[35]

This expanding service aristocracy was an alien element in the town not only on account of occupation, but also as a result of geographical origins and separate life-style. Garrison officers were periodically restationed with their regiments, just as naval officers were directed to different bases. In the case of the latter comprehensive career dossiers reveal that only 15 per cent of those serving in 1789 had been born in Toulon.[36] Almost 30 per cent hailed from Provence, some of them scions of the region's most famous houses: de Grasse, de Castellane, or de Sade (a brother of the notorious marquis was enlisted at Toulon). The remaining half were drawn from further afield, mostly from the seaboards of Languedoc, Brittany and Normandy.

Apart from sub-lieutenants (*sous-lieutenants de vaisseau*), who were engaged in a newly-created rank designed to attract recruits from the merchant navy, seagoing officers at Toulon had undergone an exclusive form of training. Noble families, well connected with the service and endowed with a modicum of wealth, applied for their teenage sons to join the navy as cadets. Entrants were schooled in the theory and practice of seamanship before following a privileged route to the upper deck and becoming junior officers in their early twenties.[37] Promotion to lieutenant and then captain was virtually assured with the passage of time, though life on the ocean wave, even as an officer, could prove extremely unpleasant. The progress of many aspiring lieutenants was cut short by death or disability, both in and out of battle.

Such shared experience tended to foster loyalty to the service rather than to the port or town of Toulon. The absence of any real local affiliation was exacerbated by the generous periods of leave which allowed officers ample time to repair to their distant estates. Fewer than 10 per cent of all active members of the military aristocracy resided in Toulon with wives and family and an even smaller proportion owned land or houses in the vicinity.[38] Instead they usually rented apartments as single persons and, accompanied by a valet or servant, congregated in the salubrious *quartier* of Saint-Roch, in close proximity to the Arsenal. Their lack of interest and involvement in urban affairs is indicated by the fact that their representative never bothered to attend meetings of the municipal council, spurning the opportunity for participation afforded by the new town charter of 1776.[39] Only forty-six retired officers, military or administrative, are recorded in the census of 1765 as having put down permanent local roots. When they took their pensions the great majority of their colleagues completely severed any connection with Toulon.

Whatever their internal differences, which will be examined in the next chapter, the various members of the service aristocracy cultivated a strong and separate identity. As Lauvergne suggests, the urban bourgeoisie was held at arm's length, 'excluded from naval circles and all the festivities and honours associated with the upper classes'.[40] This social apartheid is most clearly revealed in the pattern of affiliation to the masonic lodges that flourished in Toulon towards the end of the *ancien régime*. The two military lodges, which were set up in the wake of the American War, never enrolled more than a handful of local bourgeois among well over 150 adherents.[41] Conversely three of the five civilian lodges inscribed only the odd military officer or leading administrator.[42] At *La Double Union*, one of the other Toulonnais lodges, some naval cadets had joined but their attendance was described as 'infrequent', while at *Les Elèves de Mars et de Neptune* it was army sergeants who mixed with clerks and artisans.[43] The cream of military society held aloof from the urban elite. It is, therefore, hard to credit an allegation made by the naval *commandant* in 1786, that some of his officers were meeting with 'magistrates, merchants and retired officials' to read journals and newspapers together.[44] All those he named were masons, but at separate military and civilian lodges.

The forty-six retired officers and administrators enumerated in the census of 1765, who had fixed their domicile in Toulon and usually owned substantial amounts of local property, were much better integrated into the community than their erstwhile colleagues. As keen contenders for municipal office they helped to provide a point of contact between town and dockyard or garrison. For this reason the monarchy was especially anxious that such individuals should assume leadership in the town and they frequently headed the municipality during the closing decades of the *ancien régime*. These former royal servants became a vital component of the urban elite at Toulon. In company with indolent noblemen and those professions which Lauvergne labelled '*le haut tiers*', they possessed the occupational credentials that were required for admission to the ruling municipal oligarchy.[45] Just as the service aristocracy contained a small minority of non-nobles, so one in seven members of the Toulonnais patriciate was of noble extraction. Altogether, in 1765, these urban notables were 400 strong and represented 8.5 per cent of the heads of family listed by census-takers.[46]

This section of society was delineated, in considerable detail, by the town charter of 1776. Its regulations consolidated the existing pattern of recruitment into the oligarchy, both reflecting and reinforcing contemporary perceptions of the social hierarchy. According to the rubric municipal consuls, like councillors, were to be selected 'Among nobles, retired officers and officials, barristers, doctors, *rentiers* (*bourgeois vivant noblement*) . . . merchants (*négociants en gros*) . . . and the more important retailers.'[47] In practice notaries were included too and, along with nobles, retired royal officers and administrators, barristers and doctors, they could be chosen to serve as 'first' consuls. This leading position, at the very summit of the municipality, was not open to *rentiers* and merchants who held inferior status within the elite and could only be nominated as consuls of second rank.

Financial qualifications were added to these corporate occupational criteria: 'No-one can be proposed or elected as *consul* who does not personally, or via his wife, own fixed assets of 20,000 *livres* which must be located in the town or *terroir*; as for councillors, it will suffice that they possess 10,000 *livres* of the same type of property.' A number of notables fell foul of this proprietary hurdle, *rentiers* in particular.[48] However, the elite as a whole owned some 70 per cent of real estate in the town and territory of Toulon at the end of the *ancien régime*. No other professional group outside the military aristocracy could match any of its constituents in terms of average, *per capita* holdings.[49]

A dozen or so barristers were also barred from municipal office, but this was a consequence of their venal positions at the three tribunals situated in Toulon: *sénéchaussée*, *amirauté* and dockyard *prévôté* courts.[50] These officials owed their primary allegiance to crown rather than to municipality and sometimes found themselves in conflict with colleagues in private practice who served on the town council. A handful of doctors were likewise ineligible as *consul* or councillor because they were employed in the armed forces. Documents deposited at the dockyards reveal the level of their remuneration; Barbaret, for example, principal medical officer at the recently-opened naval hospital, received 4,000 *livres per annum* on the eve of the Revolution.[51] Salaries had increased during the preceding decade, though it was usual for medical and legal personnel to enjoy a private as well as a professional income. Marc-Antoine Granet, scion of a well-heeled middle-class Toulonnais family, was president of the *sénéchaussée* tribunal, but he also commanded independent resources which yielded in excess of 3,000 *livres* a year. Altogether forty barristers, notaries and doctors appeared in the census of 1765 and, a quarter of a century later, seven of them were listed among the thirty wealthiest property-holders at Toulon.

A legal qualification was not always actively employed. François-Thomas Jaume, a third-estate delegate to the Estates General who had spent most of his life in the naval town, practised only on a sporadic basis. He much preferred to indulge his antiquarian tastes and purchased a large library with his inherited wealth.[52] Jaume's career neatly personifies the close links between the liberal professions on the one hand and the *rentier*, or '*bourgeois*', on the other. The term *bourgeois* has proved a troublesome one for historians because of its Marxist connotations, but eighteenth-century administrators also produced some conflicting definitions.[53] An addendum to the town charter of 1776 stated: 'Under the heading *bourgeois* his Majesty wishes to embrace all those citizens who exercise with distinction a non-manual profession.'[54] This is a broad notion which could cover the entire spectrum of non-manual occupations, yet local documentation at Toulon generally reserved the appellation *bourgeois* for individuals who exercised no active occupation at all and were 'living like nobles'.

Achard, who compiled a contemporary dictionary of regional terminology, agreed that the label should only be utilised in this more restricted sense, to categorise: 'All those who live indolently, without exercising a profession; all those commoners who have no resources other than unearned income and who pursue no money-making activities.'[55] These '*bourgeois*', or *rentiers*, were easily assimilated with the inactive noble, or retired military officer and administrator, whose life-style they shared. Although a minority invested in government bonds, or in commerce, most *bourgeois* turned to real estate as reliable repository for their accumulated wealth.[56]

A good many *rentiers* were former merchants, or *négociants*.

Indeed, many of those engaged in long-haul trade put money into property long before retirement. No less than five *négociants* appeared in the top half of the list of the thirty most highly taxed property-holders in 1791. Perhaps this reflected the relatively limited commercial opportunities available to them at Toulon, besides the prestige which property ownership conferred. Trade in naval stores and grain supplies might yield big profits, but it could not secure the highest rank in society. The very label, *négociant*, was a relatively recent addition to the social vocabulary, denoting an individual who transacted substantial business beyond the immediate locality.[57] At Toulon the *négoce* was stretched to include entrepreneurs, like soap manufacturers, distillers and the town's leading printer, Jean-Louis Mallard. Numbers were growing, from thirty-seven in 1765 to well over forty in 1789.[58]

The designation *bourgeois* often set the seal upon a successful career from which the individual had retired in order to live off the proceeds. Many *rentiers* were thus men of advanced years. François Richaud, whose son Louis was to write a first-hand account of the revolt of 1793, is a good case in point.[59] Richaud *père* quit active commerce in 1780 and allowed the *fils* to assume control of the family business. As a *bourgeois* the father now enjoyed the leisure to take a fuller part in the municipality. He served as a councillor in 1783 and 1784 and then became rector of the town's hospital. *Rentiers* like Richaud were able to play a prominent role in local administration and they were much more assiduous in their attendance at council meetings than any other group.[60]

Those occupations which afforded access to the position of consul and councillor in the municipality constituted the core of the urban elite in the naval port. But the charter of 1776 also recognised the existence of an outer ring of notables, recruited among the minor liberal professions and the retailing branches of commerce, who served as deputy councillors:

Among these eighteen deputy councillors, two will be chosen from nobles and military officers, either active or retired ... one from the order of barristers, one from that of the doctors, one each from the communities of notaries and procurators, surgeons and apothecaries, three among the drapers, clothiers and haberdashers and one each from the silk retailers, grocers and goldsmiths.

Nobles, retired (but not active) military officers, barristers, doctors, notaries and merchants who could serve as consuls and councillors had hitherto monopolised the role of deputy-councillor too. After 1776 procurators, surgeons, apothecaries, cloth and silk retailers, grocers and goldsmiths, who had only occasionally served as deputies in the past, were guaranteed a place. Clearly the monarchy was underwriting their social status by granting them a greater say in municipal matters.

Procurators, who numbered ten in 1765, were responsible for collating documentary evidence for court proceedings and several served at the trio of Toulonnais tribunals. Surgeons, of whom thirty were listed in the census, were especially thick on the ground on account of their employment by the navy as seagoing medical officers. Their remuneration ranged from 800 to 3,000 *livres* per annum at the end of the *ancien régime*.[61] The apothecary attached to the naval hospital earned 1,600 *livres*, although most of his professional colleagues were involved in urban retail outlets, catering for a growing demand for medicine. This allied apothecaries to the big retailers who formed the bulk of those becoming eligible as deputy councillors after 1776. Seventy-nine of them were listed in 1765 and their numbers had risen to over 100 on the eve of the Revolution. At Toulon, as at Paris and other great provincial cities, the *grand corps des marchands* constituted a privileged group at the head of the local trade guilds.[62] Besides a municipal role their particular status earned them additional delegates to the urban electoral assembly of 1789.[63]

From outer ring to inner core the Toulonnais notables formed a heterogeneous elite. Differences of class, order and status are easily discerned, but without any obvious sign of the internal divisions that Perrot has discovered among similar categories at Caen.[64] At Toulon all members of the patriciate shared much in common. Besides their monopoly of municipal office and the tight grip they maintained over fixed wealth, few failed to enjoy the leisurely life style afforded by the presence of domestic servants. Well over half of them lived in the heart of the town, clustered around the old *cité*. This neighbourhood solidarity grew out of deep native roots and a propensity to inter-marriage.[65] It was reinforced by mutual association in the realms of freemasonry. Merchants predominated at *Les Amis Constants* in the early 1780s, but they rubbed shoulders with individuals exercising a liberal profession and several *rentiers*.[66] This pattern of sociability was repeated at the *Saint-Jean de Jérusalem* lodge, an equally exclusive preserve of the urban elite.[67] By contrast the lower-class lodges, *La Double Union* and *Les Elèves de Mars et de Neptune*, enrolled only the occasional *bourgeois* among serried ranks of shopkeepers and master craftsmen.[68]

The lines of social demarcation were not completely clear-cut for, in the case of *Les Elèves de Minerve*, some cross-membership did occur. A third of the masons who joined between 1781 and 1785 were drawn from lower end of the elite, while the majority were members of the popular classes. Significantly enough this was a lodge which recruited several individuals who became prominent radicals during the Revolution.[69] The mixed composition of *Les Elèves de Minerve* is also a reminder of the links between those notables of lesser standing, who were involved in the wholesale trade, and the manifold groups of shopkeepers and artisans which encompassed so many of the popular classes.

The *classes populaires*, those who lacked wealth, status and authority, made up some 75 per cent of Toulonnais heads of household in 1765. However, there was considerable variation within this section of society, which ran the gamut from master craftsmen and shopkeepers to indigents and invalids. As Ernest Labrousse has written:

> The artisanate of pre-industrial societies was involved at almost every level of the economy. It embraced most of the productive and distributive activities of both the secondary and tertiary sectors. At the lower end and in its crudest forms it constituted a quasi-proletariat. In its upper echelons, in the realms of small business, it was associated with the commercial bourgeoisie; it was indeed a quasi-bourgeoisie.[70]

Individual master craftsmen were often modest property-holders and their status was recognised by their occasional inclusion as delegates at special meetings of the municipal council. As leaders of the town's fifty guilds, which represented over 100 different trades and roughly one-third of the popular classes, they wielded substantial authority.[71] For the artisan corporations served a number of purposes, social and devotional as well as purely economic.[72] Their basic *raison d'être* was to regulate the production and sale of goods to the public, but in assuming such a function they also operated as moral communities with confraternities and patron saints, as agencies of social order.[73] Aspiring apprentices were bound for a period of training during which the master acted *in loco parentis* and this responsibility extended to qualified journeymen (*garçons* in Provence). Such paternalism is aptly illustrated by a request from the municipality of Toulon that officials of the wigmakers' guild discipline a *garçon perruquier* who was prone to drunk and disorderly behaviour.[74]

A microcosm of the wider society in which they existed, the guilds were organised along strictly hierarchical lines. Corporate administration was entrusted to masters alone though, since most of them were small employers, a high proportion of craftsmen were *maîtres*. The census of 1765 suggests, for instance, that 26 per cent of stonemasons and 46 per cent of tailors held the *maîtrise* at Toulon. It does not seem that the opportunities to graduate from journeyman to master were diminishing to the extent they are said to have been.[75] Nevertheless, a hereditary advantage was built into the system of promotion, with the offspring of master-craftsmen paying relatively little for access to the *maîtrise*.[76] A master-shoemaker's son, for example, was required to remit only eight *livres* to the guild on becoming a master, as opposed to eighty-four for those without a family connection. Marriage to a master's daughter was, however, a means of lowering the fee to sixteen *livres*.

The occupational facilities provided by the artisan corporations were not enjoyed by Toulonnais workers employed at the Arsenal. In 1765 the royal dockyards were a source of employment for 800 shipbuilders who worked as sawyers and ships' carpenters preparing the timber; drillers and caulkers assembling the hulls; sailmakers, ropers and pulley-makers who attended to the rigging; and coopers whose barrels were essential for storage purposes. They were skilled craftsmen in 'reserved' occupations and, even if they moved to private yards, they remained liable for naval call-up. Toiling beside them were numerous other artisans, such as painters and woodcarvers, toolmakers, armourers and locksmiths, not to mention victuallers. Several hundred unskilled men (*journaliers*) were also on the naval payroll, along with watchmen and gaolers on the prison hulks, a complement of gunners and a small number of sailors employed on a full-time basis (*entretenus*). When dockyard clerks are added, a total of 2,000 persons – roughly half of the popular classes – were employed at the Arsenal in peacetime. Like the service aristocracy, this huge work-force constituted an element in the Toulonnais population that had few equivalents elsewhere.

Thanks to plentiful naval archives much more can be discovered regarding the conditions of work and standards of living of dockyard workers than about other urban artisans. In the shipbuilding occupations there was a similar career structure from apprentice to

master but, unlike tailoring or shoemaking, it was the naval administration which regulated remuneration and promotion rather than
guild-masters.[77] Summoned by the same bell in the morning, all
craftsmen and allied employees in the Arsenal were subject to this
single authority. The small elite of *maîtres* and foremen who directed
operations were not owner–employers, but wage-earners like
journeymen and apprentices.

For these reasons it is tempting to view the dockyard workers as a
proletariat, concentrated in conditions which heralded the nineteenth-century factory and distinct from the rest of the popular
classes at Toulon. There is no doubt that craft loyalties were diluted
at the Arsenal although, during the *ancien régime*, attitudes towards
the management were tempered by a good dose of paternalism.[78] In
the absence of a supportive guild system, the naval administration
offered employees free hospital treatment and a contributory
insurance scheme to cater for accident, death or retirement. Workers
enjoyed the staunchly defended and much-abused right to take home
'offcuts', the *droit de copeaux*, which was no mean perk given the
local shortage of firewood. Moreover, supervision at the dockyards
was slack and the pace of work relaxed, so much so that locals
jokingly compared shipbuilders to the *sorbier*, or mountain ash, a
hard wood which was not easily 'worked'.[79]

Overmanning stemmed from the navy's concern to keep a pool of
skilled men available in the event of emergencies. Paid by the day (*à
la journée*), workers were not inclined to over-exertion. On the other
hand, rates were poor compared to those in private yards or on
merchant ships. In 1783 the average worker was earning only
twenty-six *sols* a day at Toulon, with a top rate of thirty *sols* for a
first-class carpenter and thirty-two for a driller.[80] Leading sailors
received twenty-three *sols* per day in the dockyard and twenty *livres*
a month at sea, likewise some 25 per cent below the rates for
commercial companies.[81] Levels of remuneration at the Arsenal
remained virtually static during the three decades which preceded
the Revolution and payment of both wages and benefits was
regularly delayed when the government experienced financial
difficulties.

At the very end of the *ancien régime*, however, the organisation of
labour at the Arsenal was radically altered so as to resemble conditions in private establishments. Desperate for economies and
influenced by contemporary economic thought, as well as by changes

in British shipyards, the hard-pressed naval treasury saw salvation in the commercial practice of subcontracting, *travail à l'entreprise* or *la tâche*.[82] The matter was raised for debate as early as 1776 at Toulon, when the dockyard council was asked whether 'It is better to place construction and even repair work, as well as workshop production, on a subcontracting basis, rather than continuing with wage labour.'[83] Opponents argued that shoddy workmanship and loss of skilled manpower would result, but no one queried the financial savings that could be made.[84] A pilot scheme suggested that productivity would rise by at least 33 per cent and after the American War the full implementation of subcontracting went ahead. Most tasks were put out to tender and the direct labour force was reduced by two-thirds.[85]

The position of most skilled dockyard workers was thus assimilated to that of other urban artisans at Toulon, though there was no guild structure for subcontractors. The consequence of this dramatic change was to increase the sense of solidarity between *les ouvriers de l'arsenal* and the urban work-force in general. Links were already strong as many workers at the Arsenal were of local provenance and both groups inhabited the same *quartiers* of the town. Moreover, all members of the popular classes suffered from the difficulties that had prompted the shift to subcontracting at the Arsenal. Directly or indirectly the reduced flow of funds into the naval base edged many poorer families closer to the fine dividing line between independence and indigence. As a return to the National Assembly's Committee on Poverty emphasised in 1790: 'The Arsenal is the only hope for the less fortunate inhabitants of Toulon; as long as this huge workshop offers them employment and pays them regularly they have little reason to fear the bane of destitution.'[86] The dockyards held the key to the development of Toulon, but they were also a source of insecurity and division. For in dominating economy and society the Arsenal also impinged upon municipal politics, introduced social tensions and, ultimately, created a situation ripe for conflict.

Notes

1   Failure to take these considerations into account led the eminent historian Charles Pouthas to exaggerate the extent of demographic growth at Toulon during the first half of the nineteenth century. Pouthas suggests that the population doubled in the space of fifteen years, between 1831 and 1846, but he has arrived at this conclusion by inadvertently including the

'floating population' in 1846 while excluding it for 1831. C. Pouthas, *La population française pendant la première moitié du XIXe siècle*, Paris, 1956, pp. 118–19.

2   AM CC77, Dénombrement. The comments are those of E. Baratier, *La démographie provençale du XIIIe au XVIIe siècle, (avec chiffres de comparaison pour le XVIIIe siècle)*, Paris, 1961, p. 51

3   E. Esmonin, 'L'abbé Expilly et ses travaux de statistique', *RHMC*, VI, 1957, p. 279.

4   The 'fixed' population total includes the inmates of convents, civilian hospital, almshouse, boarding-school and prison, which housed 676 individuals in 1765. Some historians would list these as 'floating' elements, for example Agulhon, *Une ville ouvrière*, p. 39.

5   J. J. Expilly, *Dictionnaire géographique, historique et politique des Gaules et de la France*, 6 vols., Paris, 1762–70, t. 3, p. 922.

6   *Ibid., loc. cit.* Certainly the number of births *per annum* recorded at the end of the seventeenth century was not repeated with any regularity until the 1830s, to judge by tables based on parish registers and *Etat civil* in O. Teissier, *Inventaire sommaire des archives communales de Toulon antérieures à 1790*, Toulon, 1866–67, pp. 345–6. Indeed, AM CC46, Dénombrement des habitants sur la capitation, 1703, lists 6,500 male *chefs de famille*, a total well in excess of the figure for 1765.

7   G. Antrechaus, *Relation de la peste dont la ville de Toulon fut affligée en MDCCXI*, Paris, 1756, p. 46.

8   *Ibid.*, p. 339.

9   C. Carrière, M. Courdurié and F. Rebuffat, *Marseille, ville morte: la peste de 1720*, Marseille, 1968, p. 309 *et seq.*

10   AM CC323–55, Comptes de la trésorerie: piquet et mouture, 1734–66, for calculations based on grain consumption by the civilian population (i.e. excluding separately supplied fleet and garrison).

11   AM CC356–77, 1767–88.

12   AM L205, Liste des habitants, 1791 and, for the lacunae, L718, Tableau de la quantité d'isles, 1791, which is obviously drawn from the preceding source.

13   Baratier, *La démographie provençale*, p. 155.

14   J. Dupâquier, *La population française aux XVIIe et XVIIIe siècles*, Paris, 1979, pp. 91–2.

15   E. Baratier (ed.), *Histoire de la Provence*, Toulouse, 1969, p. 356, suggests that Toulon had also overtaken Aix on the eve of the Revolution, but this assertion is only true if 'floating' elements are included in the population of the naval town.

16   Dupâquier, *La population française*, p. 98 and, for a particular example, J. Rives, 'L'évolution démographique de Toulouse au XVIIIe siècle, *CHESRF, Bulletin*, 1968, pp. 129–30.

17   AM, Registres paroissiaux de Sainte-Marie et de Saint-Louis, 1765–91, the basic source, GG 249–50, Hôpital du Saint-Esprit, Registres des décès, 1762–91 and GG 253, Hôpital de la Charité, Registres des décès, 1763–91.

18   M. Garden, 'L'attraction de Lyon à la fin de l'ancien régime', *Annales*

de démographie historique, 1970, pp. 206–7.

19 W. Sewell, *Work and revolution in France. The language of labour from the old regime to 1848*, Cambridge, 1980, pp. 47–8 and M. Sonenscher, 'Journeymen's migrations and workshop organisation in eighteenth-century France', in S. Kaplan and C. Koepp (eds.), *Work in France: representation, meaning, organisation and practice*, Ithaca, 1986, pp. 74–96.

20 P. Dubois, *La vie pénible et laborieuse de Jean-Joseph Esmieu, marchand-colporteur en Provence sous la Révolution*, no place, 1967.

21 AP IAI 238, Intendant, 16 May 1786.

22 AM GG250, Registre des décès, 1789.

23 AM L392, Inscription pour le service de la garde nationale, 1791.

24 D. M. J. Henry, *L'histoire de Toulon de 1789 jusqu'au Consulat*, 2 vols., Toulon, 1861, t. 1, p. 42, a view recently reiterated, for example, by E. Coulet, 'Le massacre des administrateurs du Var, juillet 1792', *Actes du 89ᵉ Con. Nat.*, 1964, t. 1, p. 419.

25 M. Agulhon, 'Le recrutement du personnel ouvrier de l'arsenal de Toulon de 1800 à 1848', *Prov. hist.*, XII, 1962, pp. 93–111.

26 AP 2G1 17, 18 and 32, Matricules des ouvriers, 1779–1812.

27 D. Roche, 'Urban history in France', pp. 16–17 and see also J. Dupâquier, 'Problèmes de codification socio-professionnelle' in D. Roche (ed.), *L'histoire sociale. Sources et méthodes*, Paris, 1967.

28 R. Mousnier, 'Conclusion', in Mousnier (ed.), *Problèmes de stratification sociale*, Paris, 1968, p. 247 and see also M. B. Katz, 'Occupational classification in history', *Journal of Interdisciplinary History*, 3, 1972–73, pp. 70–80.

29 H. Lauvergne, *Histoire de la Révolution dans le département du Var depuis 1789 à 1794*, Toulon, 1839, pp. 6–7.

30 AM L710, Prêtres: états nominatifs, 1790–91 and M. Vovelle, 'Analyse spectrale d'un diocèse méridionale au XVIIIᵉ siècle: Aix-en-Provence', *Prov. hist.*, XXXII, 1972, p. 360.

31 AM L705, Suppression des voeux monastiques, 1790.

32 M. Bernos *et al.*, *Histoire d'Aix-en-Provence*, Aix, 1977, p. 188.

33 AM BB30, Mémoire sur le nombre de garçons.

34 M. Cubells, 'La politique d'anoblissement de la monarchie en Provence de 1715 à 1789', *Ann. Midi*, VIC, 1982. I am grateful to the author for providing me with additional details concerning Toulon.

35 AP 2E4 71, Revues et soldes, 1789.

36 AP 4A1 465–7, Etats de service de MM. les officiers de la marine, 1752–93.

37 M. Vergé, 'Les officiers de marine au XVIIIᵉ siècle', *Prov. hist.*, XXIX, 1979, pp. 206–8, an article based upon his postgraduate dissertation, 'Les officiers du grand corps à Toulon au XVIIIᵉ siècle', mémoire pour la maîtrise, University of Nice, 1973. See also Vergé, *La Royale au temps de l'amiral d'Estaing*, Paris, 1977.

38 AM BB19, Liste de nobles, officiers militaires de terre et de mer, possédant biens à Toulon, 1777.

39 AM BB95–6, Délibérations, 1777–88.

40   Lauvergne, *Histoire de la Révolution*, p. 5.

41   BN FM2 436, *La Nouvelle Harmonie* and 439, *La Parfaite Harmonie*.

42   BN FM2 434, *Les Amis Constants*, tableaux, 1780–83; 436, *Les Elèves de Minerve*, tableaux, 1781–85 and 441, *Saint-Jean de Jérusalem*.

43   BN FM2 434, *La Double Union*, tableaux, 1778–88 and 435, *Les Elèves de Mars et de Neptune*, tableaux, 1783–87.

44   AP 1A1 127, Commandant, 4 May 1786.

45   Lauvergne, *Histoire de la Révolution*, p. 5.

46   G. Lefebvre, 'Urban society in the Orléanais in the late eighteenth century', *Past and Present*, 19, 1961, p. 58, has made a similar calculation for the same strata at Orléans. Comparisons with the social structure of other towns is difficult because categorisation of the bourgeoisie is so variable. See Soboul, *La France à la veille de la Révolution, économie et société*, 2nd ed., Paris, 1974, p. 166.

47   AM AA3, Lettres patentes du roi, 1 Nov. 1776.

48   AM BB18, Liste des sujets éligibles aux offices de la communauté, 1777–88.

49   AM L202, Contribution foncière and, for a similar situation at Toulouse, J. Sentou, *Fortunes et groupes sociaux à Toulouse sous la Révolution, 1789–1799. Essai d'histoire statistique*, Toulouse, 1969, pp. 468–70.

50   AM BB19, Liste des avocats et procureurs possédant biens au terroir de Toulon, 1777–83.

51   AP 2E4 70, Revues et soldes, 1788.

52   E. Coulet, 'Un administrateur hyèrois pendant la Révolution, 1789–1796: François-Thomas Jaume', *VHG*, 1937.

53   R. Robin, *La société française en 1789: Semur-en-Auxois*, Paris, 1970, p. 39 and M. Agulhon, *La vie sociale en Provence intérieure au lendemain de la Révolution*, Paris, 1970, pp. 481–2.

54   AM AA3, Modifications aux lettres patentes du roi, 18 Sept. 1777.

55   C. F. Achard, *Dictionnaire de la Provence et du Comté-Venaissin*, 4 vols., Marseille, 1785–87, t. 2, pp. 113–14.

56   D. Roche and M. Vovelle, 'Bourgeois, rentiers et propriétaires: éléments pour la définition d'une catégorie sociale à la fin du XVII siècle', *Actes du 84ᵉ Con. Nat.*, 1959, pp. 419–21 and M. Agulhon, 'Mise au point sur les classes sociales en Provence', *Prov. hist.*, XX, 1970, p. 103.

57   Carrière, *Négociants marseillais*, t. 1, pp. 238–52.

58   AM L68(1), Délibérations du conseil municipal, 17 Mar. 1789.

59   R. Busquet, A. J. Parès and L. Roberty (eds.), *Mémoires de Louis Richaud sur la révolte de Toulon et l'émigration*, Marseille, 1930, pp. iii–iv.

60   AM BB95–6, Délibérations, 1777–89.

61   AP 2E4 70, Revues et soldes, 1788.

62   Soboul, *La France à la veille de la Révolution*, p. 186.

63   AM L39, Assemblées des corporations, Mar. 1789.

64   J. C. Perrot, 'Conflits administratifs et conflits sociaux au XVIIIᵉ siècle', *Annales de Normandie*, XIII, 1963, pp. 132–8 and G. V. Taylor, 'Non-capitalist wealth and the origins of the French Revolution', *AHR*, 72, 1967, pp. 484–6.

65   AM L392, Inscription pour le service.

66   BN FM2 434, *Les Amis Constants*.

67   BN FM2 441, *Saint-Jean de Jérusalem*.

68   BN FM2 343, *La Double Union* and 435, *Les Elèves de Mars et de Neptune*.

69   BN FM2 436, *Les Elèves de Minerve*.

70   C. E. Labrousse, 'Préface' in *Colloque d'histoire sur l'artisanat et l'apprentissage*, Aix, 1965, p. 2.

71   L. Mongin, *Toulon ancien et ses rues*, 2 vols., Draguignan, 1901, t. 1, pp. 71–2. Sadly much has been lost from AM since Mongin wrote. Only a few remnants of the once copious guild archives, listed in Teissier, *Inventaire*, pp. 357–64, have survived during the past century.

72   Sewell, *Work and revolution*, pp. 25–37 for a recent survey of this neglected subject, together with an older classic, E. Coornaert, *Les corporations en France avant 1789*, 2nd ed., Paris, 1968. Fortunately research is now being conducted in this area by several scholars: see Kaplan and Koepp (eds.), *Work in France* and M. Sonenscher, *Work and wages. Natural law, politics and the eighteenth-century French trades*, Cambridge, 1989.

73   AM L39, Cahier, for this interesting phrase. See also S. Kaplan, 'Réflexions sur la police du monde du travail, 1700–1815', *RH*, 261, 1979, pp. 17–77.

74   AM HH, Corporation des perruquiers, 16 Jan. 1770.

75   Sewell, *Work and revolution*, p. 30 but, more recently, see E. J. Shepherd, 'Social and geographic mobility of the eighteenth-century guild artisan: an analysis of guild receptions in Dijon, 1700–1790', in Kaplan and Koepp (eds.), *Work in France*, pp. 97–130.

76   Mongin, *Toulon ancien*, t. 1, pp. 71–2.

77   AP 2G1 17 and 18, Matricules and 3A1 3–6, Conseils de marine, 1776–89.

78   Loir, *La marine royale*, pp. 138–4 and N. Hampson, 'Les ouvriers des arsenaux de la marine au cours de la Révolution française, 1789–1794', *RHES*, 39, 1961, pp. 289–93.

79   AP 1A1 230, Intendant, 28 Nov. 1784 and Agulhon (ed.), *Histoire de Toulon*, p. 12.

80   AN B3 751, Etat des ouvriers; AP 2E4 70, Revues et soldes, 1788 and 2G1 17 and 18, Matricules.

81   BP, Règlement sur les payes et les avancements des gens de mer, 1 Jan. 1786; Loir, *La marine royale*, p. 132 and P. Boulanger, 'Salaires et revenus des équipages des navires marchands provençaux durant le XVIIIᵉ siècle', *Prov. hist.*, XXX, 1980, pp. 415–16.

82   J. M. Haas, 'The introduction of task work into the Royal dockyards, 1775', *Journal of British Studies*, VIII, 1969, pp. 44–53.

83   AP 1A1 228, Intendant, 7 Jan. 1776.

84   AP 3A1 3, Conseil, 11 May 1776.

85   AP 1A1 127, Commandant, 30 Apr. 1786 and 1A1 238, Intendant, 25 Jan., 26 Feb. and 2 Apr. 1786.

86   AM L740, Renseignements fournis . . . relativement à la mendicité, 1790.

Table 2　*The occupational structure of Toulon in 1765 and 1791*
(a) 1765

Category	Sections								Total	% In structure
	1	2	3	4	5	6	7	8		
1	12	10	27	8	92	92	42	139	422	8.7
2	5	4	7	3	16	20	10	20	85	1.8
3	0	3	0	2	2	2	0	2	11	0.2
4	4	9	12	21	15	5	10	4	80	1.7
5	1	5	10	5	6	4	5	1	37	0.8
6	3	12	7	12	8	9	12	15	78	1.6
7	4	5	7	4	21	13	5	0	59	1.2
8	4	4	4	32	42	9	9	3	107	2.2
9	15	24	22	23	39	27	23	31	204	4.2
10	9	19	33	66	37	24	29	34	251	5.2
11	21	45	44	55	71	54	47	28	365	7.5
12	37	54	52	31	18	31	41	20	284	5.9
13	11	35	28	27	46	34	32	29	242	5.0
14	0	2	10	2	3	2	17	4	40	0.8
15	16	24	0	19	13	11	9	8	100	2.1
16	138	88	114	63	67	113	109	112	804	16.6
17	205	65	64	70	39	82	43	26	594	12.3
18	26	66	55	48	11	16	22	19	263	5.4
19	79	48	63	82	58	95	40	96	561	11.6
20	16	29	21	42	32	38	43	37	258	5.3
Total	606	651	580	615	636	681	548	628	4,845	

Source: AM CC77, Dénombrement, 1765.

(b) 1791 (six sections only)

Category	Sections						Total	% in structure
	1	2	3	4	5	6		
1	5	20	16	15	17	33	106	2.3
2	3	7	6	1	5	7	29	0.6
3	4	6	7	3	4	11	35	0.8
4	15	31	33	18	25	16	138	3.1
5	2	4	10	10	13	5	44	1.0
6	3	11	8	7	18	10	57	1.3
7	7	5	6	12	15	12	57	1.3
8	5	14	4	32	30	12	97	2.1
9	18	38	33	41	42	49	221	4.9
10	15	72	54	74	61	39	315	7.0
11	29	82	64	85	76	52	388	8.6
12	29	59	69	43	26	36	262	5.8
13	10	26	14	15	36	19	120	2.7
14	4	16	9	12	19	15	75	1.7
15	30	50	25	37	34	13	189	4.2
16	171	122	105	90	80	150	718	15.9
17	180	73	46	80	52	70	501	11.1
18	11	58	44	32	19	10	174	3.9
19	75	111	97	90	79	138	590	13.1
20	85	80	27	55	56	93	396	8.8
Total	701	885	677	752	707	790	4,512	

Source: AM L205, Liste des habitants, 1791.

3

Tension, conflict and change, 1750–1788

'This was a time of persecution, when all the local agents of monarchical despotism, from sub-delegate to clerk, battened on the people of Toulon like tyrants.'

The naval renaissance that raised the tempo of activity at the Arsenal after the mid-eighteenth century generated economic opportunities and brought rapid demographic growth to Toulon. These develop-ments were absorbed by the urban community, but only at the expense of strained relations both within and between the major segments of society. At first glance the years following 1750 do seem to present a stable contrast to both the difficulties of earlier decades and the revolutionary upheaval that lay ahead. Yet, if there was little to suggest the impending doom of the established order at Toulon, the surface calm was deceptive. Closer examination reveals under-lying conflicts, which arose from the changing balance of power in the city. The military and municipal elites were at odds with each other and protests from the latter provoked unprecedented interven-tion on the part of central government. Meanwhile the popularity of new forms of sociability and the circulation of secular ideas were producing a significant shift in collective attitudes.

The effects of naval expansion were felt, first and foremost inside the service, among its leading personnel. The great programme of reconstruction set in train during the 1750s was accompanied by a series of reforms which reflected the innovatory spirit abroad in government circles.[1] At that point the French navy still bore the imprint of its chief architect, J. B. Colbert. Dockyard administration was regulated by his Ordinance of 1689, which accorded full sway to the naval *intendant* and restricted the authority of seagoing officers to ships under sail. This separation of powers was intended to minimise the occasion for dispute inside the Arsenal, but it only served to draw lines of battle between *la plume*, or pen-pushers, as administrators were often called, and *l'épée*, the sword-wielding or military arm. Choiseul, first in the series of reforming eighteenth-century naval ministers, believed that the division of sovereignty had inhibited co-operation and impaired efficiency. In 1765 he awarded naval officers a share of responsibility in the construction and maintenance of the ships they commanded. The balance swung decisively in favour of *l'épée* in 1776, when Sartine extended military authority and confined *la plume* to the relatively minor role of purveying materials, paying wages and funding ancillary services such as the hospitals or prison hulks. The naval *commandant*, or commander-in-chief ashore, thus supplanted the *intendant* as head of the dockyard hierarchy.

These changes severely damaged the career prospects of administrative officials, as well as lowering their status inside the Arsenal. At Toulon the corps of thirty *commissaires* was reduced by half in the space of a decade.[2] Though *plume* personnel remained relatively well paid, their hostility towards overbearing military officers impeded the development of a harmonious working relationship at the dockyards. According to the naval historian, Vincent Brun, who refers to *épée* and *plume* as 'two different breeds of men', violence between individuals from the rival branches was not uncommon.[3] Friction was certainly evident in the administrative arena. Dockyard councils, established after 1765 as a formal point of contact for military and civilian officials, were sometimes the scene of bitter disputes.

Feelings ran especially high during the late 1780s when plans for expansion had to be scaled down due to financial difficulties. In the autumn of 1785, for example, a sub-committee was appointed to consider economy measures at Toulon. Not only did representatives of *plume* and *épée* disagree over the nature of savings to be made, but a civilian *commissaire* and a *lieutenant de vaisseau* vied for the honour of reporting back to the full council. The presiding *commandant* ruled in favour of the lieutenant on the grounds that 'military personnel always take priority over civilians'.[4] Malouet, the *intendant*, was outraged and asked the naval minister whether this ruling rendered him personally subordinate to the most junior rating. Were that the case, he concluded, France would quickly degenerate into a 'military despotism'.

Malouet, later elected to the Estates General where he argued in favour of a restoration of civilian ascendancy in the royal dockyards, was no impartial observer. Yet there was much truth in his claim that the new administrative system at the Arsenal 'increased costs . . . and caused endless disputes between officials of the two branches, which hinder operations'.[5] Since he was a commoner, like many of his pen-pushing colleagues, it is tempting to attribute tension between *plume* and *épée* to differences in social origin: noble officers opposing non-noble officials. But closer inspection suggests that departmental rivalry between robe and sword elements within the service aristocracy offers a more convincing explanation. Over half the *commissaires* at Toulon in 1789 were nobles and Malouet's successor as *intendant de marine*, J. P. Possel, was a local nobleman with relatives among the military. Whatever their birth, high-ranking civilian officials had obtained their posts via a privileged route and they were just as vulnerable to revolutionary demands for careers 'open to the talents' as seagoing officers.[6] The headway made by *l'épée* in the late eighteenth century was a recognition of their growing professionalism, the result of improved training and greater operational success. It did not constitute a clear-cut 'noble reaction' any more than similar, contemporary developments in the French army.[7]

The military branch of the navy was not socially homogeneous either and it also underwent considerable change during the closing decades of the *ancien régime*. Seagoing officers regarded harbour-masters and engineers, over whom they had recently acquired jurisdiction, as mere 'technicians' and they felt much the same about artillerymen. Most notorious of all on the upper deck was the division between *officiers rouges* and *officiers bleus*. The former, distinguished by a red detail in their uniforms, comprised the elite or *grand corps* of the French navy. Almost without exception they had been through the exclusive cadet schools where admission demanded a noble pedigree, good connections and a modicum of wealth (though naval commissions could not be purchased any more than naval administrative posts). The *bleus*, by contrast, wore an entirely blue uniform and were usually recruited among officers in the merchant marine. They generally held temporary, wartime commissions and otherwise continued to pursue a commercial career. Only a small number remained on the navy's books as auxiliaries with intermediary grades, such as *lieutenant de frégate* or *capitaine de brûlot*, and still fewer received a full commission.

Friction between *rouges* and *bleus* has been viewed as another manifestation of social antagonism between noble and commoner.[8]

In fact a significant minority of the merchant officers, like a small contingent of 'volunteers' who lacked both cadet training and commercial experience, were of noble extraction. Tension should instead be attributed to the professional *esprit de corps* that was instilled into *officiers rouges* by the cadet schools and directed against all outsiders. Those with a commercial background bore the brunt of their scorn, but noble officers who transferred from the line army and retained their grade were especially resented as 'intruders'. Hence the prejudice initially heaped upon the Comte d'Estaing, an outstanding naval commander in the American War.[9]

On the eve of the Revolution, however, the status of *officiers bleus* was transformed. The organisation of a bigger, modern fleet required a properly constituted reserve force instead of earlier piecemeal arrangements. During the American campaign unprecedented numbers of auxiliaries had been enrolled, including fifty at Toulon alone and, in 1786, the Duc de Castries completed the gradual process of integration adumbrated by his ministerial predecessors.[10] Many nobles continued to enjoy direct admission to the *grand corps* via exclusive cadet schools, but greater reliance was placed upon reservists, drawn from commerce or recruited as volunteers, who were awarded the new rank of *sous-lieutenant de vaisseau*. Equally important was the opportunity for these sub-lieutenants to ascend the hierarchy as lieutenants and captains, 'if their record or outstanding acts of bravery entitle them to such promotion'.

The *bleus* disappeared, though entry to the *grand corps* remained bifurcated, with noble cadets taking an express route to the upper deck. For the forty-eight sub-lieutenants enlisted at Toulon in 1789 promotion was a relatively distant prospect, but nine former auxiliaries had already become lieutenants, five of them non-nobles with commercial training.[11] These newcomers were few in number and none was aged under forty, yet they would not have progressed so far in the past. An occasional commoner had joined the naval establishment, like L. J. Truguet whose son became an admiral and then naval minister during the 1790s.[12] But merchant captains and volunteers now enjoyed enhanced opportunities, as did petty officers (*maîtres d'équipage*) and pilots, who also became eligible for selection as *sous-lieutenants*. Another Toulonnais who was made an admiral during the Revolution, P. Martin, had begun his rise from the lower deck as a humble *pilote*.

Martin would probably not have achieved so much in the absence of revolutionary upheaval, which overturned the new career structure before its worth had been tested. Yet, as Brun concludes, the naval hierarchy 'became more, rather than less accessible after 1786'.[13] The opening of the noble- dominated *grand corps* to wider recruitment throws additional doubt upon the thesis of a 'noble reaction' in eighteenth-century France.[14] Some aristocratic officers were moved to protest against the Castries reform, among them the Chevalier de Sade, who was based at the Mediterranean *port de guerre*.[15] On the other hand, commoners in the Atlantic ports remained dissatisfied with residual discrimination against those who had not trained as noble cadets.[16] No such grievance has been unearthed at Toulon, where the urban *cahier de doléances* of 1789 passed over the subject in silence, although civilians continued to regard naval officers as a domineering, aristocratic elite.[17]

Subsequent reactions to the Revolution do not suggest that the new arrangements significantly weakened solidarity among naval personnel. The proportion of non-noble officers who withdrew after 1789 equalled that of their aristocratic counterparts. The breakdown of discipline within the navy and mounting hostility from civilians were as much responsible for resignations as the egalitarian reform of the officer class in 1792.[18] Internecine feuds often disrupted the French navy during the great pre-revolutionary period of change, yet a service ethos had been forged which ultimately bound together all branches and grades. It is easy to exaggerate the degree of interdepartmental antagonism and to ignore the extent of co-operation and concerted effort. A shared feeling of pride and self-confidence resulted from victory in the American War. In the face of civil unrest which threatened the fabric of the navy in 1789, *intendant* and *commandant* stood shoulder to shoulder at Toulon, literally closing ranks, regardless of their occasional differences.

Relations with the local community were increasingly strained. The growth of the Arsenal and the garrison during the late eighteenth century had elevated the numbers and inflated the pretensions of the service aristocracy at Toulon. Confrontation frequently occurred with a municipality that was determined to maintain its traditional authority, in spite of the shifting balance of power. The most bitter incident arose in 1783 and concerned the local bread supply.[19] It began when *intendant* Malouet issued loaves baked in shipyard ovens to all employees of the Arsenal because he was so disgusted by the quality of bread on sale in the town. His unilateral action provoked an immediate riposte from the municipality, which could ill afford to lose a major source of revenue (for, unlike civilian imports, naval grain was not subject to local taxation). No sooner had this controversy subsided, with the municipal council promising stricter supervision of bakeries, than the naval administration sought to acquire the civilian almshouse of La Charité as a hospital. Town councillors were adamant in their refusal to exchange or sell the property and Malouet decided to convert the vacant Jesuit seminary instead.[20]

Maurice Agulhon suggests that Toulon was 'perhaps the only town in Provence where nobility and third estate were deeply divided', yet the essence of such conflicts lay in hostility between service aristocracy and urban notables, between rival military and municipal elites.[21] Dockyard and garrison had long engaged in a cold war with the *hôtel de ville*. Officers and administrators in the armed forces were unanimous in regarding the town council as a parochial body, whose narrow-minded members delighted in frustrating worthy defenders of the realm. The naval *commandant* summed up this general exasperation when he wrote in 1781: 'Those gentlemen at the council house who, for all sorts of reasons, ought to be giving us still more privileges in the town, are always seeking to reduce our rights; they would suppress them completely if they had the power to do so.'[22]

Until the Revolution afforded a brief opportunity to stem the tide, the Toulonnais notables fought a losing battle to retain the full range of their municipal powers. Since the seventeenth century towns everywhere in France had come under mounting administrative pressure from the crown.[23] Situated in a peripheral *pays d'états*, remote from Versailles, the municipalities of Provence were in a good position to resist encroachment upon their traditional 'liberties', but the centralising impetus was particularly acute at Toulon. In the naval town military considerations were used to justify a greater measure of royal intervention than elsewhere in the region. The establishment of the Arsenal began a process of attrition which was marked symbolically, in 1679, by the surrender of town keys to a resident garrison commander.[24] For the remainder of the *ancien régime* the city fathers' role in protecting and policing Toulon was purely honorific.

After the effective installation of a provincial *intendant* at Aix, in 1673, and the subsequent despatch of a sub-delegate to Toulon, further inroads were made by the crown.[25] A series of sales of municipal office, that commenced as a fiscal expedient in 1690, caused financial disarray which then served as the pretext for still closer control. In 1713, for example, an edict ordered the town council at Toulon to submit all extraordinary items of expenditure to the *intendant*.[26] The central government also began to vet newly-elected Toulonnais personnel and another threshold of intervention was crossed in 1738 when municipal regulations were altered to create a fourth consul. All these changes were later incorporated into the electoral statute of 1754, in which the monarchy justified increasing supervision as a means of ensuring 'the good of the armed forces', besides that of the urban community.[27]

The subordination of local interests to those of the military was anathema to the Toulonnais notables. They clung to the belief, trenchantly articulated in 1771, that 'The municipalities of Provence are entitled to make the administrative arrangements which suit their local circumstances best. This right is part of public law in the province and constitutes the inalienable patrimony of its communities.'[28] This *cri de coeur* represented an appeal to a Provençal particularism that was frequently asserted in opposition to monarchical centralisation.[29] During the second half of the eighteenth century, under the sympathetic intendancy of Charles Galois de la Tour, the erosion of local autonomy was more successfully resisted. For instance, the Laverdy edict of 1765, which sought to apply a uniform system of municipal administration throughout France, was rejected in Provence and fresh sales of offices were also avoided soon afterwards.[30] Yet Toulon, a port city in period of continuous naval activity, was unable to escape the crown's tighter grasp. Resistance was mounted, but it merely hastened the advent of more comprehensive controls.

The rising discontent of the Toulonnais bourgeoisie came to focus upon a local barrister named Mourchou. Though not a member of the urban oligarchy he was appointed town archivist in 1753 and thus joined the council. Six years later a royal edict made him *procureur du roi en la police* as well.[31] This judicial post had always been in the gift of the patricians and was subject to annual renewal, but it was conferred upon Mourchou for life. The newcomer was a close friend of the sub-delegate at Toulon, nominated at the behest of the *intendant*. Evidently the monarchy was seeking to undermine the municipality by the insertion of a placeman, who was entrusted with the business of record-keeping and endowed with police powers. Notables in the naval port were losing control of their own destiny, a development which was emphasised in 1768 when the unpopular archivist was allowed to select a deputy and successor.[32] It only took the difficult economic and political circumstances of the early 1770s to touch off a minor municipal rebellion at Toulon.

The protest exploded against a background of poor harvests which hit municipal finances, as taxes on grain imports declined and bread prices had to be subsidised. At the same moment the central government's draconian administrative reforms led to the suspension of both *parlement* and *intendant* in Provence.[33] When Louis XVI succeeded to the throne in 1774, a change of policy was expected and, at Toulon, grievances were brought to the fore in anticipation of a favourable response. Hyacinthe Paul, barrister and town councillor, seized the opportunity to demand the removal of both Mourchou and his deputy, Beaudin. Indeed, on 25 July, Paul persuaded his municipal colleagues to begin the process of expelling the two men but the central government, far from endorsing the initiative, ordered immediate reinstatement of the infamous pair who were now frankly described as 'our royal servants'.[34] All but a handful of Toulonnais council members were dismissed and a caretaker body was established to conduct the municipal administration until, in 1776, the crown issued a fresh town charter.[35]

Slightly modified the following year these new regulations were, so the preamble asserted, designed to 'establish greater harmony among administrators and to improve administrative procedures'. This justification was accepted at face value by Gustave Lambert, for he wrote in his monumental *Histoire de Toulon*: 'In 1774 . . . the disarray was such that Louis XVI was obliged to dismiss two consuls and ten councillors from their posts . . . self-interest and caprice dominated the administration . . . municipal business was totally neglected.'[36] A rump of two consuls and three councillors remained in office, but this was because they favoured a less abrasive approach. There is no evidence of negligence or self-seeking on the part of those dismissed, nor of any social distinction between the docile minority and the hawkish majority on the council. Paul, who led the revolt, did become the Jacobin mayor of revolutionary Toulon, but his close accomplice in 1774 was a nobleman who emigrated during the 1790s. Any disorder within the municipality must, therefore, be blamed upon an interfering government which eagerly seized on the protest as the pretext for further inroads into the town's autonomy.

The system imposed upon Toulon in 1776 retained the basic structure of its predecessors. In keeping with the traditions of the Midi the council was headed by consuls, who chaired meetings, supervised officials and represented the town in civic rituals at home and away.[37] Supplementary instructions of 1777 reduced the consular quartet at Toulon to a more customary trio, whose term of office lasted twelve months. A dozen councillors were elected for two years, one half of them to be replaced each year. It was the gathering of consuls and councillors, together with secretary, treasurer and archivist, which constituted the 'ordinary' council that dealt with most municipal business. This body was expanded into a 'general' council, to discuss more weighty matters, by the addition of eighteen *conseillers adjoints*. As elsewhere in Provence, these deputy councillors were also summoned when the general council served as an electoral college, to select fresh personnel for the coming calendar year.[38]

An important innovation of 1776 lay in the extension of access to the deputy-councillorship. It was widened to embrace occupational groups outside the charmed circle of patricians who continued to monopolise the posts of consul and councillor proper. The monarchy was evidently eager to involve the minor liberal professions and the leading retailers in the municipal administration, perhaps as a counter-weight to more established but disaffected elements. While the full councillorship demanded a high level of local property ownership, occupation alone was deemed a sufficient criterion for *conseillers adjoints*. Whereas in the past deputy-councillors had been chosen indiscriminately, a quota system now guaranted places for the newly-admitted professional categories.[39] Above all the regulations requiring the convocation of general councils were deliberately stiffened, so that *adjoints* would be summoned to meetings more frequently in future. Between 1777 and the outbreak of the Revolution over 50 per cent of all council meetings were *conseils généraux*, compared to a mere 3 per cent during the preceding twenty years.[40]

Deputy-councillors played an even greater role under the new charter than these figures would suggest because many of them were called upon to make up a quorum at ordinary council meetings

Table 3 Office-holding in the Municipality of Toulon, 1755–1789

| Occupation | Posts of Consul and Councillor | | | | | | Proportion of those eligible in 1788 (%) |
| | 1755–1775 | | 1777–1789 | | Overall | | |
	No.	%	No.	%	No.	%	
Civilian nobles	19	10.4	3	2.4	22	7.1	4
Retired military officers	17	9.3	10	8.0	27	8.8	18
Retired royal administrators	14	7.7	18	14.4	32	10.4	15
Rentiers	30	16.4	19	15.2	49	15.9	17
Barristers & notaries	27	14.8	18	14.4	45	14.6	14
Doctors	10	5.5	2	1.6	12	3.9	4
Merchants	66	36.1	35	28.0	101	32.8	28
Retailers	–	–	8	6.4	8	2.6	–
Surgeons	–	–	2	1.6	2	0.8	–
Total	183		125		308		

Note: Deputy-councillors (*adjoints*) have not been included here since their occupational composition was fixed by Letters Patent.

Source: AM BB12, Listes des officiers municipaux élus, 1754–88 and BB18, Listes des sujets éligibles, 1754–88.

convoked after 1777. Such recourse to *adjoints* had rarely been necessary before. Thus, unintentionally as well as deliberately, government legislation broadened the municipal oligarchy at Toulon; less prestigious elements of the urban elite were able to acquire administrative experience as a result. This development paved the way for further changes during the Revolution, but its immediate consequence was to increase the feeling of alienation already manifest among the Toulonnais notables. Outright protest had failed so discontent took the passive form of boycott, reflected in lower attendance at fewer council meetings. Consuls continued to participate fully, but the average for councillors fell below 50 per cent, compared to almost 80 per cent prior to 1776. Deputy-councillors were often equally remiss and on several occasions former councillors had to be summoned to *conseils généraux*. Disinclination to serve on the remodelled municipality is also evident in the failure of notables to register their eligibility for office on the civic roll, or *Livre d'Or*.[41] Less than half of those who were inscribed took any active part between 1778 and 1789, for the various offices were held by less than 100 different individuals.

Members of the Toulonnais elite naturally resented being downgraded into 'unpaid civil servants'.[42] As much in spite, rather than because of more rigorous governmental guidelines, municipal business at Toulon continued to be despatched with efficiency. Until the very end of the *ancien régime* income kept abreast of expenditure and some 500,000 *livres* were handled each year without a trace of peculation.[43] Besides maintaining existing commitments the council also undertook several initiatives in the 1770s and 1780s. Support was given to manufacturing, education and poor relief, while a strenuous effort was made to improve the urban environment. More might have been achieved had the monarchy and armed forces not prevented another aggrandisement of the town, or an extension of port facilities. The suspicion that urban interests were being sacrificed to those of the Arsenal was confirmed when, in 1780 and again in 1781, the annual renewal of the municipal council was suspended in order to preserve administrative continuity at the height of the American War.[44]

In 1789, when the Toulonnais notables were given the opportunity to voice their dissatisfaction, they protested bitterly against 'the unwarranted and vicious system of 1776' and demanded the right to 'draw up a new statute more in keeping with the real interests of the municipality'.[45] Needless to say they closely identified these interests with their own. In return for losing much of their autonomy, members of the urban elite had procured one important privilege during the eighteenth century: permission to pay the town's taxes to the crown as a lump sum, or *abonnement*. From the 1730s onwards the *taille* and *capitation*, the main impositions, were recovered by a series of indirect local levies, chiefly upon foodstuffs. This system allowed wealthier inhabitants to protect property and income from all forms of direct taxation. As one regional historian puts it: 'In the guise of fiscal justice the notables were dispensed from the greater part of the burden they would have borne if the *taille* had been in force.'[46] A report to the National Assembly's committee on poverty, drawn up at Toulon in 1790, candidly admitted 'that the poor, being great consumers of bread and wine, are obliged to bear almost all of the tax load'.[47]

This regressive fiscal system was a basic cause of riots in the town in the spring of 1789. It also had unforeseen electoral repercussions during the Revolution when, in the absence of tax rolls, franchise restrictions could not be imposed. However, until the very end of the *ancien régime* the popular classes acquiesced in both the unfair incidence of taxation and their exclusion from the municipal administration. The medieval assembly of 'all heads of household' had ceased to decide municipal elections long before the regulations of 1609 explicitly restricted participation to certain occupations.[48] Yet the infamous royal charter of 1776 retained provision for an 'expanded' town council, which included delegates from various professional bodies and artisan guilds. It was actually convened several times in the late 1780s in response to the deepening political crisis of those years.

It is difficult to discern many signs of tension between popular classes and bourgeoisie at Toulon before the outbreak of the Revolution. There is, for example, no evidence that the notables actively encouraged or even desired the abolition of the trade guilds. In 1789 support for these bodies was perhaps inserted in the urban *cahier* of Toulon out of prudence, yet thirteen years earlier the municipal oligarchy had strongly resisted Turgot's abortive dissolution edict. Conflict had subsequently occurred with the bakers' guild over the quality of bread, but this was an isolated incident.[49] The Toulonnais *corporations* were certainly troubled by mounting indebtedness, which had risen to an average of over 5,000 *livres* for

each association in the 1780s.[50] Nonetheless the artisan corporations survived and even acquired a renewed, if short-lived importance in municipal affairs in 1788 and 1789, while also participating
in elections to the Estates General.

Notables in the naval town had, by contrast, been anxious to
disband another type of popular organisation, the penitent fraternity. These products of what Maurice Agulhon calls 'Mediterranean
sociability' and 'baroque piety' flourished in the seventeenth
century, when at least one *confrérie de pénitents* had been established in every Provençal community.[51] There were four at Toulon,
denoted by the colour of their robes and variously concerned with
devotional activities, charitable endeavour and mutual aid. Most
celebrated of all was their participation in festivals and funeral pro-
cessions, when they displayed their full hooded garb. As the
eighteenth century progressed the penitents were denounced as
relics of superstition by enlightened opinion, while the ecclesiastical
authorities came to consider them a distraction from, rather than a
contribution to parochial life.

The Toulonnais municipal council, which cast a jealous eye upon
the fraternities' property, sought to exploit this growing
unpopularity. In January 1789 letters patent were obtained to
dissolve 'whites' and 'blues'.[52] The intended victims put up some
spirited resistance and it is said they helped foment the disturbances
which erupted at Toulon in March (although several aggrieved
groups were alleged to have played a similar rôle).[53] The revolutionary upheaval subsequently produced a short respite but the penitents, ultimately disbanded in 1793, were in an advanced state of
decay. The black penitents had already disappeared in 1780 and the
'greys' were struggling to survive.[54]

Membership lists are not available for Toulon, but surviving
shreds of evidence support Agulhon's general conclusion that,
towards the end of the *ancien régime*, bourgeois in Provence were
deserting the penitent fraternities in favour of masonic lodges.[55] In
1789 the Toulonnais *pénitents* were led by craftsmen and small
shopkeepers, while roughly one in four of the local notables was
attracted to freemasonry. Masonry struck deep roots in Lower Provence and by the late 1780s members of the popular classes were
also adhering to the lodges in large numbers. Unlike Lyon, for
example, some 25 per cent of 495 Toulonnais masons were clerks,
master artisans and shopkeepers.[56] Ironically it was from one of the

Table 4 The occupational structure of freemasonry at Toulon in the 1780s

Lodge	Military officers	Leading admini- strators	Rentiers	Liberal professions	Merchants	Retailers	Clerks	Artisans/ shop- keepers	Soldiers	Priests	Total
Les Amis Constants	2	–	4	10	23	10	4	2	–	–	55
La Double Union	18	2	2	2	9	14	19	42	–	1	109
Les Elèves de Mars et de Neptune	–	–	7	2	3	2	5	12	40	1	72
Les Elèves de Minerve	3	–	2	6	7	16	16	18	–	–	68
La Nouvelle Harmonie	81	6	–	–	3	–	–	–	–	1	91
La Parfaite Harmonie	59	11	–	–	–	–	–	–	–	–	70
Le Saint-Jean de Jérusalem	–	2	1	8	12	–	–	1	–	–	24*
Total	163	21	16	28	57	42	44	75	40	3	489
Percentage	33.3	4.3	3.3	5.7	11.7	8.6	9.0	15.3	8.2	0.6	–

Note: * Not including 13 Dutch merchant officiers.
Source: BN FM2, Loges maçonniques de Toulon.

lower-class lodges, *Les Elèves de Minerve*, that a complaint was made concerning breaches of masonic secrecy, because membership had been 'opened to all and sundry'.[57]

Lodges were first founded at Toulon in the 1750s, but only three seem to have lasted into the 1780s, when another four affiliated to the Grand Orient.[58] Like so much else, the fortunes of freemasonry in the town were at the mercy of dockyard activity. The early spate of foundations owed much to naval influence and flourished with the increase in operations at the Arsenal after mid-century. Mobilisation for the American War brought a fresh wave of recruits, especially among military officers: no less than 40 per cent of all known masons were drawn from the service aristocracy. Masonry peaked in 1786, when reductions at the dockyards caused a decline that was sealed by the Revolution. A correspondent from *La Parfaite Harmonie* attributed difficulties at his lodge in the late 1780s to 'the absence of many members, who have no reason to remain at Toulon'.[59] Equally, as a former *élève de Minerve* put it, participation decreased because 'we had much more urgent and important matters to attend to than those of freemasonry'.[60]

Since masonry was a casualty of the revolutionary upheaval, and it had been dominated by the aristocracy, it can hardly be viewed as an overtly subversive organisation as some have argued. What freemasonry offered was sociability in a secular context; the wide network of contacts it provided was especially attractive to mobile groups in the population, like military personnel or businessmen. The constitution established by *Les Amis Constants*, for example, required members to respect magistrates and uphold the law, for monarchs were 'God's representatives on earth'; it is no surprise to find the same lodge celebrating a mass for the birth of the *dauphin* in 1781.[61] Of late, however, historians have posited an indirect masonic contribution to the origins of the Revolution, in so far as lodges constituted an independent and federated forum for the discussion of public affairs.[62] The naval *commandant* therefore had some justification for his alarm at the existence of a reading room in Toulon, which was probably of masonic origin.[63] The naval port possessed no academy nor library, nor was a newspaper produced in the town. Yet there was a local audience for new ideas: Robert Darnton has discovered twenty-one Toulonnais subscribers to the quarto edition of the *Encyclopédie*.[64]

The most striking characteristic of Toulonnais masons was not their politics but their youthfulness. In four out of five lodges, where age was recorded on entry, the overwhelming majority were in their twenties or thirties. This rising generation of Frenchmen was abandoning the values of its elders, in a manner indicated by Michel Vovelle's study of changing attitudes towards death in eighteenth-century Provence. Vovelle estimates that at mid-century some 90 per cent of Toulonnais testators, representing the same occupational groups from which masons were recruited, solicited requiem masses in their wills. The proportion fell to a mere 30 per cent at the end of the *ancien régime*, a bigger drop than the one recorded at Marseille, so often the provincial trend-setter.[65] The same slide was also apparent in the index of charitable bequests at Toulon, with the percentage of testators making donations falling from a mid-century peak of over 50 per cent, to below 20 per cent on the eve of the Revolution.[66] It would be wrong to automatically equate this evolution in *mentalités* with the progress of dechristianisation. The abandonment of 'baroque' religious practice may reflect a simpler, more personal form of piety, owing as much to Jansenism as to secular influences.

Although the spirit of Catholic reform often encouraged intolerance, it had facilitated the development of popular education at Toulon. In mid-century Christian Brothers, like Christian Sisters before them, responded to the municipality's invitation to establish a free primary school in Toulon.[67] Their efforts may have contributed to the rising proportion of signatures in the parish registers: the number of males married at Toulon, who were able to sign their names, rose steadily from 49 per cent in the 1720s to 59 by the mid-1780s. While figures for women continued to lag far behind those for men, a proportionally greater increase was recorded, from 13 to 23 per cent. When immigrants are removed, and the calculation is restricted to those of Toulonnais birth, the male literacy rate rises to almost 70 per cent. This was not a 'cultural revolution' but, by the standards of a backward South of France, it represented considerable progress.[68]

Since major advances were made in the world of shopkeepers and artisans, while wage-earners and rural workers marked time, it is tempting to correlate the development of 'dechristianisation' with that of rising literacy. Agulhon suggests that both penitent and occupational fraternities were becoming secularised, while masonry found fertile soil in the same artisan *milieux*.[69] In 1770, a municipal memorandum asserted that Toulon 'has always been one of the most Catholic towns in the entire kingdom', but this was a reference to the absence of Protestantism.[70] The chronology of conceptions revealed by the parish registers suggests that sexual abstinence was greater in summer, rather than during Advent and Lent as the church recommended.[71] Weddings were rarely celebrated at these points in the Christian calendar, yet this was simply a result of priests' refusal to conduct the ceremony, not obedience to ecclesiastical teaching. When civil registration of marriages was instituted after 1792 the clerical ban was completely disregarded.

Toulon, like Lower Provence in general, was ceasing to produce many of its own clergy.[72] One explanation for the failure of the church to maintain its influence in the naval port resides in its inability to cope with a fast-growing, mobile population. Not only was manpower deficient and financial resources limited, but the small ecclesiastical establishment was plagued by internal disputes. Overworked priests in the two huge urban parishes of Toulon were all subsisting on the *portion congrue*, a meagre stipend administered by the relatively affluent cathedral chapter. During the final decade of the *ancien régime* Toulonnais *curés* and *vicaires* began to campaign for salaries more worthy of their vocation, joining forces with *congruistes* elsewhere in Provence and winning a substantial rise in 1786.[73] In the process the *curés* of Sainte-Marie had even threatened a 'work to rule' unless their pay and lodgings were improved. The disaffected pair complained that they were treated like servants by their capitular and episcopal superiors and associated themselves with widespread demands for involvement in the administration of the church.[74] Such discontent naturally found further expression during clerical elections to the Estates General in 1789.

The regular clergy at Toulon were better endowed than their secular counterparts yet, the use of their convents for public worship apart, they offered little support. Compared to John McManners' fascinating personalities in late eighteenth-century Angers Toulonnais regulars were a dull lot, neither erudite nor extrovert.[75] With the exception of those involved in education, male orders in the naval town were in pronounced decline and few monks opted to uphold their vows when given the chance to quit in 1790. Only three were under thirty years old and their average age was fifty-six.[76] Nearly all nuns, whose numbers had remained stable, resolved to stay put, but they too were generally elderly.

Even before the Revolution convents had been under threat, not only from military and municipal authorities eager to acquire their valuable intramural properties, but also from an unsympathetic bishop and chapter. It was the Bishop of Toulon who sought to shuffle around Carmelites and Capuchins in order to obtain land for the new parish church of Saint-Louis, but the Capuchins refused to be rehoused in the Carmelites' old quarters until they were forcibly evicted in 1781.[77] Apparently they took their revenge on the bishop during the disturbances of spring 1789. The Recollects were also earmarked for removal, to make way for a diocesan seminary, while the cathedral chapter was seeking to disperse the Dominicans in order to pay parish priests their increased stipend from the proceeds.[78]

With its clergy engaged in unseemly wrangles, unable to resist the tide of secularisation, Toulon had begun to rival Marseille as a lost cause for the church. Of course, the rising incidence of prostitution, illegitimate births and abandoned babies owed as much, perhaps more, to mounting poverty than to changes in attitudes and beliefs. The first of these social problems was inevitable in a port city which hosted both a naval base and an army garrison. Concern over the number of prostitutes was always especially intense during and after periods of mobilisation.[79] In the 1760s many *filles publiques* were arrested and whipped in public then, in the early 1780s, the recently appointed *chasse-mendiant* filled the prisons with such women as well as sturdy beggars. The influx of footloose sailors, soldiers and dockyard workers was also reflected in the annual numbers of pregnant girls who entered a special ward at the *Hôtel-Dieu* for their confinement. Their numbers rose steadily from twenty-seven in the early 1770s to thirty-eight a year in the late 1780s.[80] Over the same period the proportion of children born out of wedlock, or simply abandoned, increased from 11.5 to 15.5 per cent of baptisms per annum.

Poverty was doubtless as much to blame as immorality, for many *enfants trouvés* were probably of legitimate but impoverished parentage.[81] The economic crisis of the late 1780s also left its mark on the total of patients received at the Saint-Esprit hospital. From the beginning to the end of the decade admissions increased dramatically, from 500 to 800 a year.[82] Whereas some 8,000 *livres* of outdoor relief was distributed annually by the town's *bureau de charité* (or *Miséricorde*) in the 1760s, that figure had risen to 19,000 *livres* just two decades later. In 1790 some 1,500 inhabitants were apparently receiving assistance.[83] Altogether, towards the end of the *ancien régime*, even a conservative estimate suggests that one in ten Toulonnais was dependent upon some element of charitable support.

In the naval town a general recession was deepened by demobilisation after the American War, which had generated unprecedented prosperity. It was intended to continue construction work at a relatively high level, but funds were not always forthcoming and economy measures were accompanied by the implementation of subcontracting for dockyard labour. Under the *système d'entreprises* master artisans, or in some cases groups of workers, began to tender for the various shipbuilding tasks. The *intendant* expressed grave misgivings about the keeness of the competition. Some regular dockyard workers were forced to 'submit bids at completely unrealistic prices' in a vain effort to remain active.[84] As anticipated, 'subcontractors employed fewer workers and they only took on the most skilful'.[85] It was decided to pay a small retainer to some 500 unemployed craftsmen and to offer a subsidy to contractors to train apprentices, 'the seedplot of tomorrow's shipwrights'. These palliatives were introduced by *intendant* Malouet partly out of paternalism ('society has a duty to support all its members'), but mainly because he feared the loss of a skilled reserve which would be needed again in the event of war.[86]

Malouet's successor subsequently admitted that 'since its inception the system of subcontracting has disaffected the greater part of the work-force'.[87] As early as 1786 it was reported that 200 workers had demonstrated angrily against subcontracting and ill-feeling grew when many contracts were not renewed the following year.[88] As government funds were exhausted, so the coffers of the Toulonnais Arsenal emptied. Remuneration at the dockyards had often been tardy but, during the closing years of the *ancien régime*, delays became intolerable. In November 1788 contractors could only be paid for the preceding July, day labourers for August.[89] Malouet was powerless to remedy the situation and he correctly predicted the consequences when he wrote, 'there is a spirit of rebellion abroad and we are incapable of controlling it'.[90]

At Toulon, as elsewhere, the pre-revolutionary period duly culminated in an explosion of popular wrath. The misery of the late 1780s pulled into focus the various problems which had been accumulating over the preceding decades. The unparalleled importance attributed to the French navy after 1763 had brought great economic and demographic growth to Toulon, but only at the cost of worsening relations between the different sections of urban society. Governmental efforts to arbitrate only served to add a further layer of conflict, at a time when established institutions of the regime like the church came under severe pressure from rising population and changing beliefs. It was the interaction of these underlying urban tensions with a national political crisis, in 1789, which unexpectedly precipitated the total collapse of the old order.

Notes

1 Loir, *La marine royale*, provides a general introduction, but see also G. Lacour-Gayet, *La marine militaire de la France sous le règne de Louis XV*, 2nd ed., Paris, 1910; Lacour-Gayet, *La marine militaire de la France sous le règne de Louis XVI*, Paris, 1905; J. Pritchard, *Louis XV's navy, 1748–1762: A study of organisation and administration*, Montreal, 1987 and, above all, Acerra and Meyer, *Marines et Révolution*.

2 AP 2E4 50–71, Revues et soldes, 1775–89.

3 Brun, *Port de Toulon*, t. 1, p. 399.

4 AP 1A1 237, Intendant, 18 Dec. 1785.

5 P. V. Malouet, *Mémoires*, 2 vols., Paris, 1874, t. 1, pp. 181–2.

6 AM L76, Doléances des commis de marine, 6 Oct. 1789.

7 D. Bien, 'The army in the French enlightenment: reform, reaction and revolution', *Past and Present*, 85, 1979, pp. 68–98.

8 J. Aman, *Les officiers bleus dans la marine française du XVIIIe siècle*, Geneva, 1976, provides an invaluable corrective.

9 L. Levy-Schneider, *Le conventionnel Jeanbon Saint-André*, 2 vols., Paris, 1901, t. 1, pp. 293–4 and Brun, *Port de Toulon*, t. 2, p. 106.

10 BP Règlement sur les états majors et équipages, 1 Jan. 1786; M. Leclère, 'Les réformes de Castries, 14 octobre 1780–23 août 1787', *Revue des questions historiques*, 128, 1937, pp. 52–6 and Aman, *Les officiers bleus*, pp. 146–51.

11 AP 4A1 465–6, Etats de service.

12 C. Morazzini, 'Truguet, amiral toulonnais', *Bull. T.*, 1929, pp. 64–5.

13 AP 3A1 6, Conseil, 1787–9 *passim* and Aman, *Les officiers bleus*, p. 150.

13 Brun, *Port de Toulon*, t. 2, p. 137 and Levy-Schneider, *Le conventionnel Jeanbon Saint-André*, vol. 1, p. 295.

14 W. Doyle, 'Was there an aristocratic reaction in pre-revolutionary France?', *Past and Present*, 57, 1972, pp. 107–14. The navy is not among the institutions discussed in this important article, but brief references are made to *la marine* in P. Goubert, *L'ancien régime 2: les pouvoirs*, Paris, 1973, p. 209 and G. Lemarchand, 'Noblesse, élite et notabilité en France: aspects sociaux et politiques', *Etudes sur le XVIIIe siècle*, VII, 1981, p. 141.

15 P. Bonnichon, 'Missions de la marine au temps de Louis XVI', *RHES*, 54, 1976, p. 556 and J. Gaignebet, 'Les loisirs du chevalier de Sade, lieutenant de vaisseau du roi à Toulon, 1789', *Bull. T.*, 1933.

16 BM F30 (11), Réclamations des sous-lieutenants de vaisseau, 10 Aug. 1789.

17 AM L39, Cahier, contains no reference, though the *cahier* for the *sénéchaussée* of Toulon does seek a general 'opening of careers to talent' (AN Ba 81).

18 AP 2E4 71–5, Revues et soldes, 1789–93 and AM L285, Officiers de marine, 15 Mar. 1792.

19 AP 1A1 235, Intendant, 1783 *passim*; AM BB96, Délibérations, 1783 *passim* and A. J. Parès, *A propos de pain: conflit entre l'intendance maritime de Toulon et le parlement de Provence, 1782–84*, Toulon, 1919.

20 AP 1A1 236, Intendant, 1784 *passim*; AM BB96, Délibérations, 25 Mar. 1784 and Malouet, *Mémoires*, t. 1, pp. 186–7.

21 Agulhon, *Une ville ouvrière*, p. 10.

22 AP 1A1 125, Commandant, 28 Aug. 1781.

23 N. Temple, 'The control and exploitation of French towns during the ancien régime', *History*, LI, 1966; G. Bossenga, 'City and state: an urban perspective on the origins of the French Revolution', in K. Baker *et al.* (eds), *The French Revolution and the creation of modern political culture*, vol. 1, 'The political culture of the Old Régime', Oxford, 1987, pp. 115–40 and M. Bordes, *L'administration provinciale et municipale en France au XVIII*ᵉ *siècle*, Paris, 1972.

24 AM BB29, Formes anciennes et modernes de l'administration de Toulon, 1765 and Lambert, *Histoire*, t. 4, pp. 17–19.

25 Baratier (ed.), *Histoire de la Provence*, pp. 305–7 and M. Bordes, 'Le rôle des sub-délégués en Provence au dix-huitième siècle, *Prov. hist.*, XXIII, 1973, pp. 402–3.

26 AM BB29, Etat des revenus de la communauté, 1765; AM BB29, Formes anciennes et modernes and Lambert, *Histoire*, t. 4, p. 351.

27 AM AA3, Règlement sur les élections, 1754.

28 ADBR C 1321, Municipalité de Toulon à l'intendant, 23 Sept. 1771.

29 F. X. Emmanuelli, 'De la conscience politique à la naissance du "provençalisme" dans la généralité d'Aix la fin du XVIIIᵉ siècle. Prélude à une recherche', in C. Gras and G. Livet (eds.), *Régions et régionalisme en France du XVIII*ᵉ *siècle à nos jours*, Vendôme, 1977. See also Emmanuelli's *Pouvoir royal et vie régionale en Provence au déclin de la monarchie. Psychologie, pratiques administratives, défrancisation de l'intendance d'Aix, 1745–1790*, 2 vols., Lille, 1974.

30 M. Bordes, *La réforme municipale du contrôleur-général Laverdy et son application, 1764–1771*, Toulouse, 1968, pp. 12–13 and p. 260.

31 AM BB32, Intendant à la municipalité, 18 June 1748 and BB92, Délibérations, 8 Jan. 1759.

32 AM BB32, M. Beaudin, sous-archiviste, 14 Mar. 1768.

33 Baratier (ed.), *Histoire de la Provence*, p. 360 and J. F. Bosher, 'The French crisis of 1770', *History*, LVII, 1972, pp. 18–24.

34 AM BB32, Mémoire de M. Paul, 25 July 1774; AM BB32, Intendant à la municipalité, Aug.–Oct. 1774 and BB94, Délibérations, July–Dec. 1774.

35 AM AA3, Lettres patentes, 1776 and Modifications.

36 Lambert, *Histoire*, t. 4, pp. 302–3.

37 M. Bordes, 'L'administration des communautés des habitants en Provence et dans le comté de Nice à la fin de l'ancien régime: traits communs et diversité', *Ann. Midi*, LXXXIV, 1972.

38 M. Derlange, 'En Provence au XVIIIe siècle: la représentation des habitants aux conseils généraux des communautés', *Ann. Midi*, LXXXVI, 1974, pp. 45–6.

39 AM BB10, Verbaux d'élection, 1754–88.

40 AM BB90-6, Délibérations, 1754–88.

41 AM BB18, Liste des sujets, 1776–88.

42 N. Temple, 'Municipal elections and municipal oligarchies in eighteenth century France', in J. F. Bosher (ed.), *French government and society, 1500–1800: essays in memory of Albert Cobban*, London, 1973, p. 87.

43 AM CC367–76, Comptes, 1778–87 and C. Ferrucci, 'La vie communale à Toulon de 1750 1788', mémoire pour la maîtrise, University of Nice, 2 vols., 1970, t. 1, pp. 133–78.

44 AM BB17, Arrêts du conseil d'état, 1780–81.

45 AM L39, Cahier and AN Ba81, Cahier.

46 F. X. Emmanuelli, 'Introduction à l'histoire du XVIIIe siècle communal en Provence', *Ann. Midi*, LXXXVII, 1975, p. 164.

47 AM L740, Renseignements fournis.

48 Lambert, *Histoire*, t. 4, pp. 296–9.

49 AM BB30, Mémoire sur le pain, 1783.

50 AM BB30, Etat des principaux corps.

51 Agulhon, *Pénitents et francs-maçons de l'ancienne Provence*, Paris, 1968, pp. 86–8.

52 AM GG13, Lettres patentes, Jan. 1789 and Agulhon, *Pénitents*, pp. 138–40.

53 Henry, *L'histoire de Toulon*, t. 1, pp. 48–50.

54 AM GG13, lettres patentes and II16, Projet par forme de règlement, pénitents gris, 1782.

55 AM L707, Confréries, correspondance, 1789–93 and AD 1L 1119–20, Confréries de Toulon, 1789–91.

56 BN FM2 434–41, Loges maçonniques de Toulon and for Lyon, Garden, *Lyon*, pp. 546–8.

57 BN FM2 436, Les Elèves de Minerve, 19 Nov. 1783.

58 A. Le Bihan, *Loges et chapitres de la Grande Loge et du Grand Orient de France (deuxième moitié du XVIIIe siècle)*, Paris, 1967, pp. 234–6 and 360–1.

59 BN FM2 439, 30 May 1787.

60 BN FM2 436, Les Elèves de Minerve, 29 Mar. 1792.

61 BN FM2 436, Les Amis Constants, 14 June 1780 and 17 Nov. 1781.

62 D. Roche, *Le siècle des lumières en province. Académies et académiciens provinciaux, 1680–1789*, 2 vols., Paris, 1978, t.1, pp. 257–80

and R. Halévi, *Les loges maçonniques dans la France d'ancien régime aux origines de la sociabilité démocratique*, Paris, 1984, pp. 103–6.

63   AP 1A1 127, Commandant, 4 May 1786.

64   R. Darnton, 'The Encyclopédie wars of pre-revolutionary France', *AHR*, 78, 1973, p. 1349.

65   M. Vovelle, *Piété baroque et déchristianisation en Provence au XVIIIᵉ siècle: les attitudes devant la mort d'après les clauses des testaments*, Paris, 1973, p. 130.

66   *Ibid.*, pp. 243–5 and 257–9 and M. Corda, 'Les hospices civiles de Toulon' (BMT ms, 1884), p. 196.

67   AM BB29, Mémoire sur les établissements faits à Toulon pour l'instruction, 1765.

68   M. Vovelle, 'Y a-t-il eu une révolution culturelle au XVIIIᵉ siècle? A propos de l'éducation populaire en Provence', *RHMC*, XXII, 1975, pp. 101–3; Vovelle, *Piété baroque*, pp. 605–7 and F. Furet and J. Ozouf, *Reading and writing. Literacy in France from Calvin to Jules Ferry*, trans. Cambridge, 1982, p. 58 *et seq.*

69   Agulhon, *Pénitents*, p. 70 and p. 89.

70   AM BB29, Mémoire pour l'histoire.

71   J. P. Bardet and J. M. Gouesse, 'Le calendrier des mariages à Rouen. Rupture et résurgence d'une pratique (XVIIIᵉ–XIXᵉ siècles)' *CHESRF*, *Mémoires et documents*, 35, 1978, pp. 63–78.

72   Vovelle, *Piété baroque*, pp. 219–24.

73   ADBR C4311, Mémoire pour les curés de Provence, 1 July 1779.

74   AM II15, Mémoire pour H. Revest et J. Daumas, curés, 1780; E. Préclin, *Les jansénistes aux XVIIIᵉ siècle et la constitution civile du clergé*, Paris, 1929, pp. 390–1 and T. Tackett, *Priest and parish in eighteenth-century France*, Princeton, 1977, p. 225 *et seq.*

75   J. McManners, *French ecclesiastical society under the ancien régime; a study of Angers in the eighteenth century*, Manchester, 1960, pp. 26–56.

76   AM L705, Suppression des voeux.

77   AM BB95, Délibérations, 1781, *passim* and Lambert, *Histoire*, t. 4, p. 379 *et seq.*

78   AP 1A1 234, Intendant, 22 Oct. 1782 and AM L714, Demande pour la suppression des Frères Prêcheurs, June 1789.

79   E. Davin, *La prostitution à Toulon*, Toulon, 1940 and Agulhon (ed.), *Histoire de Toulon*, p. 129.

80   AM GG unmarked, Registre contenant les noms des filles enceintes reçues à l'entrepôt de l'hôpital, 1772–1808.

81   O. Hufton, *The poor of eighteenth-century France, 1750–1789*, Oxford, 1974, pp. 329–34 and Perrot, *Caen*, t. 2, pp. 842–53.

82   AM L725, Rapport de mm. les commissaires nommés pour examiner l'exposé de l'hôpital du Saint-Esprit relatif à ses besoins, 1790 and Corda, 'Les hospices civiles', p. 72.

83   AM BB29, Mémoire pour l'histoire and L727, Hôpital de la Miséricorde, revenus et dépenses, 1789–91.

84   AP 1A1 240, Intendant, 26 Nov. 1788.

85   AP 1A1 127, Commandant, 24 Jan. 1789 and AM L68(1),

Délibérations, 23 Jan. 1790.
  86 AP 1A1 238, Intendant, 2 Apr. 1786.
  87 AP 1A1 241, Intendant, 5 Dec. 1789.
  88 AP 1A1 238, Intendant, 24 Jan. 1786.
  89 AP 1A1 240, Intendant, 9 Nov. 1788.
  90 AP 1A1 240, Intendant, 23 Oct. 1788.

4

1789: the outbreak of the Revolution

'The time has come . . . you must seize this opportunity, because there will never be a better one.'

At Toulon, as in other towns of Provence, the spring months of 1789 were accompanied by an upsurge of unrest. The popular classes grasped the opportunity presented by a series of elections to the Estates General to express their grievances by rioting. These widespread disturbances do not indicate a conspiracy, as many contemporaries believed; they originated instead in high bread prices, unemployment and poverty. This explosive situation was detonated by unprecedented political activity, which began in 1787 when the central government permitted the Estates of Provence to reconvene after a lapse of nearly 150 years. The long-dormant provincial assembly was revived by the monarchy as part of a desperate attempt to bolster its ailing authority. In the event resurrection of the *Etats de Provence* was a divisive issue which polarised the Provençal elites, raised popular expectations and turned into a dress rehearsal for Revolution.

The recall of the provincial estates, which had last met in 1639, appeared to signal victory for the fief-owning nobility.[1] They were entitled to sit in the assembly at the expense of other nobles and in numbers which enabled them to dwarf the smaller contingents of clergy and commoners. These enfeoffed noblemen had persistently campaigned for restoration of the Estates on a traditional basis, yet their eventual success was only won at the price of unleashing the pre-revolution in Provence. A determined opposition, brilliantly led by the dissident nobleman, Mirabeau, quickly emerged to challenge reactionary fief-holders.[2] When the unreformed body met at the end of December 1787 substantial changes in the composition of the Estates were proposed, which attracted support from all quarters. Most delegates from the thirty-six towns which were represented at the assembly lent their weight to demands for reform, but the Toulon deputy, a retired naval officer, refused to be associated with them.[3] When he returned to Toulon, after the Estates had ended in uproar and deadlock, Captain de Gineste was severely censured for the stance he had adopted. The Toulonnais notables nominated a more compliant delegate to a special meeting of municipal representatives, called in the spring of 1788 to discuss tactics; he was firmly mandated to seek 'a majority of votes' for the *tiers* at future reunions of the *Etats de Provence*.[4]

Little progress was to be made during the months that followed, but the task of restructuring the provincial estates acquired added urgency in the autumn when it was announced that the Estates General of the realm were to meet the following year. According to time-honoured precedent Provençal deputies to the *Etats-généraux* were elected at the provincial assembly. For third-estate representatives it thus became more important than ever to wrest power from the hands of enfeoffed nobles and their followers. The municipal council at Toulon sought to emulate the example of neighbouring Dauphiné, where the traditional estates had been bypassed, by proposing: 'The summoning of an assembly of all three orders of the Provençal "nation", legitimately represented by deputies who are freely chosen and drawn from all the various corporations . . . to constitute a real parliament.'[5] This idea was not taken up in Provence but it stimulated a good deal of useful discussion, in the naval town as elsewhere.

The Toulonnais notables had already sought popular support for their campaign when, in December 1788, guild delegates were invited to join the debate at an extraordinary council meeting.[6] This proved to be a dangerous innovation because, two months later, the corporations put the issue before their own members. Master craftsmen, like those in the liberal professions, declared unanimously in favour of a substantial remodelling of the provincial estates.[7] However, they proceeded to request popular participation in the election of third-estate delegates to a reformed body and suggested reviving the ancient assembly of all heads of household at Toulon. This suggestion was totally unacceptable to more conservative notables, who were equally dismayed by comments from court ushers and shoemakers denouncing the privileges of the local urban oligarchy, as well as the pretensions of enfeoffed nobles and upper clergy.

In the event negotiations at Versailles with Jacques Necker, recently reinstated to ministerial office, upset everyone's calculations. Necker undercut intransigent groups in Provence by deciding that regional elections to the Estates General would take place in the *sénéchaussées*, rather than at the provincial Estates.[8] This represented a victory for the *tiers*, but only at the cost of overturning the constitutional traditions of Provence. The touchstone of eighteenth-century particularism, *la constitution provençale*, was effectively abandoned in order to overcome aristocratic resistance to reform, though the full implications of this historic step were not immediately recognised.[9]

The general electoral decree of 24 January 1789 was therefore applied in Provence.[10] Elections were still conducted by order and, in the case of the third estate, voting was indirect. At Toulon itself preliminary elections were needed to create a manageable urban assembly for the *tiers* from which delegates were sent to *sénéchaussée* level. A further stage of voting was also required (for clergy and nobles too) because the *sénéchaussée* of Toulon was obliged to share its representatives at Versailles with the small, adjacent *sénéchaussées* of Brignoles and Hyres. However, by virtue of the system of indirect taxation employed at Toulon, no commoners in the naval port were ruled out of preliminary elections for failing to pay tax. As the municipality later explained: 'There is no one here who pays no tax at all; on the contrary, everyone pays something as a result of his consumption of bread, wine etc.'[11]

Nonetheless, when the first round of elections for the *tiers* took place at Toulon, between 15 and 17 March 1789, ordinary journeymen and the great mass of dockyard workers were given no opportunity to assemble.[12] Only one-third of the adult males listed on a voting register drawn up early in 1790 was initially allowed to take part. Preliminaries were restricted to master artisans meeting in their guilds, though even they received fewer delegates at the town assembly than members of the liberal professions. The latter were awarded two representatives for up to 100 participants while craftsmen had to rest content with just one. The 300 or so unincorporated *rentiers* and merchants were also treated more generously.[13]

The whole procedure was heavily biased in favour of the notables but, as the urban assembly elected in this manner was gathering on 23 March, rioting brought operations to an abrupt halt. Possel, acting *intendant de marine* in the absence of Malouet, who was standing for election to the Estates General at Riom, has left a vivid account of the upheaval:

> Yesterday afternoon, at the moment when the commissioners nominated by the *tiers état* to draw up a *cahier de doléances* were reporting back to the assembly at the council house, the people appeared in force and went up to the council chamber. There they demanded the handing-over of M. Lantier, former mayor-consul and M. Beaudin, town archivist, both of whom managed to escape, though with considerable difficulty and only after having endured some extremely rough treatment. Their flight failed to calm the crowd, which was armed with axes, sticks and stones, so the garrison commander readied all his soldiers, while Albert de Rions (the naval *commandant*) did the same with his troops. I summoned workers back to the Arsenal, in an effort to diminish the number of rioters on the streets. These precautions and the decision taken by municipal officials to order an immediate reduction in the price of bread, meat and olive oil went some way to appeasing the crowd, which now confined its attention to the episcopal residence and threw the bishop's carriage into the harbour. Houses belonging to Lantier, Beaudin and Mourchou (the former town archivist), were pillaged throughout the evening . . . Next day the municipal customs house was demolished and the sub-delegate's office was threatened. All this damage was done without any blood being spilled.[14]

The prolongation of these disturbances into a second day obliged the municipal council to order a further reduction in the price of bread, from 2 *sols* 6 *deniers* for a local pound loaf to just 2 *sols*.[15] This final concession, along with the summoning of the bourgeois militia, eventually succeeded in restoring order, although many dockyard workers continued to absent themselves from the Arsenal on 25 March. It was the wealthy Toulonnais printer, J. L. Mallard, who brought their 'strike' to an end by offering a loan of 60,000 *livres* to the naval authorities. This timely gesture enabled the dockyard administration to settle wage arrears outstanding since the close of 1788.[16]

In its inquiry into the disturbances the municipal council ascribed a leading role to dockyard workers and bemoaned their malign influence upon other inhabitants.[17] There is no doubt that other members of the popular classes were also involved. Some idea of the composition of the crowd at Toulon, which included women and children, can be derived from the list of those tried and convicted for alleged participation.[18] The sentences were severe, though none was actually implemented: six men were condemned to death; two to the prison hulks; one to a whipping; and another to exile. At least four of these individuals were dockyard workers and one of the acquitted was a shoemaker. The latter, Louis Lemaille alias Beausoleil, was executed as a 'terrorist' by anti-Jacobins during the rebellion of 1793. Indeed, according to Louis Richaud who wrote a memoir on the revolt of Toulon, it was during the *émeute* of 1789 that 'future leaders of the band of Toulonnais brigands made their first public appearance'.[19]

The presence of an apothecary among those who were sentenced for riotous behaviour points to the involvement of individuals on the periphery of the urban elite. It also suggests there was a grain of truth in the naval *commandant*'s accusation that persons in authority ought to 'blame themselves for having encouraged, or even provoked the outburst'.[20] Patrician elements may have turned the crowd against the town archivist, Beaudin, and his hated predecessor Mourchou. This notorious pair, who had survived efforts to dislodge them in 1774, were finally forced out in 1789.

Once the disturbances had begun discontented groups, like stonemasons in contractual dispute with the municipality, or Capuchin friars nursing grievances against the Bishop of Toulon, were given a golden opportunity to exploit the confusion. Yet theirs were clearly secondary conflicts and the municipal administration rightly insisted upon the essence of the uprising as an '*émeute de faim*'. Its report emphasised that 'the populace was especially agitated by the high prices of basic foodstuffs'.[21] The sharp rise in bread prices stemmed from the poor harvests of the late 1780s. At Toulon, subsidies notwithstanding, the cost of a loaf reached 3 *sols* 1 *denier* (4 *sols poids de marc*) in the early spring of 1789, an increase of roughly 20 per cent compared to the same season in 1787.[22] Moreover, the destruction of the olive crop during the harsh winter of 1788–89 produced a similar rise in oil prices, while meat was in equally short supply. The combination of bad weather and commodity shortages was responsible for a huge death toll during the spring months of 1789.

The attack on the customs house and the beneficial result of lowering price levels both confirm the causal importance of the high cost of living. Yet increases in bread prices in the late 1750s, mid-1760s and early 1770s were all steeper, without producing any comparable disorder. Undoubtedly the economic crisis underlying this outbreak of *taxation populaire* at Toulon was exacerbated by particular difficulties and developments at the Arsenal. The naval *intendant* saw 'arrears of pay' as a significant cause of upheaval and the settlement of arrears as essential to the return of peace.[23] The impecunious dockyard authorities were three months behind in the remuneration of employees and had to distribute ships' biscuit in lieu of pay. Economy measures included a five instead of a six-day week and closure of the Arsenal when it rained.[24] The adverse effects of subcontracting on the labour force must also be taken into account, but post-war difficulties had not led to violence in the past.

A leading place in the hierarchy of causation must therefore be awarded to the unprecedented political crisis of the late 1780s. It was no coincidence that disturbances should erupt just as delegates were meeting to discuss the town's *cahier de doléances*. As the municipal inquiry stated: 'The series of assemblies held to nominate deputies generated tremendous excitement among the populace.'[25] Unrest had been brewing for a few days before the crowd commenced its rampage with a calculated assault upon the debating chamber. Those leading the onslaught were said to have styled themselves as 'representatives of the people', articulating popular demands. By doing so they were challenging the monopoly which notables and craftsmen were exercising over the electoral process. In other words, 'the people wanted to insert its own grievances' in the *cahier*, which was altered to incorporate the abolition of indirect taxes on foodstuffs and an end to the subcontracting of dockyard labour.[26]

Not only the demands but also the delegates of dockyards workers were accepted by the assembly when discussions on the draft *cahier* resumed five days after the riot. In the interim 1,264 sailors and craftsmen from the shipbuilding trades, who had not previously been consulted, had met to elect twenty-two additional deputies.[27] This virtually doubled the number of persons who had been able to take part in preliminary elections and brought representatives of nearly all social groups into the political reckoning. The Toulon *cahier* had already been drafted by an eight-man committee dominated by the notables and even in its amended form it clearly bore their imprint.[28] Some 50 per cent of the ninety-six articles dealt with constitutional, judicial and administrative matters in general terms. A new constitution, fiscal equality and regular meetings of an Estates General endowed with legislative powers, where voting would be conducted 'by head', were all prominent issues. They were accompanied by proposals designed to establish individual freedom, end administrative abuses and foster equality of opportunity. Many revolutionary enactments such as the abolition of the intendancies and venal office-holding, the redemption of feudal dues, improved status for parish priests and liberty of the press were included.[29]

This relatively high degree of radicalism doubtless owed a good deal to the pre-revolutionary political campaigns in Provence. By contrast, a lengthy section on commerce, comprising 20 per cent of the content, reflected essentially local preoccupations and sought assistance for economic development at Toulon. It was taken for granted that some form of regional Estates would exist in the future, despite the fact that the traditional Estates of Provence had been bypassed in the elections of 1789. This echo of particularism is perhaps less surprising than the absence of any concrete proposals for overcoming aristocratic resistance to change. The third estate *cahier* for *sénéchaussée*, so similar to the cahier of Toulon that contemporary officials confused them, injected an extra note of hostility towards noble and clerical privileges, yet it was equally devoid of any political strategy.[30] Perhaps its authors regarded conciliatory gestures by the other two orders, which met for the first time in the *sénéchaussée* on 31 March, as a sufficient guarantee. Clerical and noble *cahiers* have not survived, but both orders supported the principle of fiscal parity.[31]

Of the three assemblies at *sénéchaussée* level, that of the clergy was the most deeply divided.[32] Some two-thirds of the sixty clerics who gathered in Toulon were parish priests, determined to assert their numerical superiority and obtain the recognition denied them in the past. The bishop was purposely excluded, both from a committee elected to draft the *cahier* and from the delegation later sent to confer with deputies from the *sénéchaussées* of Brignoles and Hyères. At the joint assembly, held in the naval port on 6 April, parish priests retained a crushing majority which they employed to send two *curés* to Versailles.[33] Though neither hailed from Toulon, both had been outspoken opponents of the ecclesiastical hierarchy. Here, as elsewhere in Provence, parochial clergy conversant with the anti-episcopal movement of the preceding decade were firmly in control.[34]

Nobles in the *sénéchaussée* of Toulon were also obliged to contend with internal dissension, but sharp disagreement between fief-holders and the unenfeoffed, who had been at odds over the composition of the provincial estates, was resolved more amicably.[35] The twenty-four individuals who gathered in the naval port were evenly split between those who did and those who did not own fiefs, though most were active or retired military officers.[36] Those who subsequently joined them from the adjacent circumscriptions of Brignoles and Hyères had similar career backgrounds and both the noble deputies sent to Versailles had military connections with Toulon. The predominance of officers from the armed forces was typical of Provence as a whole and was equally marked at the Estates General.[37]

Third-estate assemblies at *sénéchaussée* level showed a high degree of social homogeneity despite the diversity of the order; here, as elsewhere in France, popular elements had been reduced to a small minority.[38] The Toulonnais delegation, forty strong, did contain twenty-three master craftsmen but the other seventy-seven *sénéchaussée* deputies, who hailed from the hinterland, were all notables. The selection of delegates to meet with those from the associated *sénéchaussées* of Brignoles and Hyères acted as a further filter and only two artisans survived. Three of the four individuals sent to Versailles to represent the combined circumscriptions were barristers, two of whom had been deeply involved in the pre-revolutionary struggle in Provence. Only Meifrund, the solitary Toulonnais among these deputies, possessed any business experience and even he had retired from commerce.[39]

In spite of a procession through the streets of Toulon, in which deputies of the clergy, nobility and *tiers* mingled together in a demonstration of unity, fresh disturbances were only narrowly avoided. On 6 April another Toulonnais, a merchant turned magistrate, was elected as a deputy to the Estates General to prevent further rioting.[40] The individual immediately resigned, but his 'election' by the popular classes reflected an atmosphere still highly charged with emotion. Bread prices had been raised again, while lower-class representatives had been excluded from the final stage of the electoral proceedings. The incident was an unpleasant reminder to the notables that social tension, so evident in the *émeute* of 23 March, had scarcely diminished. Officials were forced to admit that 'the people had become increasingly critical of abuses and unfairness in the municipality'.[41]

Dockyard workers and journeymen remained disaffected but most master craftsmen, whose representatives had been admitted to council meetings before March, supported the elite. It was they who formed the backbone of the urban militia which, together with regular troops, was policing the streets of Toulon. Guild delegates remained involved in municipal business throughout the spring of 1789.[42] Their help was desperately needed to rebuild the town's financial resources, which had been exhausted in the course of the riots. The extra food subsidies that bought peace on the streets could not be met out of existing income, but the notables were unwilling to levy a rate on property because the burden would fall mainly upon themselves. This left no alternative save recourse to reductions in ordinary expenditure and, most of all, a gradual relaxation of controls on the price of bread. It was also decided to reintroduce the local tax on foodstuffs, which enjoyed a final lease of life until its suppression by the National Assembly a year later.

The reimposition of indirect taxation at Toulon in the summer of 1789, in spite of a demand for its abolition in the *cahier*, was guaranteed to provoke more unrest. Unhappily it coincided with the date set for the execution of participants in the March riot and renewed disturbances were only averted because news of a general reprieve arrived on 23 July.[43] The notables were clearly shaken by the continuing threat of disorder and they purposely chose the next day to publicise their approval of the revolutionary events taking place at Versailles. Whatever members of the urban elite might privately think of the transformation of the Estates General into the National Assembly, or the storming of the Bastille in Paris, their political survival in the town demanded some association with it.[44]

When, a month later, a further resignation left only one consul in office, it was decided to refashion the municipal administration at Toulon. On 24 August more than 500 assorted 'heads of household' packed a gathering to determine how this should be done. Roubaud, the remaining consul, proposed the creation of some kind of committee to provide assistance and add legitimacy to his hard-pressed council.[45] His suggestion won immediate approval. It was a logical extension of the consultation with guild delegates that had been conducted since the end of 1788, but there were heated exchanges over how a committee should be formed. Two divergent proposals were circulating. One, sponsored by Brun Sainte-Catherine, a retired naval official and current councillor, called for no more than the co-option of additional notables. The conservative tenor of this proposal was evident in Brun's longer-term objective: a restoration of the municipal charter of 1754. A radical alternative was submitted by J. S. Barthélemy, a procurator. He took the local oligarchy to task for its exclusivity and contended that the new committee should be elected by popular vote. Furthermore, the 'permanent committee', as he called it, should take precedence over the present council which was only qualified to 'administer business encompassed by old regime statutes', not a revolution.

After a noisy debate it was agreed to elect a committee of forty-eight in the general assembly of citizens. When this was done, two days later, less than half the membership was entrusted to notables. Barthélemy himself was chosen and so was Hyacinthe Paul, leader of the municipal rebellion in 1774. Both men belonged to a radical faction emerging within the old elite, especially from its lower reaches, but newcomers formed a clear majority on the *comité*. Master craftsmen predominated; in many cases, like the cutler S. Foucou or the tanner F. Fisquet, they had recently participated in preliminary elections to the Estates General.

Maurice Agulhon has underestimated the importance of the *comité permanent* at Toulon. The naval port, he says, was one of those towns 'which had no need of a "municipal revolution" to put revolutionary bourgeois in control'.[46] Yet its manner of election and the composition of the committee both represented a setback for the Toulonnais patriciate. As the monarchy collapsed, instead of reasserting its traditional autonomy, the old elite was obliged to share power with shopkeepers and artisans. There was a clear division between conservative notables and other groups within the *tiers état*, which resulted in a significant transfer of power during the summer of 1789. The *comité* was initially subordinate rather than superior to the existing council but, within three months, committee and council had coalesced to form a single, municipal administration.

This later development, which occurred at the beginning of December, was the product of deteriorating relations between townspeople and service aristocracy. Even reactionary notables at Toulon were suspicious of military officers, who were viewed as potential counter-revolutionaries. During August rumours had circulated of 'a plot to destroy the town and massacre its inhabitants'. Fears such as these had prompted the search for an arms cache said to be located at the château Missiessy, the local home of a prominent officer family.[47] Although nothing was found the threat of counter-revolution persuaded the municipal council to boost the urban militia to a complement of 1,000 men.[48] The notables remained firmly in command of this enlarged force, which was renamed the *milice nationale*, but militiamen were keen to demonstrate their revolutionary commitment and over-zealous in their policing of Toulon.

Altercations with regular troops were not slow to occur and in mid-November a major incident arose.[49] A picket of militia arrested a regimental officer who was sporting the black cockade of Austria, a symbol of allegiance to the *ancien régime*. The officier was incarcerated, for protection rather than punishment, while municipal leaders sought an accommodation with the military authorities. Commanders at the garrison and the Arsenal, however, brushed aside the olive branch that was offered to them and instead demanded an abject apology from the *milice*. Albert de Rions, the naval chief, was instrumental in orchestrating an 'aggressive response' from the service establishment. This 'distinguished sea-captain . . . full of bravery . . . but deeply imbued with aristocratic prejudices', was soon embroiled in a similar, but more serious dispute.[50]

De Rions was fundamentally opposed to the citizen militia, which he saw as a rival to his authority. He also felt that guard membership had encouraged insubordination among dockyard workers, besides disrupting schedules, as men took time off for patrol duty.[51] On 30 November matters came to a head when the impulsive *commandant* sacked two petty officers, ostensibly because they were trouble-makers. Townspeople preferred to interpret the dismissals as retaliation for the pair's enrolment in the *milice*.[52] Fearing untoward consequences the municipal council begged de Rions to reverse his decision, but he refused. He had, earlier in the year, complained to the naval minister that 'kindness equals weakness' and added, 'a commander cannot change his mind without being humiliated'.[53]

The next day few workers appeared at the Arsenal; most gathered with other members of the popular classes in front of de Rions' residence on the Champ de Bataille. Inside municipal councillors were desperately seeking an accord with the *commandant*. Outside clashes occurred between demonstrators and soldiers, some of whom refused to ready their arms when ordered to do so and exposed their officers to assault. Rions' belated promise to reinstate the two employees failed to appease the riotous assembly and it was left to the civilian militia to save the day by taking six *militaires*, including the *commandant* himself, into protective custody.

This celebrated *'affaire de la marine'* raised the spectre of anarchy in one of the kingdom's military bases and naturally caused great alarm at the National Assembly.[54] As Malouet, the former naval *intendant* of Toulon correctly discerned, the coexistence of the new militia with royal troops was a recipe for disorder.[55] Legislation was urgently required to determine where responsibility for internal security ultimately lay. Yet efforts to resolve this thorny issue proved unsatisfactory and conflict between the military and civilian authorities continued to bedevil peace-keeping at Toulon. After an acrimonious debate the Assembly ordered the release of the imprisoned *militaires*, but refused to prosecute municipal leaders on a charge of treason. This was a further blow to the morale of a service aristocracy which was undermined by indiscipline in the ranks and resignations among its officers. The municipality meanwhile strengthened its hand by raising membership of the citizen militia to 4,000, thereby inscribing practically all male heads of household.[56]

Calm was rapidly restored and peace prevailed when municipal elections were held in February 1790. According to the system of local government established by the National Assembly, the municipality or *commune* of Toulon (which retained its old-regime boundaries), was integrated into a uniform, national hierarchy of administrative bodies.[57] The new municipal council was to comprise a mayor, a *procureur* and his deputy as town clerks, fourteen councillors and thirty *notables*, or deputy-councillors. As in the past the presence of deputy-councillors was required to turn an ordinary into a general council meeting, for the consideration of more weighty matters. In structural terms the revolutionary council thus bore a good resemblance to its predecessor, although the traditional Mediterranean consuls had disappeared, along with secretary and archivist, to be replaced by a mayor, *procureur* and *substitut-procureur*.

The manner in which the council was elected represented a rather more radical break with the old order. No longer did a tiny oligarchy of notables decide the outcome; the right to vote and to stand for election at Toulon was effectively extended to all adult male inhabitants. Now, the Assembly had decreed that the franchise should be restricted to 'active citizens', that is to say to those men, aged twenty-five and over, who paid direct taxes to the value of at least three days' local wages. The *journée de travail* at Toulon was duly set at 18 *sols*, so the right to vote required an annual tax payment of 54 *sols*. However, the Toulonnais administration added, 'given the current method of raising revenue this qualification will be waived'. The levy of indirect taxes upon foodstuffs meant that 'every adult male was paying enough to vote and also to compete for office' (ten days' wages).[58] The regressive fiscal system from which the notables had benefited in the past thus backfired upon them, for no less than 5,634 Toulonnais, or one in four of the population, appeared on the first voters' register.[59] Elsewhere, in 1790, some 30 per cent of French males were denied the franchise but, at Toulon, universal manhood suffrage operated from the outset of the Revolution. By the time that direct taxes were levied, in 1792, restrictions upon voting and eligibility for office had been swept away.

Yet, initially, the democratic franchise inflicted little damage upon the old elite. Only 22 per cent of the huge electorate actually voted for a new municipal council in February 1790. Low turnout was the rule in the Midi, though not everywhere in France.[60] At Toulon there was a sharp contrast with elections to the Estates General, held the previous year, when over 50 per cent of an equally large electorate had participated. In 1790 polling was conducted in assemblies of the eight *sections*, or urban divisions, into which the town was split for administrative purposes. It took time to generate political activity on a neighbourhood basis, rather than in the familiar context of the guild.[61] The lengthy electoral procedure instituted by the National Assembly was equally off-putting. It entailed meeting in assemblies, where the preliminary election of president, secretary and scrutineers was required before a series of separate, exhaustive ballots for mayor and councillors could even commence. Only 18 per cent of the electorate voted for the mayor and, when it was the turn of deputy-councillors a fortnight later, only a handful of persons remained in attendance.

Notables comprised over a third of the participants in February 1790 and they continued to attend as the polls were deserted by those with less time at their disposal. It was they who served as officials in the assemblies and, not surprisingly, they swept the board as elected municipal officials. In February J. F. Richard, a *rentier*, was chosen as mayor. His *procureur* was a merchant-turned-magistrate and the *substitut* a barrister. Of fourteen councillors no less than six practised a legal profession, while two were *rentiers*, two merchants and the remaining four a doctor, ironmonger, pasta retailer and clockmaker. All but the last two were substantial property-holders and had served on the old-regime municipality prior to 1789.

Thus far the elections had produced a council little different from its predecessors and, although there were no less than 461 nominations for the thirty posts of deputy-councillor, two-thirds of these places were also captured by the elite. Direct representation for the popular classes, who had bulked so large on the defunct *comité permanent*, was now confined to a small group of deputy-councillors who included just one dockyard worker. It is true that a few of the notables elected in February 1790, like H. Paul or J. S. Barthélemy, were radical in outlook, but they had been chosen well down the list, Paul as twelfth councillor and Barthélemy as a deputy-councillor. The first elections of the Revolution, like those which followed later in 1790, therefore constituted a great triumph for conservative notables. They had survived the crisis of 1789 and reasserted their ascendancy in the municipality by winning a fresh mandate from the vastly expanded electorate.

As the rest of the new administrative system was put into place notables also went on to achieve unprecedented influence over the hinterland. The municipality of Toulon was situated at the base of a hierarchy of unitary authorities, with elected members, which replaced *intendant*, *sub-délégués* and the patchwork administration of the old regime. Above the communes stood *districts*, that were themselves segments of the eighty-three *départements* into which the kingdom was divided. Provence, like all the ancient provinces, disappeared as an administrative entity in 1790 and three departments emerged instead: the Bouches-du-Rhône in the east, the Basses-Alpes to the north and the Var in the west (taking its name from the river which marked the French frontier with the Comté of Nice).[62] Toulon became chief town (*chef-lieu*) of the Var, though only after a long struggle with three other contenders. All the larger towns were anxious to secure the status, commercial opportunities and employment, that would accompany headship of the new department. Toulon was undeniably the major city in the Var, but it was awkwardly located in the south-western corner of an extensive area. It took a great deal of lobbying at Paris, supported by the naval authorities, before the claims of Toulon finally prevailed over those of Brignoles, Grasse and Draguignan.[63]

Defeated rivals obtained some satisfaction when a departmental administration was chosen by the electoral college (*assemblée*

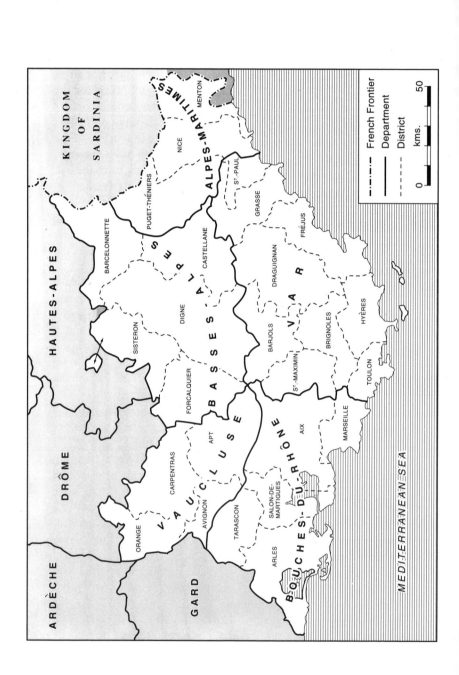

KINGDOM OF SARDINIA

HAUTES-ALPES

ARDÈCHE

DRÔME

GARD

ALPES-MARITIMES

MENTON

NICE

PUGET-THÉNIERS

BARCELONNETTE

ST.-PAUL

GRASSE

CASTELLANE

DIGNE

SISTERON

FORCALQUIER

FRÉJUS

DRAGUIGNAN

VAR

BARJOLS

BRIGNOLES

HYÈRES

ST.-MAXIMIN

TOULON

S
E
P
L
A
-
S
E
S
S
A
B

AIX

MARSEILLE

VAUCLUSE

APT

CARPENTRAS

ORANGE

AVIGNON

TARASCON

SALON-DE-MARTIGUES

ARLES

BOUCHES-DU-RHÔNE

MEDITERRANEAN SEA

French Frontier
Department
District

0   kms.   50

départementale) of the Var during the summer of 1790. This assembly comprised 550 delegates from the *cantons*, local units employed for the purpose of 'primary' elections to the electoral college. On account of its large population Toulon itself was split into two cantons, one of which included the nearby hill-village of Le Revest. The Toulonnais turnout in June 1790 amounted to a mere 15 per cent of the electorate and half the participants were notables, who comfortably dominated the low poll everywhere in the department.[64] The fifty-seven delegates from Toulon were thus drawn from the same social groups as others at the electoral college, but they were deliberately snubbed when the choice of administrators was made. The departmental directory, or executive, of eight persons contained no one from Toulon and only three Toulonnais were elected to the twenty-eight member council. Opponents of Toulon thus won the initial battle for political control of the Var.

In 1790 the electoral assembly of the Var had also established directories and councils for nine district administrations interposed between *départements* and *communes*.[65] At this level Toulonnais influence was less resistible. Toulon was the uncontested *chef-lieu* of a district formed by its hinterland and delegates from Toulon duly took the lion's share of a dozen posts on offer. When a district tribunal was set up at the end of the year members of the legal professions from Toulon also obtained all five places on the magistrates' bench.[66] Notwithstanding their failure to win many prizes at departmental level Toulonnais notables could draw considerable satisfaction from their share of the revolutionary spoils. The courts and administrative headquarters now situated in the town were much grander than their old regime predecessors in terms of both territorial extent and judicial authority.

On the other hand Toulon lost its long-standing episcopal status. When, in 1790, the four small bishoprics that fell within the Var were amalgamated into a single, departmental diocese, the seat went to Fréjus.[67] Other provisions in the Civil Constitution of the Clergy, which reformed the French church, stripped Toulon of its cathedral chapter and also of most of its monasteries. Since the town was not an ecclesiastical metropole like Aix or Angers, these sweeping changes made little political impact. Some vituperative pastoral letters from the bishop-in-exile and resistance from the chapter cut

The reorganisation of Provence, 1790–1793

little ice withthe parish clergy at Toulon, who had little to lose and scant respect for their superiors.[68] *Curés* and *vicaires* were therefore quick to swear the oath of allegiance to the Civil Constitution. There was only one refusal in the town, a typical response in the Var where 90 per cent of parish priests became jurors.[69]

Under the new order, as of old, Toulon retained its naval base and army garrison, twin bedrocks of the local economy. Yet, inevitably, the armed forces were brought into the reforming purview of the National Assembly, with profound repercussions for port and city. Legislators reassessed the division of power in the Arsenal between *plume* and *épée* and came down firmly in favour of the former. The decree, which eventually received royal sanction in September 1791, began with the blunt assertion that 'the administration of the dockyards will be in the hands of civilians; it is incompatible with the exercise of a military role'.[70] This marked a return to the Colbertian formula, removing the *commandant* from any function inside the shipyards. At Toulon the acting *intendant*, Possel, was reappointed as *ordonnateur* or director (the civilian chief's new title). The extension of his authority met with little resistance, because the energy of frustrated *militaires* had already been exhausted by a bitter dispute over reform of the officer corps itself.

The issue was not simply one of opening careers on the upper deck to men of ability rather than birth, as in the army, but also defining the role that commercial captains would play in the revolutionary navy.[71] The existence of civilian specialists raised the possibility of amalgamating the merchant and military marines though, after much heated debate, this radical option was rejected. It was decided instead to retain a separate military force, albeit with a substantially reduced nucleus of full-time (*entretenu*) officers, and to draw more heavily upon commercial personnel in wartime. Opportunities for merchant captains, who carried a commission on a reserve basis (*non-entretenu*), were consequently increased, a further enhancement of the added status these officers had achieved in 1780s. Admission and promotion in the permanent force was also thrown wide open. Yet established aristocratic officers had no immediate cause for dismay since some time would elapse before these egalitarian reforms had any effect. Indeed, the number of commoners on the upper deck was initially reduced due to the retirement of elderly non-noble officers, who had taken years to advance under the discriminatory system of the *ancien régime*.[72]

A substantial number of promotions from the lower deck was eventually necessary at Toulon, but this was because voluntary resignations removed so many noble officers from the ranks. The assault upon de Castellet, a naval captain who had been arrested with *commandant* de Rions after the riots of December 1789, is indicative of the insubordination and intimidation which induced members of the aristocracy to quit the service. On 10 August de Castellet was chased through the streets and badly beaten by a posse of dockyard workers who declared him an 'enemy of the people'.[73] The officer narrowly escape with his life but, needless to say, he did not reappear at the Arsenal. A census available for six of the town's eight *quartiers* reveals that only 100 military officers remained in residence in 1792, compared to nearly 250 in 1765.[74]

The dockyards at Toulon were disrupted by the continuing need for reductions in the work-force, as well as by suspicions of counter-revolutionary activities among aristocratic personnel. The financial situation had further deteriorated to the extent that in January 1790 promissory notes were issued to workers in lieu of pay.[75] Although three new ships were to go on to the stocks during the year, the recently appointed *commandant*, de Glandevès, who remained in charge of the Arsenal pending fresh legislation, saw no alternative but to impose redundancies. Despite protests from the town council he gave notice of forty-six dismissals to be made at the end of April.[76] On 3 May dockyard workers riposted with a huge demonstration on the Champ de Bataille. With some protection from a detachment of national guardsmen Glandevès was dragged off to the *hôtel de ville*. There he reluctantly agreed to withdraw on redundancy notices and calm was restored to the town.[77]

Once again shipyard workers had humiliated the naval authorities and fresh disturbances followed, later in May, this time over rates of pay.[78] Some progress was subsequently made as regards wages and, above all, a compromise was struck over the vexed issue of subcontracting. In October 1790 the National Assembly finally decreed that it would substitute 'day-labouring for subcontracting where repair-work was concerned, while retaining tendering for new vessels'.[79] Equally important, the government allocated an extra 200,000 *livres* to the port of Toulon during the summer of 1790, as fears of renewed conflict with Britain in the North Atlantic prompted a small-scale mobilisation of the French fleet.[80]

As the price of bread held steady at 2 *sols* 9 *deniers* a pound, and then fell by 5 *deniers* in the second half of 1790, the authorities at Toulon could afford to relax a little.[81] On 14 July the *fête de la fédération*, commemorating the fall of the Bastille, was celebrated in grand style at the naval port. The widespread rejoicing that accompanied this first revolutionary festival seemed to indicate that the time of upheaval was over. Yet 1790 was not exactly the 'quiet year' that some historians, taking their cue from a relatively quiescent French capital city, have described.[82] In the case of Toulon difficulties at the dockyards and disaffection among military officers combined to maintain a state of considerable uneasiness during the spring and summer months. If there was a lull in the latter part of the year, then it was no more than that, a deceptive calm before the storms to come. Deep-rooted and precocious divisions within the third estate would soon re-surface. The Revolution was only just beginning.

Notes

1 J. Egret, 'La pré-révolution en Provence, 1787–1789', *AHRF*, XXVI, 1954, p. 98 and M. Cubells, *Les horizons de la liberté. Naissance de la Révolution en Provence, 1787–1789*, Aix, 1987, p. 8 *et seq.*

2 G. Guibal, *Mirabeau et la Provence en 1789*, Paris, 1887, p. 38 and G. Chaussinand-Nogaret, *Mirabeau*, Paris, 1982, pp. 129–32.

3 AM BB96, Délibérations, 7 Mar. 1788.

4 AM AA4, Instruction donnée au député, 28 Apr. 1788.

5 AM L36, Demandes au Roi, 13 Feb. 1789.

6 AM BB96, Délibérations, 2 Dec. 1788.

7 AM L68(1), Délibérations, 17 and 25 Feb. 1789 and L38, Délibérations des corporations, 26 Feb.–8 Mar. 1789.

8 Egret, 'La pré-révolution', pp. 121–2.

9 Emmanuelli, 'De la conscience politique', pp. 133–7.

10 A. Brette (ed.), *Recueil de documents relatifs à la convocation des Etats-Généraux de 1789*, 4 vols., Paris, 1894–1915, t. 1, pp. 66–87.

11 AM L740, Renseignements fournis.

12 AM L39, Procès-verbaux des assemblées des corporations, 15–17 Mar. 1789.

13 AM L68(1), Délibérations, 16–18 Mar. 1789.

14 AP 1A1 241, Intendant, 24 Mar. 1789.

15 AM L347, Procès-verbal de l'émeute populaire, 30 Mar. 1789. The local pound of bread, *poids de table*, weighed only thirteen ounces compared to the standard sixteen ounces, *poids de marc*.

16 AP 1A1 241, Intendant, 26 Mar. 1789 and AN B3 797, Commandant, 21 Apr. 1789.

17 AM L347, Procès-verbal. For extracts from this document and a more delailed discussion of these disturbances see M. Crook, *Journées*

révolutionnaires à Toulon, Nîmes, 1989, pp. 7–17.

18   ADBR B3680, Registre des délibérations du parlement, 13 July 1789.

19   *Mémoires de Louis Richaud*, p. 4.

20   AP 1A1 125, Commandant, 25 Mar. 1789.

21   AM L347, Procès-verbal.

22   Morin, Le problème des subsistances, pp. 8–9; M. Vovelle, 'Les troubles sociaux en Provence, 1750–1792', *Actes du 93e Con. Nat.*, 1968, t. 2, p. 337 and M. Cubells, 'Les mouvements populaires du printemps 1789 en Provence', *Prov. hist.*, XXXVI, 1986, pp. 309–23.

23   AP 1A1 241, Intendant, 26 Mar. 1789.

24   AP 3A1 6, Conseil, 4–6 Mar. 1789 and AM L94(1), Municipalité, 10 Dec. 1788.

25   AM L347, Procès-verbal.

26   AN BIII 146, Lieutenant-général de la sénéchaussée au ministre, 24 Mar. 1789.

27   AM L39, Procès-verbaux des élections des ouvriers de l'arsenal, 28 Mar. 1789 and Lambert, *Histoire*, t. 4, pp. 395–6.

28   AM L68 (1), Délibérations, 18 Mar. 1789 and L39, Cahier.

29   G. V. Taylor, 'Revolutionary and non-revolutionary content in the cahiers of 1789: an interim report', *FHS*, VII, 1972, pp. 497–9.

30   AN Ba 81, Cahier. This document is correctly reproduced in B. F. Hyslop (ed.), *A Guide to the general cahiers of 1789*, 2nd ed., New York, 1967, pp. 419–29, rectifying the error in *Archives parlementaires*, t. 5, p. 788 *et seq.*, where the Toulon town *cahier* has been mistakenly transcribed instead of that of the *sénéchaussée*.

31   AN Ba 81, Lieutenant général, 31 Mar. 1789.

32   AM L39, Assemblées de la sénéchaussée de Toulon, 31 Mar. 1789.

33   AN Ba 81, Assemblées des trois sénéchaussées de Toulon, Brignoles et Hyères, 6 Apr. 1789.

34   O. Teissier, *Les députés de la Provence l'Assemblée nationale de 1789*, Draguignan, 1897, *passim*; P. Fraysse, *Jean-Joseph Rigouard, évêque constitutionnel du Var, 1735–1800*, Marseille, 1928 and J. McManners, *The French Revolution and the Church*, London, 1969, pp. 17–18.

35   AN BIII 146, Nobles non-possédant fiefs Toulon au ministre, 22 Feb. 1789.

36   Lambert, *Histoire*, t. 4, p. 434.

37   J. Murphy and P. Higonnet, 'Les députés de la noblesse aux Etats-généraux de 1789', *RHMC*, XX, 1973, p. 241.

38   Cubells, *Les horizons de la liberté*, pp. 141–5 and M. Crook, 'Les élections aux Etats-généraux de 1789 et les origines de la pratique électorale de la Révolution', in R. Chagny (ed.), *Aux origines provinciales de la Révolution*, Grenoble, 1990, pp. 420–5.

39   A. J. Parès, 'Un Toulonnais Alger aux XVIIIe siècle. Meifrund, Pierre-Joseph, 1723–1814', *Bull. hist.*, XVI, 1931.

40   AM BIII 146, Lieutenant général, 7 Apr. 1789.

41   AM L347, Procès-verbal.

42   AM L68(1), Délibérations, Apr. 1789 and L171, Délibérations des corporations, Apr. 1789.

43   AM L68(1), Délibérations, 22 and 23 July and Henry, *L'histoire de Toulon*, t. 1, p. 58.

44   AM L68(1), Délibérations, 24 July.

45   AM L74, Formation du comité permanent, 24–26 Aug. 1789.

46   Agulhon, *Une ville ouvrière*, p. 10 and D. Ligou, 'A propos de la révolution municipale', *RHES*, 38, 1960, p. 171. See also L. Hunt, 'Committees and communes: local politics and national revolution in 1789', *Comparative Studies in Society and History*, 18, 1976, pp. 327–32.

47   AM L349, Visite au château Missiessy, 24 Aug. 1789 and L350, Le comte d'Orvès, Aug. 1789.

48   AM L68(1), Délibérations, 3 Aug. 1789 and L379, Milice bourgeoise, Aug. 1789.

49   AM L351, Affaire de la cocarde noire, 13 Nov. 1789 and S. F. Scott, *The response of the Royal Army to the French Revolution: the role and development of the line army, 1789–1793*, Oxford, 1978, pp. 77 and 100.

50   C. Lourde, *Histoire de la Révolution à Marseille et en Provence depuis 1789 jusqu'au Consulat*, Marseille, 1838, p. 152.

51   AM L352, Lettre de M. Albert de Rions, 27 Nov. 1789.

52   AM L352, Mémoire de la ville de Toulon, 27 Dec. 1789; AP 1A1 241, Intendant, 2 Dec. 1789 and see Crook, *Journées révolutionnaires*, pp. 19–29.

53   AP 1A1 128, Commandant, 1 Aug. 1789.

54   *Archives parlementaires*, t. 10, pp. 416–22 and 572–3. See also N. Hampson, *A social history of the French Revolution*, London, 1963, p. 96.

55   BM F1006(2), Opinion de M. Malouet sur l'affaire de M. le comte d'Albert, Paris, 1789, and S. F. Scott, 'Problems of law and order during 1790, the "peaceful" year of the French Revolution', *AHR*, 80, 1975, pp. 862–3.

56   AM L68(1), Délibérations, 2 Dec. 1789.

57   J. Godechot, *Les institutions de la France sous la Révolution et l'Empire*, 2nd ed., Paris, 1968, pp. 108–12.

58   AM L68(1), Délibérations, 1 Feb. 1790 and L94(1), Municipalité, same date.

59   AM L573, Affiche and M. Crook, 'The people at the polls: electoral behaviour in revolutionary Toulon, 1789–1799', *French History*, 5, 1991.

60   AM L572, Procès-verbaux d'élection, 10–27 Feb. 1790. For some instructive comparisons, see M. Edelstein, 'Vers une "sociologie électorale" de la Révolution française: la participation des citadins et campagnards, 1789–1793', *RHMC*, XXII, 1975, pp. 513–17.

61   M. Crook, 'Un nouvel espace politique sous la Révolution: les sections de Toulon, 1790–1793', in P. Joutard (ed.), *L'espace et le temps reconstruits. La Révolution française, une révolution des mentalités et des cultures?*, Aix, 1990, pp. 54–6.

62   Godechot, *Les institutions*, pp. 102–7. These arrangements were revised in 1793 when the Comtat-Venaissin was integrated into France and the department of the Vaucluse was carved out. The department of the Alpes-Maritimes did not include any Provençal territory when it was first

established between 1793 and 1815, though it does today.

63   AM L114, Fixation du chef-lieu du département, Jun–Aug. 1790 and
E. Poupé, *Le département du Var, 1790–an VIII*, Cannes, 1933, pp. 1–21.

64   AD 1L218, Procès-verbaux des assemblées primaires, 13–14 June
1790.

65   E. Poupé, *Les districts du Var*, Draguignan, 1898, pp. 26–7.

66   AM L68(3), Délibérations, 28 Jan. 1791.

67   F. Laugier, *Le schisme constitutionnel et la persécution du clergé
dans le départment du Var*, Draguignan, 1897, pp. 202–22.

68   BMT, Castellane-Mazauges, Lettres pastorales, 1790.

69   AD 1L1086, Serment constitutionnel, Dec. 1790; AM L708,
Serments des ecclésiastiques, 1790–91 and T. Tackett, *Religion, revolution
and regional culture in eighteenth-century France. The ecclesiastical oath of
1791*, Princeton, 1986, p. 359.

70   BP, *Recueil des lois relatives à la marine et aux colonies*, t. 2, 21 Sept.
1791 and M. Wyott, 'De l'ordonnateur au préfet maritime, ou l'administrateur du port de Toulon, 1789–1800, *Prov. hist.*, XXI, 1971, pp.
3–5.

71   N. Hampson, 'The "comité de marine" of the Constituent
Assembly', *HJ*, 2, 1959, pp. 141–7 and Acerra and Meyer, *Marines et
Révolution*, pp. 113–19.

72   AP 2E4 74, Revues et soldes, 15 Mar. 1792 and AM L285, Officiers
de marine.

73   AM L355, Affaire de M. de Castellet, Aug. 1790; AP 1A1 242,
Intendant, 12 Aug. 1790 and Henry, *L'histoire de Toulon*, t. 1, pp. 140–3.

74   AM L205, Dénombrement.

75   AM L68(1), Délibérations, 23 Dec. 1789 and Brun, *Port de Toulon*,
t. 2, pp. 161–5.

76   AM L321, Etat nominatif des ouvriers, 15 Mar. 1790 and L68(2),
Délibérations, 28 Apr. 1790.

77   AM L354, Procès-verbal de l'affaire Glandevès, 4 May 1790; AP
1A1 242, Intendant, 4 and 6 May 1790 and Henry, *L'histoire de Toulon*, t.
1, pp. 118–23.

78   AM L321, Demande des calfats, 18 May 1790.

79   AM L321, 7 Oct. 1790.

80   AP 1A1 242, Intendant, 6 Sept. 1790 and Brun, *Port de Toulon*, t. 2,
pp. 160–1.

81   AM L68(2) and (3), Epreuves de pain, 1790, *passim*.

82   F. Furet and D. Richet, *La Révolution française*, Fayard ed., Paris,
1973, p. 99.

5

The Jacobins seize power, 1790–1792

'Toulon remained calm until the establishment of a Jacobin club in the town, then our descent into anarchy began.'

Conflict between notables and popular classes, which had erupted in 1789, re-emerged with a vengeance in Provence at the beginning of 1791. Agitation surrounding the oath of allegiance to the Civil Constitution of the Clergy and fear aroused by the local activities of *émigré* agents have been identified as the principal causes of renewed civil strife.[1] Yet, in the department of the Var as elsewhere in the South-East, the overwhelming majority of parish priests swore to uphold reform of the church, while the threat of counter-revolution tended to unite rather than polarise opinion. It was the formation of political clubs in virtually all of the towns and villages of Lower Provence which seems to have been responsible for provoking fresh discord. These patriotic societies became engines of unrest, employed by their leaders as a means of challenging the existing authorities and seeking to replace them. Thus began a dramatic struggle for power which divided communities and plunged the region into more violent disorder.

A club entitled *La Société patriotique des vrais Amis de la Constitution* was founded at Toulon on 21 June 1790.[2] It was commonly known as the *Club Saint-Jean* because during its heyday meetings were held at the Recollects' convent in the urban *quartier* of Saint-Jean. Historians have usually referred to it as the Jacobin club, since the Toulonnais society quickly affiliated to the parent body in Paris and worked hand in glove with influential counterparts already established at neighbouring Marseille and Aix.[3] Unfortunately the great bulk of the documentation generated by the club at Toulon was destroyed in 1793, when its adversaries succeeded in closing it down. A full analysis of its organisation, ideology and membership is therefore out of the question.

The initial impetus for Jacobin activity in Toulon is also shrouded in mystery, though the society seems to have originated in a series of informal political gatherings that were brought to the attention of the municipal authorities in the spring of 1790.[4] To judge by surviving shreds of evidence, the earliest adherents were recruited from the urban elite, primarily among the liberal professions.[5] Several of these pioneers had already participated in freemasonry, but it seems unlikely that there was any general movement from the lodges, which had become dormant before 1789, to the club.[6] Nonetheless, masonry left behind a rich legacy of 'democratic sociability' and the growth of the *Société patriotique de Toulon* was remarkably similar to its masonic predecessors: it rapidly attracted a large membership, drawn from lower and lower down the social scale, a development which rapidly led to dissension and then division.

The merchant and memoir-writer, Louis Richaud, recalled that the Toulonnais Jacobin society enrolled 'the lower class of artisans and nearly all the sailors and dockyard workers' in the town.[7] The number of signatures appended to addresses in 1791 or 1792 does suggest that the club eventually attracted well in excess of 1,000 members, but it was only during the autumn of 1790 that the popular classes began to join *en masse*. Their attendance at meetings, which took place three evenings a week, was part effect and part cause of a more radical leadership at the club.[8] Conservatively-minded members were perturbed by their loss of control and became thoroughly alarmed when the society began to intervene in local politics.

Controversy arose over a poor turnout in the municipal elections of November 1790. Fewer than 9 per cent of the electorate bothered to participate in the renewal of half the council and this enabled notables to consolidate their hold on the municipality.[9] Club leaders showed their disappointment by an allegation that National Guard officers, drawn from the urban elite, had conspired to ensure a victory for 'partisans of the *ancien régime*'. They had prevented militiamen from voting by deliberately posting them away from their own sections: 'the bulk of those who lived in one *quartier* were assigned duties on the opposite side of town'.[10] This charge rings rather hollow in view of electoral apathy earlier in the year, but militia officers were obviously offended and sought an apology. When rank and file guardsmen were asked for their opinions on the dispute, however, only two out of twenty companies were prepared to censure the club. The commanders of one company immediately resigned and others threatened to follow suit.

These differences were briefly set aside with the arrest of a Toulonnais barrister, C. Granet, on suspicion of complicity in a counter-revolutionary plot at Aix.[11] Club and municipality co-operated in the subsequent investigations, but conflict resumed in the New Year over the establishment of a local judiciary. On 26 January 1791 the town council selected a *bureau de la paix*, a lay conciliation panel which was to assist justices of the peace, newly-created lay magistrates soon to be elected in the cantons.[12] Although the council had acted quite properly in nominating the *bureau*, the Jacobin club insisted that the electorate should have been consulted. Pressing its demand further, the club called for an 'opening', or assembly of the urban sections where the matter could be publicly discussed.[13]

The presentation of a petition to this end, on 27 January, was a new departure at Toulon, though 'direct democracy' of the sort envisaged had already been practised during 1789 and 1790 at Paris and at neighbouring Marseille.[14] Club leaders in Toulon made a similar appeal to the electorate, over the heads of the city council, by invoking an article in the municipal legislation of 1789 which allowed the section assemblies to meet for the purpose of debate. The employment of the sections to override the established authorities had a profound impact upon Toulonnais politics during the turbulent years from 1791 to 1793. Indeed, the neighbourhood assemblies constituted the terrain where the battle for local power was both won and lost by the Jacobins.

Early in 1791 the appeal to popular democracy served the Toulonnais Jacobins well and their confidence in the people was rewarded by an increase in the level of political engagement. For the first meetings, on the evening of 27 January, the register of only one section has survived. It reveals a turnout of 16 per cent in Saint-Pierre, a distinct improvement upon the elections of November 1790, in a central *quartier* not noted for its Jacobin sympathies.[15] When the sections reconvened on 9 February, to address other questions, the overall attendance rose to 24 per cent and in the western *quartier* of Saint-Roch a massive 63 per cent was recorded.[16] The declining turnout of 1790 was reversed and with it the meagre participation of the popular classes, who comprised four out of every five persons now taking part. Sailors and dockyard workers in particular were heeding the call to 'use their rights as citizens' and make their numerical weight felt.

Jacobin leaders had circulated the petition requesting that the sections assemble and they were elected as chairmen and secretaries when the sections met. Radicals like J. S. Barthélemy, the *procureur*, J. L. Bonhomme, a perfume retailer and J. C. Charbonnier, a principal clerk at the Arsenal, also sat on a *comité central* of delegates which acted as a steering group for the eight sections. The powerful popular movement that was emerging was led by individuals from the lower strata of the old elite, who had recently taken control of the club. They were winning mass support from artisans disorientated by the abolition of the trade guilds and from dockyard workers dissatisfied with conditions at the Arsenal. A large following was also attracted by the sponsorship of democratic and egalitarian causes like equal inheritance, universal suffrage and opposition to the silver mark qualification that was required of deputies to the Legislative Assembly: 'You are banishing the great mass of citizens from public office . . . you are giving preference to wealth rather than character and you are telling the poor man that he is not eligible because he lacks a fortune.'[17]

Electoral returns show that support for the Jacobins was concentrated in the outlying *quartiers*, especially in the eastern districts where dockyard workers and sailors were thick on the ground. Resistance emanated principally from the central sections, which formed the administrative and commercial hub of Toulon where the majority of notables resided and maintained business premises. It was there, in the section of Saint-Pierre, that a second political club was eventually founded. Attempts to establish a rival society were first made at the end of January 1791, but bore no fruit until the following July.[18] Nonetheless the initially abortive request for a *Société des Amis et Défenseurs de la Constitution* highlighted the polarisation occurring in the town, as Jacobin leaders took their campaign to the people and alienated the bulk of the urban elite in the process. In common with other French cities, the community at Toulon was dividing along social and neighbourhood lines.

At Toulon, as at Aix or Strasbourg, the new club was a product of schism within the old.[19] Signatories to the later, successful request for a second society, submitted in July 1791, stated that most of them had been members of the Jacobin club until 'The violent behaviour of a handful of sedition-mongers, who had outraged the sensibilities of the membership with a hypocritical display of patriotism that masked their greed and personal interests, forced them to resign.'[20] This assertion is corroborated by a memorandum from the silk merchant Provençal, a founding father of the second club. He claimed that on 27 January all members of the Saint-Jean club were instructed to sign a resolution denouncing the nomination of a *bureau de la paix* and supporting the sections. Those who refused to comply were obliged to withdraw, whereupon they formulated plans for their own society.[21]

The establishment of *Les Amis et Défenseurs de la Constitution* at the convent church of Saint-Pierre was delayed for six months. While the local authorities, if not most sections, were sympathetic, they feared the consequences of club rivalry. But the denial of organised expression to these Toulonnais conservatives, alleged 'associates of the *Société monarchique*' at Paris, cannot obscure the emergence of stiff opposition to the Jacobins. Resistance was headed by notables who saw their political hegemony threatened by the rise of a radical, popular movement. In their eyes the Revolution had been accomplished, hence their resolute defence of the liberal, constitutional monarchy that was being created in France. They aimed to consolidate what had been achieved in 1789, through obedience to the law and respect for property. By their own admission they were chiefly '*rentiers*, merchants and men of means.'

The list of subscribers to the new club included members of the former municipal oligarchy, together with remnants of the service aristocracy. Mercantile dynasties long established at Toulon, like the Granets or Aguillons, were heavily represented, as were numerous barristers, notaries and former naval officers. Their opponents thus had some justification for labelling *Les Amis et Défenseurs*, or the *Club Saint-Pierre*, as representatives of 'the well-to-do, solid bourgeois, rich property-holders', members of the 'the old, aristocratic municipality'. Hyacinthe Paul, soon to become Jacobin mayor of Toulon, castigated his political enemies as 'the class of bourgeois and merchants . . . who . . . want to perpetuate the old order or, worse, foment a counter-revolution'.[22]

Nineteenth-century historians endorsed these contemporary perceptions of the power struggle by referring to the anti-Jacobins as 'the leading bourgeois', or 'les honnêtes gens'.[23] In truth some artisans and shopkeepers were associated with them. The social divide between the rival political factions was not an iron curtain separating all the notables from all the popular classes, although dockyard workers and sailors were conspicuous by their absence from the *Club Saint-Pierre*. Yet, while conservative forces lacked the huge following mobilised by the Jacobins, they could at least count upon the support of official bodies in Toulon. They themselves continued to lead the municipal council and the National Guard, while district and departmental directories and tribunals were staffed by men of a similar stamp and political outlook. These local administrators, who had censured the Saint-Jean club and proposed its closure as early as November 1790, were natural allies of the anxious urban elite.

In the opinion of the Jacobins both District and Department were in the hands of 'administrators tainted by association with the *ancien régime* . . . who plotted the return of the old order . . . and openly supported the bourgeoisie'.[24] In March 1791 the sections of Toulon were persuaded to petition for an immediate renewal of the electoral college of the Var, in an attempt to create more amenable administrative bodies. Since, or so it was alleged, the popular classes had been deterred from voting the previous year, it was hardly surprising that the Toulonnais delegation to the departmental assembly contained 'Practically no artisans, sailors or dockyard workers, although these men comprise the greater part of the electorate . . . In their absence, can it really be said that our delegates represent the will of the majority of the people?'[25] In 1790 district and departmental administrators had inevitably been chosen among 'staunch supporters of the old regime'.

Fresh primary elections were not held in the Var until the summer of 1791 and, when the electoral college did meet, Jacobin delegates from Toulon were overwhelmed by a conservative majority from the interior. However, at Toulon itself the popular momentum swept all before it. Control of the National Guard, which had retained much of the character of a traditional militia, was the first to fall. Reorganisation of the force into section battalions with elected officers, following the example of Marseille, was urgently demanded when the Toulonnais sections met in February 1791. It was, representatives of the eight assemblies declared, 'the duty of true citizens to root out all corrupt remnants of the *ancien régime*, especially those which tend to perpetuate inequality among men'. Because its leaders were nominated rather than elected the current organisation of the National Guard at Toulon was declared to be 'the most defective and unconstitutional of the entire realm'.[26]

Guardsmen were asked to express their opinions and all but a few companies agreed to the changes that were proposed. At the end of February elections for the command of the eight new battalions duly went ahead and attracted an overall turnout of almost 20 per cent of the electorate.[27] Though retired military officers and experienced members of the elite were placed on the general staff, there was a considerable renewal of personnel at section level. Prominent Jacobins captured the officer corps in all but the two central *quartiers* of Saint-Pierre and Saint-Philippe. Not all the *honnêtes gens* were ousted, as Louis Richaud claims in his memoirs but the guard, which was responsible for policing and peace-keeping at Toulon, was now deeply divided.[28] The loyalties of its battalions faithfully reflected the balance of forces within the town, polarised along neighbourhood lines in a manner that was to have fatal consequences during the long, hot summer of 1791.

Some municipal by-elections, held in the spring, proved equally disastrous for the notables. At the end of February an unexpected blow fell with the death of Mayor Richard. His demise led to a special mayoral election on 6 March. The contest was hard fought but Hyacinthe Paul, an experienced barrister and leading member of the *Club Saint-Jean*, emerged victorious from a 22 per cent poll. The support of the popular classes tipped the scales firmly in favour of Paul who, as the only Jacobin candidate, took 75 per cent of the vote. His opponents made little headway in the eastern *quartiers*, but continued to attract a majority in the central sections of the town.[29]

Paul, who was re-elected on two future occasions, remained mayor until July 1793. The council he led when he entered office was still dominated by notables, but this situation soon changed. Growing political pressure and the strain of constantly meeting, almost each day, brought one resignation after another. A number of councillors departed during March 1791 and deputy-councillors preferred to withdraw rather than be promoted to plug the gaps. By the end of the month the deputies' ranks were completely denuded and a fresh round of elections was required in April to fill all thirty vacant positions. On this occasion interest was relatively lukewarm and the competition for places less keen. Yet, despite a low turnout of only 13 per cent, the results yielded further municipal gains for the Jacobins who could now count upon solid backing among deputy-councillors.[30]

Far from resting content with these successes Jacobin leaders focused their attention upon forthcoming primary elections in the two cantons of Toulon. Voting was, as usual, conducted in the section assemblies, on the basis of one delegate for every 100 citizens on the electoral register. However, in June 1791, the choice of delegates to the departmental college of the Var was preceded by the election of justices of the peace. This local component of the revolutionary judicial system, which was taken much more seriously by contemporaries than historians have realised, had already aroused great passion in Toulon in January when the dispute over the *bureau de la paix* had arisen. The Jacobins naturally made careful preparations to ensure the triumph of their candidates as justices. Permission was obtained for dockyard workers to leave the Arsenal for two hours at lunchtime and to finish earlier than usual in the evening, in order to vote at the opening sessions of the electoral assemblies.[31]

These efforts were rewarded by record turnout of 30 per cent and two prominent Jacobins, Barthélemy and Escudier, were declared *juges de paix* for the eastern and western cantons of Toulon respectively.[32] Primary elections were about to begin, on 21 June, when the departmental directory suspended the elections in order to investigate alleged irregularities in the proceedings of the central sections. The interruption was badly received in other neighbourhoods, where the inquiry was seen as a ploy to disqualify Barthélemy and Escudier. Several assemblies only dispersed after registering a strong protest.

In the course of demonstrations the next day *abbé* Simond, a leading club member and local councillor who wore a municipal sash over his cassock, was arrested for inciting unrest.[33] Tension was only defused when departmental administrators relented and allowed the election of delegates to the electoral college to commence on 24 June. During the next two days the level of participation reached an unsurpassed level of 38 per cent, as the competing factions strove for supremacy, but the outcome merely repeated the results of previous months.[34] Save in the *quartiers* of Saint-Philippe and Saint-Pierre Toulon's delegation was completely changed. Conservative notables elected in 1790 were cast aside as retailers, artisans, shopkeepers and a number of dockyard workers topped the polls.

It was widely rumoured that the departmental directory was contemplating further intervention and additional arrests, in an effort to reverse these Jacobin gains. The sections had yet to dissolve and tempers were fraying. Then news of Louis XVI's flight to Varennes arrived and an ugly confrontation was avoided, at least for the time being. It was generally believed that the king's 'abduction' was the signal for an *émigré* invasion from the nearby frontier. Once again an external threat proved salutary, prompting a *union sacrée* as the warring factions united in mutual defence. Municipal, district and departmental bodies met in joint assembly and their spirit of solidarity was reflected in a resolution from the Jacobin-dominated section of Saint-Vincent: 'At such a critical juncture it is essential that all citizens come together and sink their differences, that each person sacrifices party preferences for the good of the nation.'[35] The *directoire du départment* was able to report that 'all personal animosities were put aside and all the citizens agreed to concern themselves solely with issues of national security'.[36]

This respite was prolonged by the celebration of the *quatorze juillet* and still more by the relief which greeted decrees maintaining the monarchy later in the month. There was no trace of republican sentiment at Toulon. On the contrary, the Jacobin club not only condemned the 'troublemakers' who had 'provoked' the Champ de Mars incident at Paris by drawing up an anti-monarchical petition, but went on to rival district and departmental directories with a flowery tribute to the National Assembly and its 'majestic decrees'. An address from a self-styled 'majority of inhabitants' was even more glowing and exulted: 'These resolutions are the despair of those lawless individuals who only spread republican ideas because they want anarchy', before concluding with the standard assertion that monarchy was the only form of government suitable for France.[37] The provenance of this document is significant: it emanated from a gathering sponsored by conservative elements, full of new-found determination and confidence.

The reaction which followed the king's flight encouraged anti-Jacobins at Toulon to present a fresh petition in favour of their own political club on 26 July.[38] This time the municipal council reluctantly gave way and the *Amis et Défenseurs de la Constitution* began to meet at the former Augustinian convent two evenings a week. The eventual establishment of the Saint-Pierre society coincided with the Feuillants' secession from the Jacobin club at Paris. This schism had disorientated affiliated Jacobin organisations everywhere and offered a particularly good opportunity for Toulonnais conservatives to launch their counter-attack.[39] Two well-defined and well-organised 'parties' now existed in the town and a violent clash occurred between them as soon hostilities resumed over the election of local *juges de paix.*

A lengthy departmental inquiry into proceedings at the original assemblies had revealed contraventions of electoral law, albeit rather minor ones, and three sections were ordered to repeat their operations on 31 July. Although Barthélemy and Escudier were given another big majority allegations of ballot-rigging provided a further pretext for investigation by the authorities. This goaded the Jacobins into calling a mass meeting at the former Minims convent, on 4 August, which drew up a petition urging the departmental directory to ratify the election. The submission of this address to departmental headquarters on the Cours d'Arbres was made in the presence of a large crowd, composed mainly of the popular classes, who broke into the building and forced administrators to give way.[40] The *Club Saint-Pierre* and its allies in the hinterland mounted a counter-demonstration the next day, but the election of Barthélemy and Escudier was allowed to stand and voting for their assistants (the *assesseurs*) went ahead in the sections during the following week. All these elections were subsequently quashed by the central government; it was late December before the saga ended, with a different pair of Jacobin justices eventually receiving official endorsement.[41]

The rival factions carried their electoral differences on to the streets of Toulon in August 1791. Contemporaries were shocked by the brutality of what municipal leaders characterised as a class war, 'with clear lines of battle between the bourgeoisie and the popular classes'.[42] Law and order broke down under the strain, while the town council was undermined by another series of resignations, which Jacobins claimed was a consequence of deliberate intimidation. Even more alarming was division within the peace-keeping forces: 'two well-defined factions existed within the National Guard at Toulon'.[43] The departmental administration sought to suspend the militia and replace it with regular troops, but this was anathema to the municipality which regarded the proposal as another reactionary gambit. Attempts by the district tribunal to arrest citizens involved in street brawls were viewed as shameless provocation, part of the same anti-Jacobin conspiracy; civil war was being stirred up to facilitate counter-revolution. The tribunal was regarded as dispensing one-sided justice, protecting the notables while 'dockyard workers and artisans . . . are being insulted all the time'.[44] It was the issue of warrants to incarcerate three Jacobins held responsible for disturbances on 18 August which precipitated a pitched battle five days later.

It is not easy to establish exactly what happened on the evening of 23 August at Toulon.[45] It would appear that a crowd of armed individuals, many of them dockyard workers, gathered on the aptly-named Champ de Bataille to object to the arrest of their colleagues. The municipal council refused to summon garrison troops and chose instead to rely upon the National Guard to disperse the demonstrators. However, some of the militiamen fraternised with the crowd and then, in the confusion, shots were fired. As the departmental directory put it: 'It proved impossible to prevent the two parties which had formed within the National Guard opening fire on each other.'[46] The resulting *mêlée* left seven dead and several persons badly wounded, before martial law was imposed and garrison soldiers succeeded in restoring order. There seems no doubt that 'martial law was proclaimed . . . too late'.[47] A traditional reluctance to surrender up authority to the army, rather than any sympathy for the rioters, led to an inadequate and indecisive response on the part of the municipal council. Opponents of the Jacobins were not slow to capitalise upon the mistake.

The National Assembly was horrified that 'civil war' should erupt in its Mediterranean naval port. Martial law was not lifted until 8 September and proposals were made, though not implemented, to disband the Toulonnais National Guard and both political clubs.[48] Meanwhile the district tribunal initiated proceedings against twelve members of the town council, who were accused of criminal incompetence in mismanaging the disturbances. Jacobins like Barthélemy fled to the safe haven of Marseille to escape prosecution, but the indictment was later dropped as a gesture of reconciliation when the Constitution of 1791 came into effect in the autumn. An abortive attempt was also made to exclude Toulonnais radicals from the electoral college which met in the Var in September to choose deputies for the new Legislative Assembly and to replenish the departmental administration. 'Tribunals and administration have combined to prevent the best citizens being elected to the Assembly', wrote the Saint-Jean club to its parent body in Paris.[49] In fact Jacobins remained in a minority at the *assemblée électorale*. An anti-Jacobin from Toulon, the former magistrate M. A. Granet, was elected as one of the Varois deputies, who were mostly conservatives, while a like-minded team was chosen for the departmental executive.[50]

Notables also retained control at district level and briefly recovered Toulon itself. More resignations from the municipal council in September, in addition to the removal of members deemed guilty of misconduct, enabled the departmental directory to nominate replacements.[51] The contrast between a dozen commissioners named by the directory and the handful of elected councillors allowed to remain in post was a sharp one. The former included a military officer, two retired naval captains, two *rentiers*, a merchant, a doctor, a barrister and a soap manufacturer; the latter comprised a merchant seaman, a customs official, a joiner, a house painter and a naval pilot.

In other words, representatives of the *Club Saint-Pierre*, 'les honnêtes gens', resumed authority in the town, but they were obliged to surrender it again when the annual round of municipal elections was held in November. This contest was fiercely fought and the level of participation was high, at 30 per cent of the electorate.[52] Opposing candidates were clearly defined and on this occasion Paul faced a single rival in his bid for re-election as mayor. Though he failed to win in the central sections, and his overall majority was reduced, Paul emerged as victor, like his Jacobin colleagues on the council. Radically-minded notables were returned as councillors, while clerks, shopkeepers and artisans predominated as deputy-councillors. Supported by the bulk of the popular classes the Jacobins had triumphed once again at the polls. Yet their share of the vote had slipped somewhat and they were evidently chastened by the behaviour of over-zealous followers, which had cost them dear in the summer. Thus they entered office with a call for unity upon the bases of 'nation, king and law'; the people of Toulon were asked to rally behind the revolutionary settlement enshrined in the 1791 Constitution.

The calm that ensued, in the winter and early spring of 1791–92, suggested that these appeals were succeeding, to the extent that in February 1792 members of the two political clubs fraternised at a public banquet.[53] Those issues which did cause concern threatened the town's security and tended to bring the inhabitants together rather than divide them. For example, the passage of the refractory Ernest-Suisse regiment through Toulon was opposed by all shades of opinion and these suspect troops were duly diverted elsewhere.[54]

Likewise, though fresh elections in February 1792 saw the Jacobins strengthen their control over the National Guard, there was general agreement that the militia should be better armed.[55] The various local authorities joined in criticising garrison and dockyard officials for their failure to supply the Guard with sufficient weapons and ammunition to defend the town.

As war with monarchical Europe loomed ever larger civilians from both ends of the political spectrum voiced similar misgivings about the reliability of the armed services. While *commandant* de Flotte was exaggerating when he reported that only two lieutenants and not a single captain were enrolled at Toulon, a review of the fleet in March 1792 did reveal that half of the officer corps had refused to re-enlist in the revolutionary navy.[56] The departure of so many of their colleagues inevitably cast suspicion upon those who remained, especially if they were former noblemen. The naval *commandant* himself was arrested in March for allegedly writing a letter that subscribed to counter-revolutionary opinions. De Flotte's residence was subsequently searched but, since no incriminating evidence was unearthed, he was released. The following month the elderly garrison chief, de Coincy, was treated in a similar fashion. It was significant that the departmental directory approved these precautionary measures, which were instigated by an ever-vigilant municipal council.[57]

Co-operation in security matters was matched by mutual efforts to contain popular anger over a substantial rise in prices. During the second half of 1791 the cost of living began a steep upward movement. By February 1792 a pound loaf in the naval port was 30 per cent dearer than a year before.[58] A below-par harvest was partly to blame, but the major factor was the appearance of paper money, or *assignats*. Dockyard workers were immediately affected because the naval administration sought to insert the fast-depreciating currency into its employees' wages. In November 1791 one 5-*livre* note was used to make up salaries of more than 30 *livres*. The treasurer at the Arsenal intended to increase the proportion of *assignats* every month until, in February, he encountered strident protests and was obliged to withdraw them altogether.[59]

The chief naval administrator (*ordonnateur*) decided that no further attempt to employ *assignats* would be made until improved pay scales were introduced later in the year. A potentially explosive conflict was shelved because the outbreak of war, declared in April

1792, made stability at the dockyards the main priority. In another effort to appease workers at the Arsenal the dockyard administration established a bread dole, which enabled wage-earners to satisfy their families' needs below cost price. A system of child benefits, already operating in the Atlantic ports, was also extended to Toulon in the spring of 1792.[60] Mobilisation simultaneously reactivated the shipyards and promised an upturn in the flagging urban economy. Even before the maritime powers joined the coalition against France, at the beginning of 1793, a Mediterranean fleet was being fitted out at Toulon, generating a good many jobs and contracts in the process.[61]

Rising inflation, however, undermined this change of fortunes and with it the fragile political equilibrium that had been struck over the winter months. Plummeting paper money prompted the departmental directory to write in desperation to the Finance Committee at Paris: 'we dare not envisage, still less cater for the catastrophe which may ensue'.[62] By early summer 1792 the *assignat* was losing 50 per cent when exchanged for goods and the district tribunal had not helped by ruling that the refusal of retailers to accept notes was perfectly legal. There were disturbances outside bakers' shops in April, but it was only when such discontent merged with serious reverses on the military front that political divisions at Toulon rose to the surface.

On 26 May 1792, prompted by their counterparts at Marseille, the Toulonnais Jacobins called for the despatch of volunteers to help defend Paris against the enemy.[63] The departmental directory was unwilling to concede this demand, but it agreed that a token force should travel to the capital to participate in Bastille Day celebrations. Like the 600 volunteers who set out from the Bouches-du-Rhône, the eighty Varois militiamen were committed Jacobins, drawn from the artisan–shopkeeper strata.[64] They too 'knew how to die' and they were also involved in the momentous events of 10 August which brought down the monarchy. Indeed, one of the sixteen recruits from Toulon, the glazier J.B. Gueit, subsequently returned to the Midi and was executed by royalist rebels in September 1793 for 'desecrating the king's palace'.[65]

The departmental administration in the Var regarded the levy of volunteers as a fresh Jacobin offensive, rather than a reflex action in face of national defeat and danger: 'At this very moment intrigue and factionalism is dominating the popular societies . . . In some of these clubs the talk is all of destroying property and cutting off aristocrats' heads. And who is designated by this infamous word? In the towns wealthy merchants and substantial property-owners; in rural areas those whom we call *rentiers* (*bourgeois*).'[66] The reluctance of District, Department and their related tribunals to take firm measures to tackle the crisis convinced Jacobins that these administrators were sympathetic towards counter-revolution. Nowhere was this divergence more apparent than in their respective attitudes towards the monarchy.

Louis XVI had angered Toulonnais Jacobins in January 1792 when he had used the royal veto to block legislation against the *émigrés*. Condemnation by the club had stopped short of the king himself – 'you are surrounded by traitors, your majesty . . . their wicked advice may lead you astray' – but when Louis dismissed his Girondin ministers in June the monarch was no longer spared.[67] On 20 June, the same day that a massive anti-monarchical demonstration was mounted in Paris, a monster petition bearing over 700 signatures was drawn up at a mass meeting in Toulon: 'Is it true that the head of state . . . is a perjurer who is conniving at the misfortune of his people?', it asked.[68] Although they referred to Louis XVI as 'Monsieur de Varennes', the Jacobins of Toulon remained reluctant republicans. It was another month before they dared seek the king's suspension, not on ideological grounds, but because 'Louis XVI no longer respects the Constitution.'[69]

The departmental directory in the Var took an entirely different attitude. It demanded severe punishment for those Parisians who, on 20 June, had invaded the Tuileries and 'violated the constitution in the person of the hereditary representative of the nation'. As defenders of king and established order departmental officials claimed they were threatened as much by 'anarchists' as by 'aristocrats'. They concluded with a promise to stand firm, whatever the consequences: 'Only by marching over our corpses will these factions succeed in overthrowing the Constitution.'[70] Little did the authors of this address realise how prophetic their words would be. The following month a national emergency was declared and, in the ensuing panic, the Var was plunged into bloodshed.

Jacobins argued that only 'patriotic excesses' were penalised at Toulon, while counter-revolutionary crimes went unpunished.[71] On July 1792 the *Club Saint-Jean* proceeded to petition for suspension of departmental administrators who, it was stated, 'have not provided the slightest proof of loyalty since the outset of the Revolution'. This was followed by another tirade a few days later: 'The country is really in a state of crisis, but less on account of the enemies who are pouring over our frontiers than as a consequence of those evil citizens who ravage the interior.' The Toulonnais Jacobins went on to demand a purge of the enemy within, beginning with the king and encompassing departmental and district directories, as well as judicial bodies and leaders of the armed forces.[72]

These objectives were achieved, at Toulon as elsewhere in the Midi, by popular revolutionary violence which took radicals by surprise, though they had rhetorically fanned the conflagration. On 19 July the Toulonnais Jacobins, who were sending out agents to set up clubs everywhere in the region, established a central committee for affiliated societies in the Var. Fourteen Varois clubs sent delegates to Toulon, where they assembled under the chairmanship of J. L. Bonhomme.[73] The purpose of this gathering was ostensibly to defend the frontier department against invasion yet, meeting in defiance of the local authorities, it sponsored petitions against the King and generally heightened tension in the town. A week later the mobilisation of the popular classes was further advanced by a request from the *Club Saint-Jean* that the sections assemble every day (*en permanence*), like other elected bodies.[74] Even the municipal council jibbed at this proposal, but to no avail, for the sections began to convene without official sanction. As Toulon became ungovernable so a wave of upheaval smashed the conservative opposition and overwhelmed administrators who stood in its way.

The dreadful days of summer 1792, 'l'horrible trimestre' which so embedded itself in the Toulonnais consciousness, began on 27 July with the murder of a refractory priest at nearby La Valette.[75] In the town itself the home of Reboul, a prominent anti-Jacobin merchant, was ransacked that same evening. Next morning hostile demonstrators massed outside the departmental headquarters on the Cours d'Arbres. When four members of the administration emerged to appeal for calm they were seized, beaten and hung from lamp posts. In the evening Reboul himself was put *à la lanterne* and on the three following days, 29 to 31 July, two anti-Jacobin manufacturers, two judges and two more administrators were brutally massacred, together with a *concierge* at the *palais de justice*. One of these poor victims was discovered hiding in a convent church, while another was dragged to his death from hospital, where he had been taken after sustaining injury in a vain effort to flee by scaling the city walls.

These grisly events were to continue sporadically during August and September, despite an attempted reconciliation where it was declared that 'the rival names Saint-Jean and Saint-Pierre would be forgotten'.[76] A district administrator and another merchant were next to be slaughtered by the crowd, which then turned its wrath upon military personnel. A retired sea-captain was killed on 18 August as he was being brought to prison at Toulon. In September a serving naval officer was murdered, on the same day that *commandant de marine* de Flotte was lynched near the Arsenal, while the *ordonnateur*, de Possel, narrowly avoided a similar fate. Finally, towards the end of the month, two militiamen from Le Beausset were hauled from gaol and battered to death. They had been imprisoned for their involvement in releasing some 1,000 convicts from the dockyard prison hulks on 23 August. In this most bizarre of incidents escaped prisoners ran amok on the streets of Toulon, dancing the *farandole* and shouting *Vive la Liberté*, until all of them were recaptured.[77]

More than twenty persons perished in the course of this carnage, which preceded the notorious September massacres in Paris. For nineteenth-century historians the violence at Toulon stemmed from 'the bestial instincts of the people', released in a blind fury. Yet the victims of these atrocities were, in the main, well-known opponents of the Toulonnais Jacobins. Their selective murders can be attributed to a psychosis of fear and betrayal, generated by a climate of war and counter-revolution. Among the remarks uttered by assailants were frequent references to the political and social affiliations of their prey. 'Aristocrate' or 'patriote soupçonné' were the words most often employed in this bloodthirsty discourse. One assassin is said to have added: 'Thus the poor are avenged on the rich and powerful . . . The aristocracy of nobles and clergy has already been overthrown . . . but the strongest aristocracy of all remains in place – that of the bourgeoisie.'[78]

The perpetrators of the massacres cannot be easily identified as no arrests were made at the time and it was left to the anti-Jacobin regime to exact revenge a year later, in circumstances hardly conductive to judicial impartiality. Between July and October 1793, no less than twenty-one individuals were arraigned before a 'popular tribunal' and put to death for political crimes committed at the end of July 1792.[79] Several of the condemned men were well-known

Jacobin militants who had been active since 1789, like Beausoleil or Bonnaud (whose *sobriquet* was 'moustache'), but their background was typical of the accused in general. They were dockyard workers, artisans or shopkeepers by trade and mostly Toulonnais by birth.

Another four persons, club officials drawn from higher up the social scale, were also executed in 1793 for allegedly orchestrating the violence. In fact Mayor Paul, convicted of incitement to murder, was badly injured trying to save a victim from the crowd. The commander of the National Guard was actually killed in a vain effort to halt the slaughter, though once again the town council had been reluctant to declare martial law. These Jacobin casualties might suggest the blood-letting was essentially a wild outburst of popular anger, rather than a settlement of political accounts. Yet J. J. Silvestre, a Jacobin official, had led a 'civic procession' through Toulon on 27 July 1792, on the eve of the massacres, threatening 'aristocrats' and 'carrying a noose instead of a flag'. In the aftermath of these terrible events a report to the Jacobin Club at Paris expressed little remorse, glibly stating that 'a popular uprising, provoked by attacks from aristocrats, has resulted in a number of deaths'.[80] Sympathetic administrators added: 'In the dreadful circumstances facing us, the Jacobins of Toulon preferred tough to tender action; *Feuillants* and reactionaries received their just deserts.'

Ambivalence towards the victims, rather than direct responsibility for the outrage, reflects the political advantages which the Toulonnais Jacobins derived from these terrible *journées*. Leading opponents had been liquidated, the rival Saint-Pierre club was closed and conservative elements withdrew from all public activity. Administrative bodies which had resisted Jacobin pressure lay in ruins. The Department could muster a mere nine administrators from a total of thirty-six, the District was reduced to just two members and their respective tribunals had also been devastated by death or desertion. A transfusion of new blood was urgently required to maintain the system of local government and assist the over-worked municipal council at Toulon. Survivors from the departmental and district administrations accordingly met to nominate a dozen commissioners to replenish their depleted ranks.[81] The machinery of justice took rather longer to repair; only in September was a temporary criminal court created, by means of special elections in the sections of Toulon.[82]

Prominent Jacobins from Toulon, emanating for the most part

from the minor liberal professions and the retailing trades, filled the administrative vacancies for a few months until regular elections were held in the late autumn. Their brief tenure of these important local offices represented the high-water mark of Toulonnais influence in the Var, unhindered by central government and surrounding communities alike. The power wielded by the Jacobins in the chief town was even greater than the composition of the various commissions would suggest, because all decisions were made by the three local authorities (*les trois corps administratifs*) acting in concert. Department, district and municipal councils assembled daily in joint session, often assisted by delegates from club, sections and Arsenal, where workers followed the prevailing fashion and established their own *comité central*.[83]

According to opponents the *Club Saint-Jean* controlled 'all administrative bodies and disposed of all the opportunities for employment', even at the Arsenal.[84] The dockyard had been reduced to chaos in September with the loss of both *commandant* and *ordonnateur* in the disorders. Thivend, the only remaining naval commissioner, was obliged to become provisional director and he summoned the dockyard council, on a daily basis, in an effort to restore some semblance of authority. It was no easy task and, writing to the ministry on 23 September, Thivend described the disarray confronting him: 'There are no leaders left; the principal administrators are either on sick leave or with the fleet, while the rest are in deep despair or frightened to death.'[85] A new *ordonnateur* named Pache was appointed at the beginning of October, only to resign a week later when he was made Minister of War. To fill the breach the local authorities intervened and decided to install Paul, the Mayor of Toulon, as his successor. For a month even the Arsenal, which had so often dictated to the municipality, came under civilian and Jacobin sway. Vincent, the official replacement, had considerable difficulty establishing himself when he arrived in November.[86]

None of the initiatives taken to restore stability at Toulon had actually been approved by government ministers. On the contrary, news of the July massacre was expected to elicit an extremely hostile response from the Legislative Assembly in Paris. For this reason two envoys had been despatched to the capital to explain the extraordinary series of events and to plead for a sympathetic hearing. It was fortunate that by the time the pair arrived in Paris the revolutionary events of 10 August were under way, thrusting upheaval at

Toulon firmly into the background. The overthrow of king and constitution provided a *de facto* sanction for the violence which had already occurred in the naval town; the rump of the Assembly simply declared its satisfaction with the way the Toulonnais municipality had handled a difficult situation.

At the end of August an expanded electorate was invited to create a fresh departmental assembly in the Var. It was to choose deputies for a National Convention, entrusted with the task of founding the First French Republic. The abolition of restrictions on the franchise for these primary elections had no great effect at Toulon, where the suffrage was already universal, but lowering the voting age to twenty-one did make a slight impact. Turnout in the town was roughly 25 per cent, compared to 15 per cent in the department as a whole.[87] In the absence of any real opposition Jacobin candidates swept the board. No less than forty-four of the fifty-six Toulonnais delegates were drawn from the popular classes and everywhere radicals were returned. When the electoral college met at Grasse in September Charbonnier and Escudier, two well-known Jacobins from Toulon, were elected to the Convention at the top of a list of mainly *montagnard* deputies, who included the infamous Paul Barras.

Two months later the electoral college reconvened to appoint a regular administration for the Var.[88] Victories on the battlefield, especially the capture of Nice in October, brought a relaxation of political tension. In these circumstances the departmental council regained a more familiar appearance. Notables returned to the helm and Toulonnais representation was significantly reduced. Nonetheless authority resided with new men who were Jacobin in outlook and, since the council continued to assemble in company with district and municipal councils at Toulon, the influence of the town remained very strong. The local district council was inevitably dominated by Toulonnais, who scored a further success in December when one of their number, J. S. Barthélemy, was chosen as president of the restored departmental criminal court.

As 1792 drew to a close it was the turn of the municipalities to hold elections. At Toulon the level of participation was relatively poor, with a turnout of only 15 per cent but, because their opponents abstained, Jacobins from the *Club Saint-Jean* triumphed easily.[89] Paul was re-elected mayor with 95 per cent of the votes cast and, since leading club members had found places on superior bodies, the

Table 5 Office-holding in the Municipality of Toulon, 1790–Year VII (1799)

Category	Feb. 1790		Nov. 1790		Apr. 1791		Nov. 1791		Dec. 1792		Jul. 1793		Nominated Years II–III		Elected Years III–VII	
	No.	%	No.	%	No.	%	No.	%	No.	%	No.	%	No.	%	No.	%
Military officers & officials	–	–	–	–	–	–	–	–	–	–	3	6.3	–	–	–	–
Rentiers	7	14.9	11	23.4	8	17.0	2	4.3	–	–	4	8.3	–	–	1	4.3
Liberal professions	17	36.2	10	21.3	8	17.0	3	6.4	2	4.3	5	10.4	1	2.5	4	17.4
Merchants	5	10.6	7	14.9	4	8.5	1	2.1	–	–	7	14.6	5	12.5	2	8.7
Retailers	8	17.0	10	21.3	9	19.1	9	19.1	5	10.6	7	14.6	8	20.0	5	21.7
Clerks	1	2.1	–	–	5	10.6	5	10.6	8	17.0	2	4.2	2	5.0	2	8.7
Artisans & shopkeepers	8	17.0	8	17.0	11	23.4	18	38.3	23	48.9	6	12.5	22	55.0	6	26.1
Dockyard workers	–	–	–	–	–	–	4	8.5	7	14.9	9	18.7	–	–	2	8.7
Sailors	1	2.1	1	2.1	2	4.3	3	6.4	2	4.3	5	10.4	–	–	–	–
No profession indicated	–	–	–	–	–	–	2	4.3	–	–	–	–	2	5.0	1	4.3
Total	47		47		47		47		47		48		40		23	

Source: AM L68 (1-9), Délibérations du conseil municipal, 1790–an VII (1799).

town council exhibited a more popular complexion than ever before. Of fourteen councillors one was a grain merchant, another a wine retailer and the third a tanner; the remainder comprised two shopkeepers, two clerks, two naval gunners, four carpenters and a ships' painter. Few of these individuals had any previous administrative experience and most of the deputy-councillors, among whom dockyard workers and artisans predominated, were similarly inexperienced.

Louis XVI's execution in January 1793, like the abolition of the monarchy a few months earlier, was warmly applauded by local administrators at Toulon. The only complaint was that 'the tyrant' had been spared for so long.[90] However, strong republican sentiment was accompanied by an increasing emphasis upon the need for order and obedience. Firmly ensconced in office, Jacobin leaders issued repeated warnings against lawlessness and demanded restraint from their followers. As early as 25 August 1792, in the wake of the mass escape from the prison hulks, municipality, district and department issued a joint proclamation to the populace: 'These excesses must end . . . if the law is not observed then the country has fallen into the gravest of dangers.'[91] The renewed outbreak of disturbances in September prompted a sterner rebuke: 'Liberty and equality can only exist if all citizens submit themselves to the laws in a constant and wholehearted fashion . . . you will only be happy when you accept the rule of law.'[92]

The murder of a constitutional priest at La Valette, on the outskirts of Toulon, at the end of October, caused considerable anger among Jacobin leaders. One of them, Jean-Louis Bonhomme, who was a justice of the peace, mounted the rostrum at the club to insist that 'without the exercise of virtue your revolution will be in vain'. He finished his speech by threatening 'any individual reckless enough to sanction such acts of brutality' with loss of membership.[93] This was no empty harangue. The first sentence of death recorded by the departmental tribunal was pronounced in January 1793, against a Toulonnais stonemason called Figon. He was condemned to the guillotine for acts of 'terrorism' and had been prosecuted with the full co-operation of the local Jacobin club (recently renamed the Republican Society). As he delivered his verdict the public prosecutor declared: 'May this example serve as a warning to all wrongdoers, bring them to a respect for property and remind them of the duties they have abandoned, so that we can at last enjoy that tranquillity and repose which we have sought for so long.'[94]

Once in office victorious Jacobins were anxious to end the turmoil which had engulfed Toulon. Their quest for power had proved extremely bloody, the consequence of deep-rooted political and social tensions which had been released but not resolved in 1789. The urban notables briefly reasserted their authority in 1790, before they were swept away by a powerful popular movement in which sailors and dockyard workers predominated. Leaders at the Jacobin club had mobilised their supporters in the sections to win municipal supremacy by electoral means, but it was the 'primitive' violence of an unruly crowd which ultimately defeated their opponents in the fearful summer of 1792. Though they immediately sought to restore stability and suppress disorder the Jacobins could not cast off an aura of anarchy and extremism. Their pursuit of respectability, moreover, risked alienating expectant and undisciplined followers; no sooner had the Toulonnais Jacobins triumphed than popular disaffection began to pave the way for their downfall.

Notes

1 Baratier (ed.), *Histoire de la Provence*, pp. 405–7 and Poupé, *Le département du Var*, p. 74.

2 AM L68(2), Délibérations, 18 June 1790 and H. Labroue, *Le club jacobin de Toulon, 1790–1796*, Paris, 1907, pp. 3–6.

3 M. Kennedy, *The Jacobin club of Marseilles*, Ithaca, 1973, pp. 212–13 and Kennedy, *The Jacobin clubs in the French Revolution*, 2 vols., Princeton, 1982–88, t. 1, p. 16.

4 AM L68(2), Délibérations, 22 and 24 Apr. 1790.

5 AN DIV 66, 1997, Citoyens de Toulon à l'Assemblée nationale, 25 Apr. 1790.

6 Agulhon, *Pénitents*, pp. 262–5 and Halévi, *Les loges maçonniques*, pp. 103–6.

7 *Mémoires de Louis Richaud*, p. 17.

8 AM L68(3), Délibérations, 25 Nov. 1790 and L509, Extrait du registre, 22 Nov. 1790.

9 AM L574, Procès-verbaux d'élection, 14–20 Nov. 1790.

10 AM L386, Dissentiment avec la société patriotique, Nov. 1790.

11 AM L356, Affaire Granet, Dec. 1790.

12 AM L68(3), Délibérations, 26 Jan. 1791 and Godechot, *Les institutions*, pp. 148–9.

13 AM L68(3), Délibérations, 27 Jan. 1791.

14 AM L509, Club patriotique, 6 Feb. 1791; R. B. Rose, *The making of the sans-culottes. Democratic ideas and institutions in Paris, 1789–1792*, Manchester, 1983, especially chapter IV, and Crook, 'Un nouvel espace

politique', pp. 57–8.

15   AM L78, Assemblées des sections, 27 Jan.–1 Feb. 1791 and L592, Procès-verbal de la section Saint-Pierre, 27 Jan. 1791.

16   AM L79, Assemblées des sections, 9 Feb.–22 Mar. 1791.

17   AN DIV 66, 1990, Amis de la constitution à l'Assemblée nationale, 10 May 1791; AM L81, Adresse des citoyens actifs, 29 Apr. 1791 and Labroue, *Le club jacobin*, p. 18.

18   AM L512, Les Amis et Défenseurs de la Constitution, 31 Jan. and 26 July 1791.

19   Kennedy, *The Jacobin clubs*, vol. 1, pp. 26–8 and H. Gough, 'Politics and power: the triumph of Jacobinism in Strasbourg, 1791–1793', *HJ*, 23, 1980, pp. 341–3. At Aix however, the schism produced a more popular, rather than a more conservative, second club.

20   AN DIV 66, 1990, Adresse à l'Assemblée nationale, 23 July 1791.

21   AM L512, Mémoire de M. Provençal, 31 Jan. 1791.

22   AN DXXIX 79, 186, La Société patriotique à l'Assemblée nationale, 19 Aug. 1791 and AM L368, Mémoire de H. Paul, 13 Aug. 1791.

23   Henry, *L'histoire de Toulon*, t. 1, p. 162 and Brun, *Port de Toulon*, t. 2, p. 171.

24   AN DXXIX 79, 186, La Société patriotique à l'Assemblée nationale, 18 Dec. 1790, and BMT 4059, Adresse de la société patriotique, 31 Jan. 1791.

25   AM L576, Adresse des sections, 21 Mar. 1791.

26   AM L387, Commissaires des sections au conseil municipal, 13 Feb. 1791.

27   AM L388, Procès-verbaux d'élection, 24 Feb.–2 Mar. 1791.

28   AM L68(4), Délibérations, 29 Mar. 1791 and *Mémoires de Louis Richaud*, pp. 12–13.

29   AM L576, Procès-verbaux d'élection, 6 Mar. 1791.

30   AM L577, Procès-verbaux d'élection, 10–15 Apr. 1791.

31   AD 1L1727, Délibérations du directoire du district de Toulon, 22 June 1792.

32   AD 1L1848, Procès-verbaux dèélection, 19–20 June 1791.

33   AM L357, Affaire de l'abbé Simond, 22 June 1791.

34   AD 1L218, Procès-verbaux d'élection, 24–25 June 1791

35   AM L338, Adresse de la section Saint-Vincent, 26 June 1791.

36   AN FI CIII Var 11, Département au ministre, 26 June 1791.

37   AM L80, Adresses à l'Assemblée nationale, 23–27 July 1791. Coulet, 'Le massacre des administrateurs', p. 442, is wrong to suggest that 'a "republican party" was set up by the Jacobins at the end of 1790'.

38   AM L512, Les Amis et Défenseurs, 26 July 1791.

39   AM L510, La Société patriotique aux Jacobins de Paris, 9 Aug. 1791 and Kennedy, *The Jacobin clubs*, t. 1, pp. 287–92.

40   AD 1L104, Délibérations du directoire du département, 3–5 Aug. 1791 and AM L358, Procès-verbal de l'affaire des Minimes, 4 Aug. 1791.

41   AD 1L848, Procès-verbaux, 5–12 Aug. and 26–27 Dec. 1791.

42   AM L358, Les officiers municipaux de Toulon aux députés, 9–10 Aug. 1791.

43   AD 1L277, Procès-verbal de l'émeute du 23 août 1791, 25 Aug. 1791.

44   AN DXXIX 79, 186, Amis de la constitution l'Assemblée nationale, 19 Aug. 1791.

45   AM L358, Procès-verbal de l'émeute du 23 août and AP 1A1 243, Ordonnateur, 24 Aug. 1791. See also Crook, *Journées révolutionnaires*, pp. 31–9.

46   AN F7 3693 Var 1, Département au ministre, 5 Dec. 1791.

47   AN F7 3693 Var I, Commandant au ministre, 25 Aug. 1791.

48   Kennedy, *The Jacobin clubs*, vol. 1, p. 212, wrongly suggests that the Saint-Jean club was closed. Other historians, like Coulet, 'Le massacre des administrateurs', p. 424, have mistakenly attributed this fate to the Saint-Pierre society. Both clubs survived: Saint-Pierre until the summer of 1792, Saint-Jean until 1793.

49   F. A. Aulard (ed.), *La société des Jacobins*, 6 vols., Paris, 1889–97, t. 3, p. 123.

50   Poupé, *Le département du Var*, pp. 13–16.

51   AD 1L104, Délibérations, 2–6 Sept. 1791.

52   AM L579, Procès-verbaux d'élection, 13–24 Nov. 1791.

53   Henry, *L'histoire de Toulon*, t. 1, p. 212.

54   AM L361, L'affaire du régiment Ernest-Suisse, Feb.–Mar. 1792.

55   AM L392, Procès-verbaux d'élection, 8 Feb. 1792 and L68(5), Délibérations, 28 Feb. and 6 Mar. 1792.

56   AN BB3 13, Commandant, 6 June 1792 and AP 2E4 74, Revues et soldes, 1792.

57   AM L361, Arrestation de M. de Flotte, 14 Mar. 1792 and L362, Arrestation de M. de Coincy, 6 Apr. 1792.

58   AM L68(5), Délibérations, Feb. 1792.

59   AN BB3 14, Ordonnateur, 24 Jan. 1792 and BB3 13, Commandant, 9 and 10 Feb. 1792.

60   AM L322, Secours aux ouvriers, 6 Feb. 1792 and Hampson, 'Les ouvriers des arsenaux', pp. 296–7.

61   Brun, *Port de Toulon*, t. 2, pp. 188–90.

62   AN DXL 16, Département au Comité des Finances, 27 Mar. 1792.

63   AD 1L835, Fédérés varois, 26 May 1792.

64   AM L228, Fédérés toulonnais, 22 June 1792 and E. Poupé, 'Les fédérés varois du 10 août', *La Révolution française*, LVIII, 1910.

65   AM L2 X 2, Tribunal populaire martial, 18 Sept. 1793.

66   AN F7 3693 Var 1, Département au ministre, 27 May 1792.

67   AN FI CIII Var 9, Adresse des citoyens, 25 Jan. 1792.

68   AM L228, Adresse des citoyens, 20 June 1792.

69   AN DXL 16, Adresse des citoyens, 25 July 1792.

70   AM L366, Adresse du département, 3 July 1792.

71   AM L94(3), Municipalité au Tribunal, 19 July 1792.

72   AN DXL 16, Adresses de la société patriotique, 17, 21 and 25 July 1792.

73   AN DXL 16, Département à l'Assemblée, 21 July 1792 and Kennedy, *The Jacobin clubs*, vol. 2, p. 20.

74   AM L68(5), Délibérations, 27–28 July 1792.

75   AM L68(5), Délibérations, 28 July–1 Aug. 1792; L363, Le massacre des administrateurs, Aug. 1792 and *Mémoires de Louis Richaud*, pp. 19–22, for a contemporary account.

76   AM L364 and 366, Troubles, Aug.–Sept. 1792 and Henry, *L'histoire de Toulon*, t. 1, pp. 258–66.

77   AN BB3 13, Commandant, 24 Aug. 1792 and AM L365, Déchaînement des forçats, 23 Aug. 1792.

78   AM L2 X 2, Tribunal populaire martial, jugements, July–Sept. 1793.

79   A. J. Parès, 'Le tribunal populaire martial de Toulon, juillet–décembre 1793', *Bull. hist.*, XIII, 1925.

80   Aulard (ed.), *La société des Jacobins*, t. 4, p. 178.

81   AD 1L108, Délibérations, 31 July 1792 and 1L 1729, Délibérations, 31 July 1792.

82   AM L596, Tribunal criminel populaire provisoire, 12–14 Sept. 1792.

83   AM L50(1), Délibérations des trois corps administratifs réunis, Aug. 1792.

84   AM L2 I 5, Adresse au nom des sections de Toulon, 13 Aug. 1793.

85   AN BB3 14, Ordonnateur, 23 Sept. 1792.

86   AN BB3 14, Ordonnateur, 8 Nov. 1792 and Brun, *Port de Toulon*, t. 2, pp. 186–8.

87   AD 1L 223, Procès-verbaux d'élection, 26–27 Aug. 1792.

88   Poupé, *Le département du Var*, pp. 249.

89   AM L580, Procès-verbaux d'élection, 9–23 Dec. 1792.

90   AM L50(2), Délibérations, 30 Jan. 1793.

91   AM L365, Proclamation aux citoyens, 25 Aug. 1792.

92   AM L366, Proclamation aux citoyens, 14 Sept. 1792.

93   AD IL2024, Discours prononcé au club, 29 Oct. 1792.

94   AM L521, Le procès Figon, Jan. 1793.

6

The revolt of 1793

'Toulon has abjured the principles which it professed so energetically . . .
This *volte-face*, inspired by agents from Marseille, with the collaboration of
bourgeois and naval officers, constitutes a Counter-revolution.'

The infamous rebellion of Toulon was the last in a series of urban
insurrections which erupted in provincial France during the late
spring and summer of 1793.[1] Historians have usually labelled these
upheavals 'federalist revolts' and viewed them as an anti-centralist
reaction to events in Paris. Yet, first and foremost, the uprising at
Toulon must be situated in the context of a local struggle for
supremacy that had been waged since the outbreak of the Revolution.[2] In July 1793 the Toulonnais bourgeoisie exploited mounting
discontent with Jacobin policies, won a popular majority in the
sections and turned the tables on their opponents. Once in power,
the main concern of the anti-Jacobins was to consolidate a new
municipal regime, but a rupture with central government soon
followed. The Montagnard faction, which now dominated the
National Convention, responded vigorously to the challenge and
despatched the army to deal with the rebels. The revolt at Toulon
was only saved from collapse by a great act of treason: rather than
surrender to General Carteaux's troops, the Toulonnais allowed the
British and their allies to occupy the naval base and defend the town.

This astonishing betrayal was entirely unforeseen when anti-
Jacobins staged their 'municipal revolution' six weeks earlier. They
did so in the section assemblies, employing the same democratic
vehicle their rivals had used to drive them from office in 1791 and
1792. Their local *coup* of 12–13 July was widely supported and
virtually bloodless. Any explanation for the triumph of the
'federalist' or sectionary movement at Toulon must, therefore, begin
by examining the profound isolation of the incumbent Jacobin
administration. Undoubtedly the Jacobins had disappointed their
followers by behaving in an increasingly conservative manner once

they were firmly established in power. Their insistence upon law and
order was not accompanied by any significant material rewards for
the popular classes, because they were no more able to curb inflation
and combat scarcity than their predecessors. Discontent over falling
standards of living, which had previously helped unseat the notables,
was now directed against the Jacobin regime itself.

In the spring of 1793 the cost of bread, a reliable indicator of
economic circumstances in general, increased to 6 *sols* a pound at
Toulon, double its price a year before. There were ominous disturbances outside bakers' shops in April and one individual was arrested
for declaring: 'we need a king, because under the monarchy bead
only cost 2 *sols*'.[3] The price-rise stemmed partly from difficulties in
supply, as enemy warships began to interrupt maritime commerce.
Equally problematic was the continuing depreciation of the *assignat*,
which had fallen below 30 per cent of its face value. Many retailers
were unwilling to take paper money and a black market in hard cash
was consequently flourishing. As the director of the dockyards
(*ordonnateur*) commented, 'shopkeepers will only accept specie'.[4]
Barras and Fréron, two representatives 'on mission' from the Convention, who were in the vicinity but had not actually visited Toulon,
claimed that dockyard workers were won over by reactionaries,
'who suddenly paid three-quarters of their salaries in hard cash'.[5]
There is, however, no archival evidence to suggest that the men were
remunerated any differently during the latter part of July (although a
quarter of their pay was delivered in coin at the end of September,
after the British occupation).

These 'Toulonnais sans-culottes', whose support was so crucial to
the Jacobins, much preferred specie to the *assignats* they had
received in their pay since the end of 1792. A salary increase of some
30 per cent was granted to them in January 1793 and they were
collecting a daily bread ration. Yet their real wages were
deteriorating so rapidly that Baille and Beauvais, a pair of representatives despatched directly to the naval port, had awarded a
further rise of 110 per cent in June.[6] This draconian measure was
prompted by a workers' petition to the Convention at the end of
May: 'We want peace in our cities and bread for our families. Your
unseemly divisions, however, demonstrate clearly what we know
only too well, that we cannot expect much on either score.'[7] Despite
the doubling of their pay the men remained disaffected. They wanted
remuneration wholly in kind and a full ration of foodstuffs, both of

which the *ordonnateur* refused to concede. A few days before their overthrow in July, local Jacobins were given a final warning by the *comité central* at the Arsenal: it was time to end 'the scourge of speculation'; prices of all goods must be fixed immediately and shopkeepers forced to sell in exchange for paper money.[8] The municipal administration, unwilling to abandon 'freedom of trade' in items other than bread, simply ignored the ultimatum.

Dockyard workers were also alienated by the additional pressures placed upon them after the entry of the maritime powers into the war against the French Republic early in 1793. Spain and the Dutch Republic, former allies of France in the American War, joined in coalition with Britain. A series of deputies was accordingly sent to Toulon from the National Convention to urge greater effort from the work-force and to end the anarchy that had prevailed in the dockyards since 1789. This campaign was seconded by Jacobin club and local councillors, who sanctioned the dismissal of delinquent employees and the reimposition of discipline. In an attempt to reduce absenteeism workers and sailors were also obliged to resign from the National Guard.[9] This had been a long-standing aim of the naval administration, but its belated achievement only served to undermine Jacobin control of the militia, a vital factor in the events of July 1793.

Meanwhile, the composition of the dockyard labour force itself was altering rapidly with the arrival of conscript craftsmen and seamen recruited along the Mediterranean and Atlantic littorals. In the spring of 1793 the total of workers rose above the 6,000 mark and the newcomers seem to have influenced political attitudes both within the Arsenal and the local community. One Basque conscript wrote in disgust to the naval minister to say how shocked he was at seeing 'so many people doing nothing in the shipyards'. 'Once the roll-call has been taken', he added, 'many workers enjoy a nap or leave the docks to earn money in the town.'[10] It was perhaps critics like this who inspired the hostile petition sent to the Convention on 31 May and disseminated anti-Jacobin opinions which were gaining ground elsewhere in the Midi.

The downfall of the Jacobins in the sections of Marseille, towards the end of May, dealt a grave blow to their counterparts at Toulon. The revolution in both ports had followed a similar trajectory and their respective political clubs collaborated closely. Resurgent Marseillais notables were soon encouraging the inhabitants of

Toulon to create their own sectionary movement and take control of the town.[11] Toulonnais Jacobins in turn blamed the malign influence of 'the aristocracy of rich and greedy merchants' at Marseille for their growing discomfort (a charge later echoed by Barras and Fréron among others), but they could do little to resist.[12] What Michel Vovelle calls 'the sudden transformation of a radical into a reactionary Midi' began in the Bouches-du-Rhône and quickly swept into the Var.[13] By the end of June Toulon had become a refuge for 'persecuted patriots', completely cut off from the rest of the region.

The disorientation experienced by the Toulonnais Jacobins is reflected in an *exposé* of their situation written towards the end of June: 'Intrigue is at work, uncertainty reigns, mistrust is spreading, opinions are diverging . . . men who share an equal affection for *la patrie* are accusing one another of wishing to re-establish the monarchy, of wanting to federalise the Republic . . . errors abound . . .'[14] This state of confusion was intensified by events in Paris. Both Toulonnais *conventionnels* (Escudier and Charbonnier) were committed *montagnards* and only one Varois deputy (Isnard) was actually proscribed, but Jacobins at Toulon were profoundly dismayed by the purge of the national assembly at the beginning of June 1793. They consequently expressed their sadness that members of the Convention had been unable to resolve their differences in a less draconian fashion; 2 June might be regarded as 'a day of mourning rather than rejoicing'. M. J. Leclerc, a Toulonnais club member who had travelled to the capital to take his seat as a reserve deputy (*suppléant*) for the Var, had in fact returned, appalled by the intimidating atmosphere in Paris.[15] In company with several Jacobin colleagues he defected to the sectionary movement.

It was remarkable that Jacobins in Toulon resisted the tide of reaction for so long. Weakened by defections and plagued by uncertainty, they had little alternative but to cling to the discredited Convention regardless of recent developments. A long-awaited republican constitution was on its way and they felt the assembly still represented the best hope of 'saving France', as well as themselves.[16] Nonetheless, by mid-July, public opinion had become thoroughly hostile and demands for a 'reopening' of the sections of Toulon, closed since October 1792, were widely broadcast. Opponents of the Jacobins saw recall of the eight neighbourhood assemblies as a means of achieving the sort of 'municipal revlolution' that had already occurred in several other cities. The Toulonnais Jacobins were so unnerved that on 12 July they committed a fatal blunder: in an attempt to buttress their waning authority they staged an armed procession through the town, shouting 'Death to all sectionaries'.[17] However, by re-enacting the prelude to the terrible massacres of a year before, they merely precipitated their own downfall.

This desperate show of force provoked an apparently innocuous gathering of national guardsmen into drawing up a request for the sections to meet that very evening. A leading part in these proceedings was played by J. B. Roux, a master saddler and militia officer. He has been cast in the role of counter-revolutionary agent yet, since he was a club member and current town councillor, he is more likely to have been a sudden convert to the anti-Jacobin cause.[18] He was not the executor of a carefully planned coup, as some historians have argued; he seems instead to have reacted spontaneously to wild threats on the streets. The notables who profited from his initiative were not signatories to the petition that was drafted at his instigation. This was supported by 227 anonymous individuals from the artisan–shopkeeper strata, precisely the kind of persons who had dominated the National Guard since the withdrawal of dockyard workers.[19]

The demand for a reopening of the sections was submitted to the municipal council at 9.00 p.m. on the evening of 12 July, but the council deferred a decision until the next day. By the time permission was officially granted, the following morning, councillors who autographed the minute with shaky hands had lost control of the town.[20] There is plentiful evidence to suggest that, under the protection of sympathetic militia units (the Jacobins had sought the reintegration of dockyard workers into the Guard the same evening, but too late) some, if not all sections had already reassembled during the night of 12 to 13 July. Several scuffles were reported, particularly in the Jacobin stronghold of Saint-Jean, but there was little bloodshed. Unable to mount any concerted opposition, the Jacobins quickly conceded defeat and stood down. The ease with which they were eventually overthrown emphasises their vulnerability. Several observers underlined the rapidity of the process: 'The revolution at Marseille was protracted while that of Toulon was made in a flash'; or, as the sectionaries themselves put it, 'we took charge overnight'.[21]

As soon as all eight sections had reconvened they were recognised as sovereign authority in the town, to remain in session, on a day-to-day basis, for the foreseeable future. The following day, which happened to be 14 July, was celebrated with a fraternal *fête* and a general committee (*comité général des sections*) was elected to act as a co-ordinating and executive body for the sections. The committee comprised thirty-two delegates (four from each section) and was renewed by half each month. Unfortunately it is no easier to monitor its activities than those of the sections themselves, because archives were deliberately destroyed or disappeared when the revolt was finally crushed at the end of 1793. The *comité général* was clearly the linchpin of the new regime and, as the sections came under pressure both from inside and outside Toulon, it outgrew the modest role it was allotted at the outset.[22] Nevertheless surviving fragments and numerous memoirs suggest that in July, and for much of August, the initiative remained very much in the hands of the eight section assemblies.

The sovereignty of the sections, where the inhabitants of Toulon were said to be exercising their democratic right of 'resistance to oppression', was quickly extended over other organisations in the town. The Jacobin club, focal point of the previous administration, was an early victim:

It was not enough to defeat the Jacobins, it was essential to stop them meeting again. The sectionaries were resolved to root out their evil deeds and went deep into the dark lair, where they had hatched their wicked plots, in order to destroy everything that belonged to them. This vampires' cave . . . was then sealed off and the emblems which decorated the walls . . . were consumed by fire.[23]

Former Jacobins were invited to participate in the neighbourhood assemblies, the sole form of public meeting to be tolerated in future: 'Those citizens who wish to assemble in another fashion . . . and who deliberate separately, correspond with one another secretly or exchange delegates, are necessarily suspect because they are forming a corporation, a caste apart, in disregard of those laws which have abolished all corporative organisations. . . .'[24]

When a municipal commission replaced the municipal council on 17 July its forty-eight members were elected in the sections and only two existing councillors were reselected as commissioners.[25] Commanding officers in the National Guard, justices of the peace and members of various committees were also 'renewed' by the sectional assemblies. By contrast, the district and departmental commissions, which supplanted existing councils at the end of July, were both nominated by the *comité général*.[26] These commissions were intended as no more than a stopgap, to be superseded by properly elected administrations when a fresh departmental electoral college met in August. However, on account of the rapid collapse of the sectionary movement, few primary elections were held outside Toulon and the departmental assembly never materialised. The temporary commissioners of district and department thus remained in post though, as Toulon became isolated from its hinterland, their authority became purely nominal.

Measures like these were adopted by all the regimes which emerged in the Midi during the summer of 1793, but the sectionary movement at Toulon was following local precedents too. When the disorders of 1792 resulted in the dissolution of the district, as well as the departmental administration, commissioners had been named by the Toulonnais Jacobins from their own ranks. Those appointed had remained in office until the electoral college of the Var met to choose successors in the autumn. Moreover, the sections at Toulon had already been involved in the organisation of the National Guard and the creation of neighbourhood committees. The history of the sectionary movement at Toulon should really be traced back to the beginning of 1791, when the Jacobins had first convened the sections in a 'deliberative', as opposed to electoral capacity. It was equally the Jacobins who had instituted the *comité central* as a means of co-ordinating the activities of the eight assemblies. During the turbulent months of 1792 the sections of Toulon had met '*en permanence*', from the end of July until the beginning of October. Local Jacobins had closed them because they were alleged to be 'obstructing normal business', but members of the *comité central* continued to attend joint meetings of municipality, district and department.[27]

Yet there were crucial elements of change as well as continuity. Anti-Jacobins at Toulon carried the principle of 'direct democracy' in the sections to an unprecedented level. In the summer of 1793 all administrative organs were subordinated to the sovereign will of the sections and their general committee. As Louis Richaud, a member of the municipal commission, commented: 'The importance of the departmental administrators was nil . . . and the municipal commissioners provided no more than a rubber stamp for decrees from the general committee.'[28] Above all, the exercise of popular sovereignty in 1793 reinstated members of the old urban elite who had been

thrust from office in the course of 1791 and 1792. The most funda-
mental difference between the sectionary regime of 1793 and the
preceding Jacobin administration lay in the political and social
affiliations of those returned to power at Toulon.

This astonishing reversal of fortunes can be gauged by examining
the fifty or so individuals elected to the *comité général* in July and
August, prior to the English occupation. They comprised sixteen
merchants, eight legal personnel, seven active or retired naval
officers, six rentiers, four naval engineers, three government officials,
three priests and just three artisans.[29] In addition, a dozen commanding officers of dockyard and garrison were invited to attend
committee meetings in an advisory capacity. Their presence underlined a new-found solidarity between civilian and military leaders.
Yet the involvement of the latter, which assumed greater importance
towards the end of August as government troops converged on
Toulon, should not disguise the domination of the notables.

One-third of the general committee's personnel were members of
the municipal oligarchy in the 1780s: J. B. Lesperon, for example,
barrister and first president of the *comité général*, had served as a
town councillor in the pre-revolutionary decade and was re-elected
to a similar post in 1790. In 1793 men like him, who had founded the
Club Saint-Pierre after being ejected from local office, regained the
upper hand over their rivals from the *Club Saint-Jean*. The
sectionary movement at Toulon was, therefore, placed in the hands
of property-owners who, in the words of the nineteenth-century
historian Lauvergne, constituted a sort of 'bourgeois aristocracy'.[30]
What they wanted was 'to enjoy their property and the fruits of their
toil in peace'.

Chairmen and secretaries of the eight section assemblies were
drawn from the same groups and this was equally true of the commissioners nominated to administer district and department. Yet the
sectionary regime at Toulon did retain a popular dimension, for the
municipal commission elected in the sections on 17 July drew one-
third of its membership from artisan and shopkeeper groups. Later
on, in mid-August, half of the Toulonnais delegates to the proposed
departmental assembly was chosen from the same strata.[31] This
proportion was comparable to the outcome of similar elections a
year before under the Jacobins, who had rarely allowed the popular
classes to hold high office. Even in September 1793, after the entry of
the allied forces, one-third of commissioners elected to conduct a

census in occupied Toulon were elected among craftsmen and small retailers.[32] This evidence suggests that the sectionary movement appealed to a diverse constituency and was broadly based in the town.

Unfortunately there are few extant statistics relating to the size of attendance, let alone the social composition of the section meetings themselves during July and August. A rare glimpse of the degree of participation is provided by numbers voting for delegates to the departmental electoral college. These indicate a turnout of roughly 20 per cent, more or less the same as figures for August 1792. Sectionaries appear to have fared no better, though no worse, than their Jacobin adversaries in securing popular political commitment, and they too had cause to condemn civic indifference. Yet one sector of the Toulonnais population was conspicuous by its absence in the summer of 1793: dockyard workers and sailors, formerly a bulwark of the Jacobin club, failed to feature at any level of the new regime. Although unwilling and unable to prevent the downfall of the Jacobin administration they did not publicly adhere to the sectionary cause, adopting instead an *attentiste* posture and waiting to see what benefits might accrue from the restoration of the old urban elite.

The sectionary regime also resembled its Jacobin predecessor by adding a fresh chapter to the chronicle of revolutionary violence at Toulon. Despite their rhetoric of unity and reconciliation victorious notables soon began to settle scores with their political opponents. Former administrators and Jacobin club officials were taken into custody, along with numerous employees from the Arsenal; almost half of these so-called 'oppressed patriots' (*patriotes opprimés*), who later received generous compensation, were clerks, sailors and dockyard workers. Fort Lamalgue and the Grosse Tour offered inadequate accommodation, so the *Thémistocle*, a redundant war-ship, was also pressed into service to house a further 300 detainees.

As in 1792 a 'popular tribunal' was elected by the sections to replace regular courts that ceased to function in the upheaval. The *tribunal populaire martial* established on 22 July 1793 was, how-ever, much more punitive than its Jacobin precursor and a 'White Terror' was soon gathering pace.[33] No less than forty sentences of death were passed between July and December 1793; under Jacobin sway, by contrast, the courts had claimed only four lives. Those executed by the sectionary tribunal were mostly dockyard workers and craftsmen deemed responsible for the massacres of summer

1792, though leading Jacobins like ex-mayor Paul or J. S. Barthélemy were treated in a similar fashion. There were few acquittals and British commissioners in the town were ultimately obliged to restrain over-zealous prosecutors.

Sectionary propaganda sought to draw a strong contrast between the new order and its Jacobin predecessor. The municipal revolution of 12–13 July had terminated 'A terrible time of wild and slanderous denunciations, protection money extorted by armed force, raids, arrests, arbitrary and illegal dismissals, brigandage, massacres and every sort of excess.'[34] This 'reign of anarchy' had allegedly been encouraged by the Jacobins, who permitted assaults upon property by men who 'possessing nothing themselves, and with no aspirations to acquire anything by dint of their own efforts, have openly embraced communist doctrines'. The conservative tenor of this discourse accurately reflects the sectionary mentality, yet it ignores the Jacobins' strong commitment to upholding law and order and the existing structure of society. Some notables were placed under surveillance by the Jacobin administration, but on the grounds of disloyalty to the Republic, not in pursuit of class warfare.

An unexpected degree of congruence characterised the relations of both Jacobins and sectionaries with central government. To be sure the sectionary movement rapidly entered into a fatal conflict with the Montagnards who had seized power in the Convention on 2 June 1793. As early as 15 July Baille and Beauvais, the two representatives on mission in the naval port, were imprisoned without charge or trial. Both became martyrs: Baille committed suicide in gaol and Beauvais expired shortly after his release when the rebellion ended. Their colleagues, Barras and Fréron, nearly joined them under lock and key, narrowly escaping arrest at Pignans, some twenty miles from Toulon. It was essentially the partisan manner in which these 'vagabond deputies' operated which condemned them in the eyes of sectionaries:

When these legislators confine themselves to their proper tasks, look after our property, guarantee our money and our lives, and preserve peace, unity, decency and virtue, then they will be inviolable and we will respect them; but, while they protect brigands and assassins, we will regard them as nothing less than traitors and villains, who deserve to be punished for their crimes.'[35]

There was an element of anti-centralism in this diatribe, but it was above all *montagnard* centralism that was at issue, the fact that these *conventionnels* emanated 'from a *montagne* which spews out a incessant flow of pestilential propaganda'. Visiting representatives had, after all, met with hostility in the past, besides bearing the brunt of critical attitudes towards Convention and capital city. In January 1793, for example, the Jacobin administration at Toulon complained: 'For much too long deputies in the National Convention have been unable to express themselves freely . . . sedition-mongers have succeeded in leading astray a minority of the Parisian populace, who hold up the proceedings and substitute their particular will for that of the French people as a whole.'[36] In response to a proposal to create a departmental guard to protect the Convention, a battalion was raised at Toulon only to be diverted, *en route* to Paris, to serve in the Vendée.[37] Already in November 1792 the Jacobin club at Toulon had lambasted 'the continual state of division and factionalism within the assembly', which consumed deputies' energies to the detriment of the provinces.[38] Representatives were reminded of the fable of the oyster, eaten by a third party while two diners engaged in argument. If nothing was done, administrators at Toulon warned, the people would 'rise up and reclaim those rights which it has delegated to you'. No wonder Toulonnais Jacobins were soon complaining that they had been 'besmirched with the dreadful charge of federalism'.[39]

Abundant evidence of this sort, drawn from elsewhere in Provence besides Toulon, led the historian Guibal to distinguish a 'Jacobin federalism' which preceded the 'Girondin federalism' later adopted by sectionary rebels.[40] Yet, however troubled their relationship with the Convention, most Jacobins ultimately maintained their allegiance to it. Toulonnais sectionaries, by contrast, had no hesitation in repudiating an assembly, dominated by Montagnards, which they claimed was no longer free and had plunged France into civil war. The people were accordingly released from any obligation to the Convention, which was to be replaced by a new body established at Bourges rather than in 'depraved and corrupt' Paris.

On 19 July, in a gesture of solidarity with their neighbours, anti-Jacobins at Toulon had disregarded an order to establish a naval blockade of renegade Marseille.[41] All legislation passed in the Convention since the end of May was subsequently declared illegal, a decision applied most notably to the hastily issued Constitution of June 1793. This document and its accompanying plebiscite rallied a good many waverers elsewhere in France, but the Toulonnais refused to have any truck with it whatsoever. At the end of July it was unanimously denounced in the sections as a cynical manoeuvre, a worthless gesture by the 'ferocious assassins' of the *Montagne*, and ceremonially burned.[42]

Autonomous activities on the part of the Jacobins at Toulon had generally received retrospective sanction from the capital; the sectionaries' rebellious behaviour received a rather different and more immediate response. Although the sectionary movement was part of a long struggle for municipal ascendancy in the naval town, from a Parisian perspective the rupture with the Convention seemed paramount. The Montagnards riposted sharply, insisting that Toulonnais sectionaries wished to 'federalise France and destroy Paris', that they were nothing less than counter-revolutionaries in sheep's clothing. These pejorative and exaggerated assertions should not invalidate Toulonnais protestations of loyalty to 'the Republic one and indivisible', nor their denials of anti-republican conduct: 'only traitors and impostors can possibly conceive of us as counter-revolutionaries, in league with the English or the religious fanatics in the Vendée . . .'[43]

Despite its refusal to endorse the *montagnard* dictatorship the sectionary movement at Toulon remained firmly committed to the cause of republican unity. Much energy was expended upon remedying defects in the coastal defences in order to resist an enemy descent.[44] Since their opponents had devastated the high command of the Mediterranean fleet in May, by the wholesale proscription of aristocratic naval officers, sectionaries could justifiably claim that their good relations with the military establishment were enhancing national security. Assistance continued to be sent to the embattled army in Italy and there was no slackening of patriotic endeavour at the dockyards.

Those decrees passed prior to the purge of the Convention were scrupulously observed; hence a refusal to permit the reformation of penitent fraternities which had been dissolved a year earlier.[45] Moreover, several speeches published during the heyday of the sectionary movement suggest that these policies represented much more than opportunism. One address, delivered by Badeigts-Laborde, an *officier de marine* who escaped from Toulon after the allied occupation, cited the ideas of Rousseau as a basis for sectionary democracy within the republican tradition.[46] Even dedicated monarchists, writing after the event with every reason to cast the movement in a counter-revolutionary light, were constrained to admit that 'the explosion had no royalist connotations at the outset'.[47]

Nonetheless both internal and external pressures induced a drift towards royalism, or at least allowed more reactionary elements to play a greater part in shaping the town's destiny. Inside Toulon a growing threat emanated from dockyard workers, who initially held aloof from politics and concentrated on the task of naval construction. Only in August, when their expectations of material improvements were not realised, did they once again grow restive. Sectionaries were no more successful than their predecessors in controlling inflation or preventing black-marketeering. Puissant, the *ordonnateur*, wrote on 2 August that 'a man with an income of 1,500–1,800 *livres* a year finds himself in dire straits'.[48] A week later a commission was created to look into the alarming economic situation. Although sectionaries had no more liking for economic controls than the Jacobins, they did impose some restrictions on profits and places of sale. In the event these by-laws proved ineffective and, during August, the price of a pound loaf rose from 4 *sols* 6 *deniers* to 5 *sols* 3 *deniers*.[49]

Demonstrations broke out at bakers' shops and demands for pay increases were made by numerous groups. At the Arsenal, where the workers' *comité central* had remained in existence, anti-sectionary propaganda and copies of the 1793 Constitution were clandestinely circulated. This growing unrest culminated in an uprising on 19 August, the day a pair of dockyard craftsmen were to be guillotined for 'terrorist' offences.[50] These disturbances, which included an abortive attempt to rescue the condemned men, were suppressed without too much difficulty, but they sounded an ominous warning: an organised opposition had evidently reappeared within Toulon. The *comité général* reacted firmly the following day by disbanding the *comité central* at the Arsenal, increasing its own authority, and, above all, by appointing a six-man *comité de sécurité* which was empowered to act without seeking prior approval from the sections.[51] Moderates despaired, while reactionary elements obtained a more decisive say in sectionary affairs. As Panisse, secretary to the *comité général* put it, 'a new order associated with a new political orientation' was emerging.[52]

This dangerous development acquired added momentum as a result of growing pressure from outside the town. In July 1793 hopes were high that the Montagnards would be defeated and a new national assembly created. Volunteers from the Bouches-du-Rhône had already set out to march on the capital (yet another repeat of the summer of 1792) and they were soon joined by a Toulonnais contingent. It was planned to rendezvous with *fédérés* from the right bank of the Rhône, relieve Lyon and eventually overawe Paris.[53] In the event Provençal forces scarcely penetrated beyond Avignon before beating a hasty and disorganised retreat. General Carteaux's troops occupied Aix on 21 August and recaptured Marseille a few days later. Toulon also faced attack from detachment of the *armée d'Italie*, a sympathetic General Brunet notwithstanding.

By the end of August Toulon was once again isolated and full of refugees. Since the town was ringed by fortifications, and possessed considerable military resources, prolonged resistance seemed feasible. However, it could only be sustained as long as food reserves lasted, because the British coastal blockade prevented the replacement of existing stocks. Although this impending subsistence crisis may have been exaggerated, as some historians suggest, fears of food shortage were understandable; the needs of inhabitants, garrison, fleet and a flood of fugitives – perhaps 50,000 persons in all – were enormous.[54] The most generous estimate suggests supplies could have been eked out for seven or eight more weeks, but certainly no longer. Confrontation was ultimately futile, while surrender to Carteaux spelled immediate doom; choosing to 'die of hunger' later, or to 'submit to the yoke of the savage tyrants' sooner, appeared the only options.[55]

An appeal to the British, who were cutting off Provence from its maritime supply routes, was to offer a means of escaping from this cruel dilemma. It was sectionaries at Marseille who took the plunge into treason when, on 18 August, some of their leaders contacted Lord Hood, who was in command of the British fleet, to request the free passage of grain. Negotiations began a couple of days later but, before agreement could be reached, Marseille was lost. The *comité général* of Toulon had not participated in these exploratory talks, despite an invitation to attend and Hood's insistence that the naval town must be involved in any arrangements. The Marseillais negotiators now suggested that Hood should go ahead and offer an alliance to the Toulonnais alone. He did so on 23 August, declaring that he would defend the town on condition that the Republic was renounced in favour of monarchy and all military installations were entrusted to him.[56]

The great act of betrayal at Toulon thus originated in an extremely haphazard fashion; there was no carefully contrived plot involving British and counter-revolutionary agents. The conservative republicanism of the sectionary regime was only abandoned in desperate circumstances which stemmed from the imminent arrival of an avenging army, fresh from the reconquest of Marseille. It was the threat of savage reprisals, not any profound commitment to royalism that led the Toulonnais to clutch at the straw which Hood's offer represented. As the Girondin M. Isnard put it, 'it was necessary either to surrender to the Montagnards or the British fleet, to yield to the tender mercies of Robespierre and Fréron or to admiral Hood'.[57] The British commander (who was then a vice-admiral) exceeded his blockading brief and took an initiative that was not only poorly supported in London, but met with little approval because of the promise to 'hold (the town) in trust for Louis XVII'. This was too specific a guarantee for the government in Britain, which remained rather non-committal where the future of France was concerned.[58]

On the Toulonnais side there were, of course, one or two dedicated royalists who welcomed this unexpected turn of events and made a virtue out of necessity. Gauthier de Brécy, for example, a nobleman who rose to prominence in the *comité général* as a result of the impending siege, later wrote that he had betrayed 'not France but merely the Republic.'[59] Less committed colleagues were more circumspect, yet they were so heavily compromised by their leadership of the revolt that any means of avoiding retribution was preferable to surrender; they might as well be hung for royalist sheep as for sectionary lambs. Whether or not the sections themselves would accept collaboration with a traditional enemy, even *in extremis*, was quite another matter. In the end the politics of panic won the day, but only after some exceptionally stormy debates on the night of 24 August. Secretary Panisse recorded that 'opinions clashed violently in some tumultuous section assemblies'. According to Louis Richaud the outcome hung in the balance until the arrival of refugee Marseillais, bearing tales of republican atrocities, tipped the scales in favour of the British offer.[60] At 5.00 a.m. on the morning of 25 August the fateful decision was finally endorsed, Louis XVII was declared King – though without the enthusiasm which royalist writers later liked to depict – and delegates departed to inform Lord Hood.

The military command at Toulon, commoners as well as former

nobles among them, had already agreed to support the sections, yet it was still necessary to win over crews on the French fleet standing in the roadstead. This was no easy matter because patriotic sentiment was especially deep-rooted among serving seamen, who threatened to turn their firepower upon the British and their allies if they dared to enter the harbour. Saint-Julien, a rear-admiral who had been involved in the Rions affair in 1789, was prepared to lead rank and file resistance to the proposed act of treason, but even his resolve did not extend to heroism. After two days of intensive talks between townsmen and sailors a mixture of threats and concessions produced an arrangement acceptable to the *comité général*. As the latter put it, 'Toulon has decided to meet force with force', by preparing to bombard any obstructive French vessels from the coastal batteries.[61] The seamen's opposition was also undermined by promises of full pay and immediate permission to return home. Sailors from the Atlantic ports, who felt little affinity with local inhabitants and had proved particularly stubborn, were encouraged to leave on four dilapidated warships; a hostile reception awaited them at Rochefort where they were treated as traitors.[62]

The allied fleet eventually entered Toulon on the morning of 28 August. Troops were disembarked and occupied the town's forts, while dockyard workers disarmed French warships and set about servicing those of their former enemies. The agreement with the British and their allies allowed the sections to continue meeting and left the *comité général* and various sub-committees in existence. A 'democratic' form of local administration coexisted with the revived monarchy, yet their relationship was an unsatisfactory one. Reference was increasingly made to the constitutional principles of 1791 (or 'the system of 1789', as the first revolutionary settlement was called). The scene was set for full-blown reaction, even for the return of elements of the *ancien régime*, and anti-revolutionary resistance to the Montagnards soon became outright counter-revolution. This radical departure was symbolised by a change of chronology as 'the first year of the reign of Louis XVII' replaced that of the Republic in official documentation.

Religion, frequently a factor in rebellions elsewhere, played little part in the sectionary movement despite the rash of *te deums* which accompanied its accession to power at Toulon. The Civil Constitution of the Clergy had received overwhelming approval from both ecclesiastical personnel and the laity, while the place of the church in society was not a divisive political issue. After the allied occupation, however, there were calls for a restoration of clerical authority. In September it was decided to return the registration of births, marriages and deaths to parish priests, who were later executed for supporting the rebellion.[63] Abolition of the 'barbaric law' permitting divorce, which had been discussed but not agreed, was effectively implemented when clerics took charge of the *Etat civil*. A proposal to resurrect the penitent fraternities, which had been refused in August, now received assent, while the former bishop of Toulon was invited to return to the city.

As moderate sectionaries withdrew or were purged from positions of responsibility, still more reactionary measures were taken. September saw the erasure of republican emblems, the hewing down of trees of liberty and the replacement of the guillotine, a revolutionary innovation, with the noose as a means of execution. These retrograde steps culminated in the abandonment of the tricolour and the adoption of the Bourbon white flag, which was hoisted with great ceremony on 1 October.[64] At the same moment a heated debate was raging over the question of aristocratic precedence in a volunteer battalion that was raised in the town and entitled 'Le Royal Louis'.[65] Equality ultimately prevailed, but the argument was a clear indication of increasing noble influence over what remained of the sectionary movement.

In December, as the revolt entered its last days, it was even proposed to revive the oligarchic system of municipal government from the *ancien régime*. The sections were to be shut and the *comité général* dissolved, but Toulon fell before the decision could be implemented. The neighbourhood assemblies had continued to meet after the occupation, but their importance was rapidly diminishing. As early as 8 September the chairman of the surveillance committee suggested closing the sections because of the 'disruptive elements' they contained.[66] This advice was ignored, but a perusal of the Panisse memoir shows that the sections progressively lost their legislative rôle and were reduced to 'a rubber stamp for the *comité général*'. In his recollections Louis Richaud bemoaned the falling attendance at section meetings and a rare document from mid-October recorded a mere fifty persons assembling in the sections of *Vrais Républicains* and *Droits de l'Homme* (which curiously enough retained revolutionary appellations).[67] This represented less than 5 per cent of the electorate, a clear indication of apathy when the vital matter of foodstuffs was under discussion.

The enemy occupation of Toulon served to reopen the seas for imports, chiefly of grain, fruit and rice from Italy. So, despite the state of siege imposed by the rapid advance of the Republican forces, the Toulonnais initially had little to fear as regards their subsistence. Fish were once again plentiful, though meat was scarce; a captain from Genoa reported in October that beef was selling for 30 *sols* a pound in hard currency.[68] The real problem was not supply, but the lack of specie to pay for it. After the arrival of the British the *assignat* had become virtually worthless and the *comité général* was forced to act to calm mounting unrest. It was decided to pay public employees 'one quarter of their wages in hard cash', back-dated to the beginning of September and, at the same time, to impose price limits on certain commodities. In this way a sort of *maximum* was published at Toulon a fortnight before similar restrictions were applied at Paris.[69] On 15 September the cost of fifty basic items was duly frozen, both in paper money and specie, but the system was short lived. Protests from commercial interests secured the repeal of the Toulonnais *maximum* after no more than a week's operation. Only bread, meat and fish remained subject to controls.

The supply of bread began to give serious cause for concern in October when republican troops succeeded in cutting off water power to mills in the *terroir*. Until then, according to Louis Richaud, inhabitants had scarcely experienced 'any of the inconveniences associated with a siege'.[70] Thereafter grain had to be shipped to the Balearics for grinding, a time-consuming business which explains why unused wheat was discovered at Toulon when the siege ended. The *comité général* was obliged to reduce the inhabitants' daily bread allowance and consumption was restricted to loaves baked at the dockyards, in three-quarter or half-pound rations. One commentator correctly predicted that 'the absence of milling facilities will reduce everyone to eating ship's biscuit', which was soon employed to top up the meagre amount of bread.[71] Naval employees continued to receive a ration as part of their remuneration, but for others the price of a loaf rose in November to 2 *sols* 6 *deniers*, payable in hard cash only; the obligation upon bakers to accept *assignats* was finally abandoned.

The subsistence issue was a major cause of disaffection from the sectionary regime in the autumn of 1793. It produced a most bizarre incident in October when two merchants were sent on an abortive mission to Italy to raise a loan of one million piastres for the purchase of foodstuffs.[72] The quality of life in Toulon was also deteriorating under demographic pressures. Roughly double the population of 1790 was crammed into the town during the three-month siege which lasted from September to December. A quarter of the total comprised allied soldiers and sailors under the jurisdiction of the occupying powers: Spain, Piedmont and Naples, as well as Britain. They took over many buildings, ejecting the poor from the almshouse of La Charité for use as a hospital, besides turning churches into billets. The civilian populace itself was swollen by refugees from other rebel towns in the Midi and burial registers record a level of mortality during the last three months of 1793 that was never surpassed during the entire period from 1750 to 1820. Weakened by food shortage and lacking medicines, while exposed to overcrowding and diseases carried by incoming troops, many inhabitants succumbed to fevers or gastric disorders.[73] As the siege drew to a close all the resources of Toulon, human as well as material, were exhausted. Major-general O'Hara, in charge of British forces, summed up the mood of despair when he wrote, 'A want of energy pervades the whole. They (the Toulonnais) seem solely to depend on the combined forces for their defence, and on their humanity for their subsistence.'[74]

The survival of the sectionary regime ultimately depended upon the successful defence of Toulon against the besieging republican army. This consideration allowed leaders of the allied troops to assume supreme authority in the town. They had no wish to rely upon indigenous personnel and only permitted the formation of a single volunteer battalion (the Royal Louis, some 600 strong), while restricting the Toulonnais National Guard to street patrols. Although the *comité général* retained an important consultative role, major decisions were taken by a British 'triumvirate' comprising Lord Hood, Major-general O'Hara and a civil commissioner, Gilbert Elliot (later Lord Minto), who arrived in November. A declaration which Elliot brought with him laid more emphasis on allied sovereignty over town and naval base than Hood's concordat had done earlier.[75] It was badly received by the Toulonnais, yet there was nothing they could do. Even Elliot found his scope limited because the essential history of this last phase of the revolt was a military one.

When the allied occupation had begun, at the end of August, the main body of republican forces was still at Marseille and sectionaries were critical of Hood's failure to extend his position into the Var. This was rather unfair, since only the neighbouring towns of Cuers and Hyères adhered to the new, royalist order and allied troops were extremely thin on the ground.[76] The allies were on the defensive from the outset, obliged to consolidate their hold on the hinterland of Toulon and await reinforcements which only arrived tardily and never in sufficient numbers. Early in September General Carteaux was able to take the crucial gorges of Ollioules, to the west of Toulon, and to advance towards the peninsula of Saint-Mandrier. This strip of land held the key to control of the roadstead, but naturally it was well defended by the British. The republican advance was halted on this front, while general Lapoype, whose wife was held hostage in the town, led a detachment from the Italian army to capture La Garde and La Valette, villages to the north-east of Toulon.

In October and November stalemate set in along the mighty arc of fortifications that protected the city. Both sides were reinforced and there was fierce fighting, both on the Faron massif and around the Balaguier outcrop which overlooked Saint-Mandrier. It was only in December when Dugommier succeeded to the republican command, with 40,000 men at his disposal, that the siege reached its climax. The genius of young major Bonaparte, who intervened decisively at the final stage, was not to conceive a new strategy – evident to anyone who glanced at a map – but to execute the plan of attack in brilliant fashion. He led the victorious assault upon the so-called Petit Gibraltar fortress, which dominated the harbour exit from Toulon, early on the morning of 17 December.[77]

The event was an important milestone in Bonaparte's rise to power, for he was rewarded with promotion to major-general, but the immediate consequence was to render Toulon untenable. The allies were well aware that escape would become impossible if they did not withdraw their fleets instantly. It was therefore decided that evacuation would begin the following day, 18 December, but as soon as the news got out pandemonium gripped the town.[78] The turmoil was heightened when Lapoype succeeded in taking the Faron heights that same afternoon and bombs started to rain down upon the city. It was a case of *sauve-qui-peut* as many Toulonnais desperately sought a safe hiding-place, or refuge on board one of the ships preparing to depart. Order broke down completely as panic-stricken inhabitants

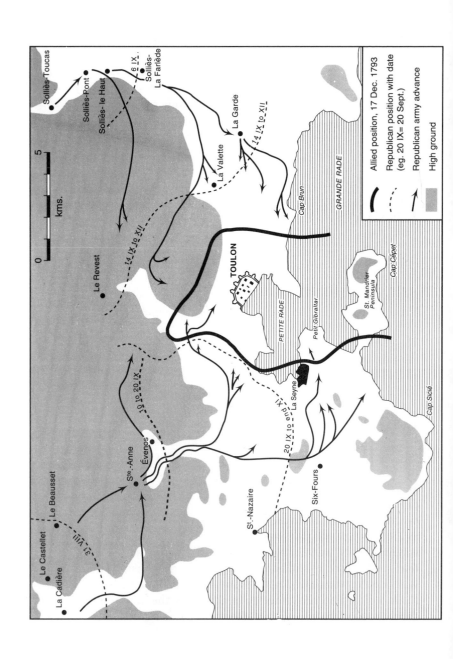

Solliès-Toucas

Solliès-Pont

Solliès-le Haut

6 IX.
Solliès-
La Farlède

Le Revest

La Valette

La Garde

14 IX. to XII

14 IX. to XII

0   5

kms.

TOULON

Cap Brun

GRANDE RADE

Cap Cépet

PETITE RADE

St. Mandrier
Peninsula

Petit Gibraltar

La Seyne

20 IX. to end

IX.

St.-Nazaire

Six-Fours

Cap Sicié

Le Castellet

Le Beausset

La Cadière

31 XII.

Ste.-Anne

Évenos

19 to 20 IX.

Allied position, 17 Dec. 1793

Republican position with date
(eg. 20 IX = 20 Sept.)

Republican army advance

High ground

converged on the quayside and piled into overloaded rowing boats.

With the benefit of hindsight it is easy to assert that resistance at Toulon was doomed from the outset. Lord Hood *in situ* and Prime Minister Pitt in London might consider the surrender of the naval port a splendid means of ending the war, but both were over-optimistic as regards the strategic possibilities and ill-informed about the internal affairs of France. Only the immediate reinforcement of Toulon might have altered the outcome by per-mitting the allies to take the offensive; confined to Toulon their prospects could only deteriorate. Slender resources were dispersed in too many directions, military objectives remained unclear and there were serious differences among the allies themselves, not to mention mistrust between them and the inhabitants.[79] Both the Spanish and the French were suspicious of the British, whom they accused of seeking to establish a 'second Gibraltar' and of having no real aim beyond the destruction of the Mediterranean base. As a royalist agent working outside France argued: 'Toulon has been occupied in order to burn it.'[80]

Barras and Fréron agreed. According to them, 'The British came here as traitors, they established themselves as cowards, and they left like scoundrels.'[81] Yet Hood himself viewed the liquidation of fleet and Arsenal as a last resort. Had he simply desired to wreck the Mediterranean fleet, French losses would have been even worse. It was only when he was obliged to quit Toulon, on 18 December, that a belated and botched attempt was made to fire the dockyards and a number of ships.[82] Spanish sailors hindered the operation and the blaze was fought by political prisoners and convicts, who heroically succeeded in dousing the flames. Only a part of the Arsenal was burned, along with twelve warships (nine ships of the line and three frigates), though the British and Spanish towed away another twelve vessels between them, for incorporation into their own navies. The damage was not irreparable, but it did constitute a more severe setback for the French than Trafalgar a decade later and the enemy had not lost a single ship in the process.

The occupying forces were fortunate that a favourable breeze was blowing on 18–19 December as, in some disarray, they left behind a town wracked by explosions and anarchy. Nearly all the leading Toulonnais rebels were able to accompany the allies, together with

The Siege of Toulon, September–December 1793

hundreds of more innocent but terrorised individuals; one pork butcher, for example, stated that he had taken flight 'because bombs were falling'.[83] Allegations that Spanish and Neapolitan seamen were more accommodating than their British counterparts seem to be ill-founded. The latter appear to have embarked their fair share of *émigrés* but, given the degree of chaos, precise totals cannot be advanced with any confidence. Fréron, one of the representatives on mission who oversaw the final stages of the siege, reckoned that some 12,000 individuals managed to get away. Most historians consider this to be a characteristic exaggeration and put their figures in the region of 7,500, though the official list falls well short of even conservative estimates.[84]

An inventory of Toulonnais *émigrés* was drawn up by the local historian Louis Honoré, as part of a painstaking survey of emigration from the Var during the Revolution. He arrived at a total of 2,519 individuals for Toulon but the figure, like his accompanying analysis, must be treated with caution.[85] In a recent survey of Toulonnais *émigrés* Colette Vitse has unearthed 100 cases which Honoré overlooked.[86] Her adjusted total of Toulonnais *émigrés* comes to just over 2,700 persons, 1,469 of whom were adult males who escaped after the revolt of 1793. All save 238 can be occupationally identified. Priests (1.5 per cent), military officers and high-ranking administrators (16 per cent) and notables (20 per cent) comprised roughly two in five adult male *émigrés*, though at the outbreak of the Revolution these groups represented less than one in five heads of household. The fact that they bulked so large reflects both their leading role in the sectionary revolt and their access to an escape route, assisted in many instances by the allied powers. The popular classes still furnished a majority of the *émigrés* (over 60 per cent), but two-thirds of them were clerks, artisans and small shopkeepers, categories heavily implicated in the rebellion. By contrast, dockyard workers and sailors, who scarcely participated in the sectionary movement, had much less motivation for flight and formed a mere 14 per cent of the total.

This emigration, which faithfully mirrored complicity in the revolt, carried Toulonnais *émigrés* all over the western Mediterranean: with the Spanish to the Balearics and the Iberian peninsula; with the Neapolitans to southern Italy; and with the British to Elba, Corsica and, above all, Tuscany where over 2,000 refugees took shelter.[87] When the tides of war engulfed the Italian peninsula many

Table 6   *The occupational structure of the Emigration from Toulon in December 1793*

	No.	% of total	% of social structure in 1765
Military officers & leading administrators	198	13.5	10.5
Rentiers	45	3.1	1.9
Liberal professions	68	4.6	2.4
Merchants & retailers	137	9.3	3.4
Clerks	128	8.7	4.2
Artisans & shopkeepers	366	24.9	26.5
Dockyard workers	87	5.9	16.6
Sailors & fishermen	87	5.9	10.9
Soldiers & gunners	51	3.5	1.4
Rural occupations	22	1.5	5.4
Unskilled workers	24	1.6	11.6
Priests	18	1.2	–
No profession indicated	238	16.2	–
Total	1,469	–	–

Source: This table relies essentially upon L. Honoré's list of Toulonnais *émigrés*. However, only those adult males who emigrated after the collapse of the sectionary rebellion have been counted here. Honor's list must be used with care because it includes fugitives from other communities, who fled to Toulon during the rebellion and it also contains individuals who were executed at the naval town for collaboration with the allied occupation force. Colette Vitse's additions to Honoré's survey have also been taken into account.

were borne away to fresh destinations, though those of lesser social stature who played only a minor role in the revolt were given an early opportunity to return to France.

It is not easy to chart the homeward flow of these *émigrés*. Honoré suggests most of them came back in 1795, as laws and attitudes were relaxed, yet their return was an extremely sensitive issue at Toulon. In the late 1790s, as the political situation fluctuated wildly, some individuals were obliged to take to their travels again, or were unfortunate enough to be arrested and executed. The Consulate, a time of growing stability and reconciliation, was a more propitious moment for repatriation. Only a small minority of Toulonnais *émigrés* continued the armed struggle against the Revolution to the bitter end. Those who served in the allied forces, like Barallier the naval engineer, had to wait until the Bourbon Restoration to come home. On the basis of a small 10 per cent sample, Colette Vitse has calculated that less than half of the Toulonnais *émigrés* were able to regain their former position in society.[88] Administrators, like military officers, could be reinstated by sympathetic regimes but those in business, such as the memoirist Louis Richaud, never recovered their assets.

A large number of *émigrés* from Toulon, whose average age in 1793 was forty, died in exile before their names were removed from the proscription lists. Yet the misery of emigration was preferable to the fate of those who remained in the city when it was retaken; they lost their lives as well as a livelihood. However, it is difficult to assess the precise impact of the Terror at Toulon. Almost 300 individuals were executed by order of a three-man military commission that was set up a week after the town fell.[89] This court judged suspected collaborators over a period of three months, from 31 December 1793 (11 nivôse according to the official, republican calendar) to the end of March 1794. Like its milder counterpart in the department, the revolutionary tribunal of the Var, it pronounced numerous acquittals and conducted a trial of sorts.

This 'legal' repression was preceded by a week of executions without a formal trial, in which Louis Richaud's elderly father perished.[90] There were some blatant atrocities immediately after the entry of victorious republican troops into Toulon, but most of these *fusillés sans jugement* were selected by a 'jury' of local Jacobin 'patriots'. The latter conducted what one observer described as 'the last judgement'. All individuals remaining in Toulon were paraded across the Champ de Mars, just outside the city walls, and submitted to scrutiny. Those singled out by the 'patriotic jury' were then led away to be shot in batches. If Fréron's bloodthirsty accounts are to be believed ('we are killing everything that moves'), there were 700 to 800 executions of this sort.[91] Overall, perhaps 1,000 persons were condemned to death by jury or commission after the recapture of Toulon.

Just over 300 individuals shot without trial are listed in archival materials, though only half of them carry any occupational details and many were not established residents of Toulon.[92] Yet the crude social profile that emerges from this source is congruent with the rather fuller analysis that can be made of those condemned by the military commission. In both cases notables and members of the service aristocracy appear in relatively small numbers, in pro-

Table 7 The social profile of executions at Toulon following the Revolt of 1793

Occupation	Shot without trial			Condemned by military commission			All executions		
	No.	% of whole	% of those identified	No.	% of whole	% of those identified	No.	% of whole	% of those identified
Military officers & administrators	19	6.1	10.2	8	2.8	3.7	27	4.6	6.7
Rentiers	0	3.2	5.4	9	3.2	4.1	9	1.6	2.2
Liberal professions	6	1.9	3.2	6	2.1	2.8	12	2.0	3.0
Merchants & retailers	12	3.9	6.5	9	3.2	4.1	21	3.5	5.2
Clerks	11	3.5	5.9	9	3.2	4.1	20	3.4	5.0
Artisans & shopkeepers	37	11.9	19.9	41	14.5	18.5	78	13.1	19.4
Dockyard workers	9	2.9	4.8	8	2.8	3.7	17	2.9	4.2
Soldiers	58	18.7	31.2	76	26.9	35.0	134	22.6	33.3
Sailors	2	0.6	1.1	11	3.9	5.1	13	2.2	3.2
Rural professions	5	1.6	2.7	26	9.2	12.0	31	5.2	7.7
Unskilled workers	8	2.6	4.3	12	4.2	5.5	20	3.4	5.0
Priests	9	2.9	4.8	2	0.7	0.9	11	1.9	2.7
No profession indicated	124	40.0	–	66	23.3	–	190	32.0	–
Total	310			283			593		

Source: Mongin, Toulon ancien, t. 2, pp. 98–116.

portions (17 per cent altogether) commensurate with their statistical weight in society. Artisans and petty shopkeepers (35 per cent of the total) were rather more prominent, while dockyard workers and sailors are scarcely in evidence. By contrast, soldiers condemned for collaborating with the allied occupation bulk very large at 33 per cent. As elsewhere, so at Toulon, the upper classes most heavily involved in rebellion were able to escape, leaving 'the smaller fry', as Fréron put it, to bear the brunt of republican retribution.

Repression and emigration exacted a terrible toll at Toulon, which ranks high on 'league tables' compiled for the incidence of the Terror in revolutionary France.[93] Yet the town did not become the charnel house of royalist legend, nor the bloodbath of terrorist rhetoric. The deputy on mission Barras (who was mightily relieved that his uncle, an artillery officer embroiled in the revolt, had escaped with the allies) believed the entire Toulonnais population deserved punishment. Fréron also recommended the massacre of remaining inhabitants and suggested razing the city to the ground.[94] Although wiser counsels prevailed, tremendous devastation had already been inflicted upon property and persons alike. The republican bombardment had smashed many buildings in the town, part of the Arsenal had been consumed by fire and the harbour was filled with wreckage. The urban population had not fallen as low as 7,000 (that is to misinterpret an incomplete register), but it had dropped dramatically to roughly 15,000.[95]

Toulon was not the only town to rebel against the National Convention, though only at Lyon were the consequences equally horrendous. The violence of the anti-Jacobin reaction in the sections during 1793 is primarily to be explained by reference to the turbulence of the preceding years. It was precisely in those cities where political and social divisions had cut deepest that the 'federalist' revolts were most deadly. The enemy occupation of Toulon was, however, a largely fortuitous turn of events, a case of the allies profiting from Toulonnais desperation in face of a rampaging republican army. This act of treason provoked terrible reprisals when the town was finally recaptured. Yet in 1794, Year II in the revolutionary calendar, the pressing needs of naval war brought a rapid renaissance. Renegade Toulon was reborn as Port-la-Montagne (a baptism derived from local topography rather than the dominant political faction at Paris) and was soon hard at work on the construction of a new Mediterranean fleet.

Notes

1   The so-called 'federalist' revolts of 1793 have received a good deal of attention of late, though H. Wallon, *La Révolution du 31 mai et le fédéralisme en 1793*, 2 vols., Paris, 1886 remains the only general survey. See W. Edmonds, ' "Federalism" and urban revolt in France in 1793', *JMH*, 55, 1983, for a brief review of more recent work on the subject.

2.   See M. Crook, 'Federalism and the French Revolution: the revolt of Toulon in 1793', *History*, LXV, 1980, a good deal of which has been incorporated into this chapter.

3   AM L50(2), Délibérations, 8 May 1793.

4   AN BB3 31, Ordonnateur, 12 July 1793.

5   F. A. Aulard (ed.), *Recueil des actes du comité de salut public, avec la correspondance officielle des représentants en mission*, 30 vols., Paris, 1889–1951, t. 5, p. 385; Barras and Fréron, 26 July 1793.

6   AP 1A2 87, Ordonnateur, 13, 19 and 20 June 1793.

067   AN AF II 183, Les ouvriers . . . à la Convention nationale, 31 May 1793.

8   AM L197, Adresse des ouvriers, 7 July 1793.

9   Aulard (ed.), *Recueil*, t. 2, p. 103; Commissaires, 9 Feb. 1793.

10   AN BB2 11, Lettre du citoyen Merci, marin, 14 May 1793.

11   AM L2 I 5, Comité général des 32 sections de Marseille aux citoyens de Toulon, May 1793.

12   Cited in Labroue, *Le club jacobin*, p. 135.

13   Baratier (ed.), *Histoire de la Provence*, pp. 422–5 and Poupé, *Le département du Var*, pp. 248–54.

14   AN DXL 23, Société républicaine, 24 June 1793.

15   AM L 50(3), Délibérations, 22 June 1793.

16   AD 1L1380, Adresse aux administrés, 7 July 1793.

17   AN BB3 31, Ordonnateur 13 July 1793; AM L2 XIX 17, Histoire des événements de Toulon en 1793, par J. L. Panisse, 12 June 1815, p. 4 and A. T. Z. Pons, *Mémoires pour servir à l'histoire de la ville de Toulon en 1793*, Paris, 1825, p. 13.

18   A. J. Parès, 'Un singulier personnage, Jean-Baptiste Roux dit Louis XVII', *Bull. Drag.*, 1937 and J. Fonvielle, *Mémoires historiques*, 4 vols., Paris, 1824, t. 2, p. 516 for a more balanced judgement. G. Vitse, 'La contre-révolution à Toulon en 1793: les agents royalistes et le faux problème des subsistances', *Prov. hist.*, XX, 1970, pp. 369–70 offers a re-statement of the conspiracy thesis, while a Jacobin view which does indicate a plot, is to be found in AD 2L362, Procès Mittre, 7 brumaire III (28 Oct. 1795).

19   AM L2 VIII 1, Ouverture des sections, 12 July 1793.

20   AM L68(6), Délibérations, 13 July 1793 for the granting of permission. For evidence that the sections had already begun to meet overnight, see AM L50(3), Délibérations, 12–13 July 1793; L2 VIII 1, Ouverture des sections and Pons, *Mémoires*, pp. 18–19.

21   ADBR LIII 10, Administration départementale sectionnaire de Marseille, 17 July 1793 and AM L2 I 5, Adresse des sections, 13 Aug. 1793.

22   AM L2 I 4, Instructions pour les sections, no date; AM L2 XIX 17,

Histoire, pp. 4–7 and E. Coulet, *Le comité général des sections de Toulon, 13 juillet–17 décembre, 1793*, Toulon, 1960, pp. 4–5, which draws heavily on the Panisse *mémoire*. See also M. Crook, 'Le mouvement sectionnaire Toulon en juillet-août 1793', in Lebrun and Dupuy (eds.), *Les Résistances à la Révolution*, pp. 151–9.

23   AM L2 XIX 17, Histoire, pp. 5–6.
24   AM L2 I 4, Instructions.
25   AM L68(6), Délibérations, 17 July 1793.
26   AD 1L112, Délibérations du conseil général du département, 27 July 1793 and A. J. Parès, 'Le directoire du dpartement du Var pendant la rébellion de 1793', *Bull. hist.*, XV, 1929.
27   AM L82, Assemblées des sections, 22 Sept. and 3 Oct. 1792.
28   *Mémoires de Louis Richaud*, p. 126.
29   Coulet, *Le comité général*, pp. 8–9 provides a list of members which has been supplemented by consulting a variety of sources.
30   Lauvergne, *Histoire de la Révolution*, p. 175.
31   AM L2 XII 1, Assemblées primaires, 11 Aug. 1793.
32   AM L2 XIII 3, Commissaires des sections, 29 Sept. 1793.
33   AM L2 XI 1, Tribunal populaire martial, 22 July 1793 and A. J. Parès, 'Le tribunal populaire martial de Toulon, juillet–décembre 1793', *Bull. hist.*, XI, 1925.
34   AM L2 I 5, Adresse.
35   *Ibid.*
36   AM L50(2), Délibérations, 8 Jan. 1793.
37   AM L228, Fédérés toulonnais, 12 Jan. 1793 and E. Poupé, 'Le 10e bataillon du Var, 1793–an V', *Bull. Drag.*, 1904.
38   AN DXL 23, Société patriotique, 26 Nov. 1792 and 4 May 1793.
39   AM L50(2), Délibérations, 31 Jan. and 6 Mar. 1793.
40   G. Guibal, *Le mouvement fédéraliste en Provence en 1793*, Paris, 1908, p. 32. For a recent discussion, see J. Bernet *et al.*, 'Existe-t-il un fédéralisme jacobin?', *Actes du 111e Con. Nat,*, 1986.
41   AM L2 I 5, Comité général, 19 July 1793.
42   AM L2 I 5, Voeu des huit sections sur l'acte dit constitutionnel.
43   AM L2 I 5, Adresse.
44   AM, Copy of Cornell University Library ms, Comité général des sections de Toulon: registre de correspondance, July–Aug. 1793.
45   *Ibid.*, 16–17 July 1793.
46   AM L2 I 4, Discours, no date.
47   M. J. Abeille, *Notes et pièces officielles relatives aux événements de Marseille et de Toulon*, no place, no date, p. 4.
48   AP 1A2 87, Ordonnateur, 2 Aug. 1793.
49   AM L2 IV 2, Comité général, 9 Aug. 1793 and E. Coulet, 'La situation économique de Toulon pendant la rébellion (juillet–décembre 1793)', *Prov. hist.*, XII, 1962, pp. 73–6.
50   AM L2 XIX 17, Histoire, pp. 28–32, and M. de Limon, *La vie et le martyre de Louis XVI, suivi d'un exposé des événements de Toulon*, Toulon, 1793, pp. 160–9.
51   Pons, *Mémoires*, pp. 59–60 and T. Imbert, *Précis historique sur les*

événements de Toulon en 1793, Paris, 1816, pp. 12–14.

52   AM L2 XIX 17, Histoire, p. 35.

53   J. E. Michel, *Histoire de l'armée départementale des Bouches-du-Rhône, de l'entrée des escadres des puissances coalisées dans Toulon et de leur sortie de cette place*, Paris, an V and Baratier (ed.), *Histoire de la Provence*, pp. 425–6.

54   P. Cottin, *Toulon et les anglais en 1793, d'après des documents inédits*, Paris, 1898, pp. 48–57 suggests that the inhabitants were deliberately misled so as to induce them to accept an enemy occupation. The allegation is repeated in Vitse, 'La contre-révolution à Toulon', pp. 370–4 but, for evidence to the contrary, see AP 1A2 80, Ordonnateur, 8 Aug. 1793 AM L185, Blés, Aug. 1793 and L2 IV 3, Grains et blés, Aug. 1793.

55   AM L2 XIX 17, Histoire, p. 52.

56   Abeille, *Notes et pièces*, pp. 9–10; Pons, *Mémoires*, pp. 62–5; J. H. Rose, *Lord Hood and the defence of Toulon*, Cambridge, 1922, pp. 19–20 and AN DXL 11 4, Affaire de Toulon, 1793.

57   M. Isnard, *Isnard à Fréron*, Paris, an IV, p. 18.

58   Rose, *Lord Hood*, pp. 20–1 and pp. 125–6. See also M. Hutt, *Chouannerie and counter-revolution. Puisaye, the princes and the British government in the 1790s*, 2 vols., Cambridge, 1983, vol. 1, pp. 110–14.

59   G. de Brécy, *La révolution royaliste de Toulon en 1793 pour le rétablissement de la monarchie*, Paris, 1814, p. 5.

60   AM L2 XIX 17, Histoire, pp. 55–9 and *Mémoires de Louis Richaud*, pp. 46–7.

61   Cornell ms, Comité général à Saint-Julien, no date. See also E. Poupé (ed.), 'Journal d'un ponantais de l'Apollon', *La Révolution française*, LX, 1911, an excellent eye-witness account of events in the harbour and, for a hostile verdict on Saint-Julien, see J. M. Puissant, *Toute la France a été trompée sur l'événement de Toulon en 1793. Voici la vérité*, Paris, an V.

62   V. Hugues, *Acte d'accusation contre les complices de la trahison de Toulon*, Paris, an II.

63   AM L2 II 1, Délibérations des sections, 17 Sept. 1793 and M. Crook, 'Une absence? Religion et contre-révolution à Toulon en 1793', in *Religion, révolution, contre-révolution dans le Midi*, Nîmes, 1990, pp. 95–102.

64   AM L2 XVIII 1, Comité général, 27 Sept. 1793 and *Mémoires de Louis Richaud*, pp. 63–4.

65   A. J. Parès, 'Le Royal Louis, régiment français à la solde de l'Angleterre', *Bull. Drag.*, 1927, pp. 12–13.

66   AN F7 3693 Var 1, Comité de surveillance, 8 Sept. 1793.

67   AM L197, Délibérations des sections, 15 Oct. 1793.

68   AN BB3 30, P. A. Adet au ministre, 13 Oct. 1793.

69   AM L2 IV 2, Comité général, 15 Sept. 1793 and AM L2 IV 2, Réglement sur les prix des denrées, 15 Sept. 1793.

70   *Mémoires de Louis Richaud*, p. 72.

71   Cited in A. J. Parès, 'La vie chère pendant la rébellion', *Congrès de l'Institut historique de Provence*, 1928, p. 239. See also AM L2 IV 7, Comité général, 27 Oct. and 9 Nov. 1793.

72   AM L68(7), Délibérations, 24 Sept. 1793; Pons, *Mémoires*, pp.

103–5 and Lauvergne, *Histoire de la Révolution*, pp. 348–57.

   73   L. G. Marquis, *Considérations médico-chirurgicales sur les maladies qui ont régné pendant et après le siège de Toulon*, Paris, an XII, pp. 10–12.

   74   PRO HO 50, 455, O'Hara to Dundas, 13 Nov. 1793.

   75   G. Elliot, *The life and letters of Sir Gilbert Elliot, first Earl of Minto, from 1751 to 1804*, 3 vols., London, 1874, vol. 2, pp. 188–90; Henry, *L'histoire de Toulon*, t. 2, pp. 103–5 and Rose, *Lord Hood*, pp. 62–5.

   76   Rose, *Lord Hood*, pp. 28–32, rebuts the allegation in Cottin, *Toulon et les anglais*, pp. 140–3.

   77   J. Tulard, *Napoléon, le mythe du sauveur*, Paris, 1981, pp. 65–6.

   78   AM L2 XIX 17, Histoire, pp. 250–1; Henry, *L'histoire de Toulon*, t. 2, pp. 123–5 and Pons, *Mémoires*, pp. 153–8.

   79   Elliot, *The life and letters*, vol. 2, pp. 202–3 and Rose, *Lord Hood*, pp. 82–91.

   80   Cited in Hutt, *Chouannerie and counter-revolution*, vol. 1, pp. 110–11.

   81   E. Poupé (ed.), *Lettres de Barras et de Fréron en mission dans le Midi*, Draguignan, 1910, p. 95.

   82   Rose, *Lord Hood*, pp. 79–81; Cottin, *Toulon et les anglais*, pp. 330–5 and Acerra and Meyer, *Marines et Révolution*, pp. 259–61.

   83   Cited in C. Vitse, 'L'émigré toulonnais de la Révolution à la Restauration: essai de caractérisation', Mémoire pour la maîtrise, University of Nice, 1972, p. 27.

   84   Poupé (ed.), *Lettres*, p. 96; Fréron, 5 nivôse II (25 Dec. 1793); Cottin, *Toulon et les anglais*, p. 325 and Rose, *Lord Hood*, pp. 77–8.

   85   L. Honoré, *L'émigration dans le Var, 1789–1825*, Draguignan, 1923, pp. 495–769.

   86   Vitse, L'émigré toulonnais, pp. 100–17.

   87   AM L2 XI 1, Secours accordés par le gouvernement britannique, 1794–96 and E. Coulet, 'Les fugitifs de Toulon et les anglais dans la Méditerranée après la rébellion de 1793', *Bull. Drag.*, 1929.

   88   Vitse, 'L'émigré toulonnais', pp. 81–90.

   89   Aulard (ed.), *Recueil*, pp. 78–80; Ricord, Barras, Fréron and Saliceti, 16 nivôse II (5 Jan. 1794).

   90   A. J. Parès, 'Une relation inédite de la fusillade du Champ de Mars à Toulon', *Bull. hist.*, XVII, 1932 and Aulard (ed.), *Recueil*, t. 9, p. 557 and p. 617; Ricord *et al.*, 30 frimaire and 3 nivôse II (20 and 23 Dec. 1793).

   91   Poupé (ed.), *Lettres*, p. 101 Fréron, 6 nivôse (26 Dec. 1793), for example. See Poupé's own verdict in *ibid.*, pp. 23–4 and also M. Vovelle, 'Représentants en mission et mouvement populaire en Provence sous la Révolution française: de nouveau sur Fréron?', *Prov. hist.*, XXIII, 1973, pp. 465–72.

   92   AD Q 1940, Liste des émigrés et punis de mort de Port-la-Montagne, an II and, for additional information, Mongin, *Toulon ancien*, t. 2, pp. 98–116.

   93   D. Greer, *The incidence of the Emigration during the French Revolution*, Harvard, 1951, pp. 35–6 and *ibid.*, *The incidence of the Terror during the French Revolution*, Harvard, 1935, pp. 36–43.

94 Poupé (ed.), *Lettres*, pp. 98–9; Fréron, 6 nivôse II (26 Dec. 1793) and p. 93 Barras, 4 nivôse II (24 Dec. 1793). In his memoirs, *Mémoires de Barras*, ed. V. Duruy, 2 vols., Paris, 1895, t. 1, pp. 128–30, Barras was at pains to deny his terrorist conduct.

95 Some accounts, such as Agulhon (ed.), *Histoire de Toulon*, p. 193, derive a low figure from AM L427, Déclarations de domicile, 24 nivôse–25 pluviôse II (13 Jan.–13 Feb. 1794), which is clearly incomplete. The movement of population in the *Etat civil* suggests a total in the region of 15,000.

Bulwark of the Republic, 1794–1799

'Toulon is a stronghold of staunch republicanism; a redoubt of true patriotism. No wonder it has come under such fierce attack from royalists.'

Toulon had been devastated, in both physical and human terms, by the ordeal that ended the 'federalist' revolt. Many Toulonnais had emigrated, numerous buildings lay in ruins and the streets were strewn with debris, but the Montagnard government was determined to create 'a workshop of national vengeance' from the wreckage. The dockyards were soon operating at full stretch to prepare a new fleet and reassert French authority over the Mediterranean. Never had the ascendancy of Arsenal over town been so great. Port-la-Montagne, as the rebellious city was officially known, became 'a place unlike any other ... a veritable naval colony', repopulated with thousands of patriotic workers and sailors who were recruited from distant provinces.[1] The departure of wealthier citizens, along with the military elites, had left behind 'nothing but a huge mass of impoverished inhabitants'.[2] Local Jacobins, supported by a series of representatives 'on mission' from the National Convention, accordingly assumed undisputed control of the municipality. Together they ensured that Toulon remained 'the bastion of the Republic' in a mostly reactionary Midi.[3]

The Committee of Public Safety, the 'war cabinet' in Paris, was determined to overcome the great naval disaster sustained at Toulon. As soon as the city had been recovered, at the end of 1793, an ambitious construction programme was put into effect. Disorder prevailed in the town, but the dockyards had been spared wholesale damage: only the general store and the hangars for masts and casks had burned down. A large portion of the Mediterranean fleet had also survived. Though all of them needed repairs, thirteen ships of the line and five frigates had been left behind by the allies; three vessels absent when the port surrendered were able to return, while three more remained on the stocks.[4] Eight of these ships fought at the Battle of Aboukir in 1799 and the Egyptian expedition would not have been feasible without them. Losses were therefore less than feared and a basis existed for rebuilding to begin immediately. Naval stores and timber were not easily obtained, but another four ships of the line and a frigate were laid down during the twelve months that followed.

The launching of a new fleet required manpower as well as materials. No senior naval officials and only five seagoing officers were to be found in the port, because 'the most experienced sailors, like men well-versed in the complex business of the dockyards, had espoused the cause of royalism' and subsequently emigrated.[5] Administrative reorganisation was thus an urgent priority. Castellan, a Toulonnais officer imprisoned during the revolt, was named commander-in-chief-ashore, while leading functionaries were drafted in from Marseille. Pomme was appointed naval agent (*agent maritime*), the new designation for the civilian head of the Arsenal. Abouzir (who had prudently changed his name from Le Roy) was made chief engineer and Thivent financial controller. This quartet met as a naval council each day to recruit a labour force and then set it to work.[6] Only a handful of dockyard workers had become *émigrés*, but the native nucleus of craftsmen required tremendous expansion if construction targets were to be met. The total of workers reached 9,500 during June 1794 (prairial Year II, according to the new republican calendar) and eventually rose to a record level of 12,000 in the autumn.[7]

Dockyard registers indicate that only 10 per cent of some 8,000 recruits originated at Toulon, with roughly 30 per cent coming from Provence and 60 per cent from outside the region.[8] Mobilisation, which soon encompassed thousands of seamen as well, had brought a great influx of immigrants before, but never in such numbers nor from so far afield. Their 'colonisation' of the town is faithfully reflected in the birthplaces of marriage partners in the Year III (1794–95), when an unprecedented total of over 600 weddings was recorded in the *Etat civil*. Only 17 per cent of bridegrooms were Toulonnais by birth, compared to over 40 per cent in the early 1780s, another period of intense naval activity. In the Year III over 50 per cent of bridegrooms actually emanated from outside Provence, while less than half the brides were of native origin and 18 per cent hailed from beyond the region. The town had been 'invaded' by 'foreigners', drawn overwhelmingly from the popular classes. Rouyer, a rather reactionary representative on mission, felt that 'a horde of savages had overrun a civilised country'.[9]

Putting such huge contingents of raw recruits to work, night and day, with only one respite per *décade* (the revolutionary week of ten days) was a formidable task. Absenteeism was rife and two *représentants* in charge of naval operations, Saliceti and Moltedo, were especially vexed by non-attendance during what had traditionally been the Easter holidays. A great deal of desertion, as well as insubordination, drunkenness and crime also occurred. Much of it could be attributed to the terrible conditions which workers had to endure in the 'colony'. Food and lodgings were hopelessly inadequate, not to mention a lack of hospital and recreational facilities.[10] Nevertheless Saliceti and Moltedo were anxious to mount a naval strike against their native Corsica, which had lately fallen to the British. In floréal II (April 1794) they reported that some 10,000 sailors were being requisitioned to serve on a rapidly assembled fleet. Seven ships of the line and five frigates subsequently set sail in messidor (June), but the sortie was premature. The French were soon forced to seek refuge along the coast in the Golfe de Juan, whence superior British forces blocked their exit for several months.

Still, an impressive start had been made to mounting a fresh challenge in the Mediterranean, despite Jeanbon Saint-André's derogatory remarks on his arrival in Toulon at the end of July 1794. As the naval specialist on the Committee of Public Safety Jeanbon was despatched to the Midi to stimulate 'the greatest possible efforts at the Toulonnais Arsenal' and he was to maintain a dominating presence for the next eight months.[11] He distrusted the Provençal officials who were currently in command of the dockyards, perhaps feeling that even they were tainted with 'federalism.' Hence he wrote: 'There are few locals who are worthy of my confidence, the naval administration here is even worse than at Brest.'[12] His penchant for men from the Atlantic ports, which he had recently visited, led him to bring several new officers and officials to Toulon: for example, admiral Martin was nominated commander-in-chief-ashore, Thévenard was made director of constructions and another Martin *agent maritime*.

It was easy to identify shortcomings in the organisation of the Arsenal, but difficult to rectify them. There was no denying the vigour which Jeanbon applied to the task, though the repetition of his decrees suggests that they were frequently ignored. His major contribution lay in his determination to improve conditions as well as to enforce discipline. He fully agreed with the municipality that 'both the work-rate and the general behaviour of dockyard employees depends upon their confidence in the food supply'.[13] However, most local grain merchants had emigrated from Toulon and Marseille, while the British were harrying shipping which plied the coastal trade routes. Urban markets in the naval port were therefore empty and, with Genoese traders refusing to exchange goods for discredited *assignats*, prices far exceeded the *maximum* or fixed price on foodstuffs. Dockyard workers were earning 75 *sols* a day, some 50 per cent above nationally prescribed pay levels, yet they still struggled to survive.[14] As in the past paper money was losing some 80 per cent of its face value and 'hard cash was the only viable means of exchange'.[15]

Jeanbon immediately grasped this nettle. On 15 thermidor (2 August) he decreed that a 'full ration', such as sailors were receiving 'in bread, wine, meat, salted fish and, when possible, vegetables', would be accorded to workers at the Arsenal.[16] The men were to be charged at prices listed in the *maximum* and the sum subtracted from their wages, effectively payment in kind. With many conscripts sleeping rough shelter was also urgently needed, so Jeanbon ejected a horde of Corsican refugees from the town and then commandeered more *émigré* property for billets. The incidence of illness among employees, as disease swept an overcrowded and unsanitary city during the summer months, was tackled with similar resolve. Jeanbon created a naval health committee to care for 1,500 workers (almost 12 per cent of the labour force) who had reported sick. The committee was instructed to establish medical facilities, attract nursing staff and procure drugs and linen.[17]

In spite of these measures and the re-establishment of a dockyard tribunal to deal with delinquents, insubordination and criminality persisted, as did desertion. According to one administrator, writing on 4 vendémiaire III (25 September 1794), 'we continue to suffer from a dreadful epidemic of desertion and misconduct'.[18] Other reports confirm that the problem was proving intractable. On 20 nivôse (19 January 1795) some 2,000 sailors were absent without leave from a complement of 10,000 men and there were apparently villages on the littoral where 'all the sailors have returned home'.[19] Given the unsatisfactory conditions at Toulon, it was hard to prevent seamen and shipwrights deserting to domestic comforts and more lucrative pursuits. Due to this chronic labour shortage *émigré* sailors and workers were allowed to return to France, provided they signed up for service.

Jeanbon felt extremely frustrated, but he could justifiably claim to have been poorly supported in his endeavours. As he commented on the eve of his departure from Toulon in mid-pluviôse (early February 1795): 'with the backing of government resources a great deal can be achieved; without them virtually nothing'.[20] Urgently required funds and supplies failed to materialise and the situation had worsened when a less *dirigiste* leadership came to power at Paris. Indeed, Jeanbon's authority was substantially undermined by the political shift in the Convention which followed the downfall of Robespierre on 9 thermidor (27 July 1794). The anti-Montagnard reaction led to his removal from the Committee of Public Safety and the appointment of Niou as deputy with overall responsibility for the navy. Jeanbon was bitterly disappointed. He agreed to stay on in the Mediterranean *port de guerre* for the time being, but his commitment to the task inevitably diminished.

By contrast Thermidor had little direct impact upon the civilian administration at Toulon. The municipal commission adhered entirely to the Montagnard version of events: 'It is quite clear that this man (Robespierre), who enjoyed the esteem and confidence of all Republicans . . . has proved to be a villain, a monster . . . he even intended to become a tyrant over his native land . . . .'[21] It was 'business as usual' in the town, where cries of 'Vive la Montagne' were still regularly heard in the autumn of 1794. In other parts of the Var, however, and more especially in the neighbouring Bouches-du-Rhône, a full-scale reaction was soon under way. It began to influence the naval colony, because many conscript workers and sailors were distracted by developments in their native communities. During the winter of 1794–95 Toulon also became a haven for refugee Jacobins whose arrival only stiffened the determination of local Republicans to retain control of the municipality, albeit under the watchful eye of resident *représentants* and a centrally appointed 'national agent.'

In the immediate aftermath of the rebellion, with Toulon still in 'a state of siege', experienced administrators from elsewhere in the department had been placed on a municipal commission, under the presidency of General Masséna.[22] Their unfamiliarity with the town ensured that surviving Toulonnais Jacobins quickly returned to the helm. Though a sprinkling of newcomers remained, such as Auguste Aurel, a printer from Avignon, or J. B. Dussap, a watchmaker from Besançon, most of the men who were co-opted on to the commission were well-known local figures. They were the surgeons, retailers, clerks, shopkeepers and master craftsmen who had risen to prominence at the *Club Saint-Jean* and enjoyed municipal office in 1791 and 1792. The sectionary revolt of 1793, when many of them were incarcerated as *patriotes opprimés*, was only a temporary setback to their political careers. The disappearance of the old ruling elite, following the rebellion, paved the way for a renewed Jacobin ascendancy, which lasted for the rest of the decade.

Not only were *émigré* notables removed from the political fray, their abandoned possessions also presented their rivals with a splendid opportunity for enrichment. Almost 40 per cent of the town's fixed assets passed to the government as *émigré* property.[23] No systematic study of sales has been undertaken, but an impressionistic analysis of the copious documentation suggests that Jacobins at Toulon were not slow to seize upon the spoils.[24] J. L. Mège and A. Guigou, for example, both naval surgeons, former club members and *patriotes opprimés*, purchased land which had belonged to *émigré* military officers; the grain merchant J. B. Boisselin bought up much of the huge Missiessy estate on the outskirts of Toulon; and even a more humble character like C. Mège, who was in charge of the fire brigade at the dockyards, participated in the plunder. These 'Jacobin notables' thus had personal as well as political reasons for preserving the Republic and preventing the repatriation of their defeated opponents.

Yet local Jacobin administrators faced enormous problems in executing the essential tasks allotted to them. During the course of 1794 the total population of Toulon, including dockyard workers, sailors and soldiers, again rose in excess of 40,000 persons. Supplying them with foodstuffs was bound to rely heavily upon the generosity and assistance of central government, army and navy because municipal finances were in total chaos. Jeanbon's decision to assume direct responsibility for naval employees had been greeted with relief at the town hall, but a fresh crisis struck in the winter of the Year III (1794–95). The harvest of 1794 was a poor one and shortages were exacerbated both by the Thermidoreans' *laissez-faire* policies and continuing inflation, which brought the *assignat* down below 10 per cent of its face value. Matters were made worse by some appalling weather. Snow was falling at Toulon at the end of February 1795; according to *représentant* Letourneur, 'no one could recall weather quite as bad as this!'.[25]

The controlled price of a pound of bread, which had stabilised at 2 *sols* 9 *deniers* during the first half of 1794, rose sharply to 3*s* 6*d* in vendémiaire (October) and then to 4*s* 6*d* in frimaire (December). Rationing was introduced at Toulon in the autumn and civilians unable to rely upon dockyard or garrison supplies were allowed to purchase 1½ lb. of bread per day. This was reduced to just 1 lb. in pluviôse (January 1795), by which time 16,000 individuals were in receipt of municipal rations. In germinal (March–April) the cost was raised first to 10 and then to 25 *sols* for a loaf of extremely poor quality.[26] Yet, since the municipality was still providing subsidies at the rate of 34,000 *livres* a day, there was a strong case for additional price increases. On 27 floréal (16 May) the commission duly requested a further rise, but resident *représentants* persuaded them to delay. Rumblings of discontent, which exploded into a major insurrection a few days later, were already apparent and there can be no doubt that the *crise des subsistances* played a part in the upheaval. Foodstuffs were pillaged during the uprising of floréal/prairial (May 1795) at Toulon, while the restoration of order was assisted by the deployment of naval grain stocks upon the urban market.[27]

On the other hand, considering the prominence of dockyard workers and sailors in the insurrection of the Year III, it would be unwise to place too much emphasis upon the cost of living, for these groups enjoyed special protection against inflation and shortage. Although the practice had been abandoned in other *ports de guerre*, naval employees at Toulon were still receiving a generous ration at a modest price. They were charged only 6 *sols* out of their wages for 2 lbs. of bread (*poids de marc*).[28] This ration was subsequently reduced to 1½ lb. a day, but the relative value of the naval allowance increased as urban prices soared in the spring. This particular factor must have blunted the impact of the subsistence crisis at Toulon and it renders comparisons with other towns rather awkward. Toulonnais civilians were paying less for their daily bread than the inhabitants of neighbouring communities which generally remained calm. Conversely the price of a smaller loaf in the Mediterranean *port de guerre* was higher than at Paris, which was the scene of rioting on two occasions, in both germinal and prairial III.[29]

At first sight there also appears to be a close correlation between the subsistence crisis and the horrendous mortality recorded at Toulon during the Year III. No less than 6,359 deaths were registered during the twelve months which straddled 1794 and 1795, almost four times the annual average for the decade. Between ventôse and prairial III (March to May 1795) there were peaks of 743, 901 and 733 fatalities respectively, which coincide exactly with the unrest that culminated in the floréal/prairial (May) uprisings. On closer inspection, however, it is evident that deaths at the naval and military hospitals were mainly responsible for these massive totals.[30] Sailors and soldiers awaiting a favourable wind for a major naval expedition bore the brunt of the casualties. Medical care for the sick was hopelessly inadequate: 3,000 naval personnel were being treated under canvas by just four doctors.[31] It is certainly true that mortality among the civilian inhabitants recorded in the *Etat civil*, or at the municipal hospital, was running some 60 per cent higher than usual, but these losses must also be partly attributed to naval mobilisation. Urban facilities were in poor shape and unable to cope with the strain of overpopulation. As in the siege of 1793 or during the late summer of 1794, when even more civilian deaths occurred, a tightly packed populace was extremely suseptible to contagious diseases.[32]

Dearth, overcrowding, disease and death provided a grim context for the last Jacobin insurrection in the Midi. Yet economic and social hardship was not the primary cause of this final revolt at Toulon, where political issues were rather more important. During the winter of the Year III (1794–95) what commentators dubbed *chouannerie*, or royalist brigandage of the sort associated with Brittany, had began to ravage Provence. This White Terror was especially marked in the Rhône valley and at Marseille which, its trade ruined by British control of the seas, had become a haven for returning *émigrés*. Jeanbon Saint-André had blamed the *port de commerce* for infecting Toulon with 'federalism' in 1793 and he warned again in 1794 that 'the tranquillity of Toulon depends upon that of Marseille'.[33] On 5 vendémiaire III (6 October 1794) an abortive Jacobin uprising was staged at Marseille in a desperate effort to overthrow the Thermidorean administration there. This had profound repercussions upon Toulon because it agitated the many Marseillais who were conscripts in the *port de guerre*, or had sought refuge in the town.

Political unrest within the naval colony itself eventually broke out

on 30 nivôse III (19 January 1795) when an army officer denounced
the 'Montagnard faction' at a weekly gathering in the Temple of
Reason (formerly the parish church of Saint-Louis). This tirade
provoked violent brawls, on the streets and in the taverns, between
Jacobin partisans and unsympathetic troops stationed at the garrison. Styling themselves 'true sans-culottes', dockyard workers and
sailors clashed with soldiers, who shouted, 'Down with the Montagne.' On 10 pluviôse (29 January) a clerk was assaulted by anti-
Montagnards at the Arsenal and a sailor was killed in the ensuing
mêlée.[34] The subsequent arrest of Montagnard supporters, but not
their opponents, seemed to indicate an incipient reaction at Toulon.
This impression was reinforced when Jeanbon, Saliceti and Espert
were recalled to the Convention at the end of pluviôse (mid-
February) and replaced by more conservative representatives on
mission. Letourneur took charge of the naval base while Chambon
and Mariette, fearing 'great unrest among the people', disbanded the
local watch committee and purged the municipal administration.[35]
They also revoked the town's now politically inappropriate
appellation of Port-la-Montagne and officially reinstated the name
of Toulon.

The Thermidorean outlook of these newly arrived *représentants*
mirrored reaction within the Convention, which had begun to repeal
legislation against *émigrés*. On 29 frimaire III (19 December 1794)
naval officers and sailors who had left France were allowed to return
if they re-enlisted. Then, the following month, an amnesty was
offered to workers and peasants who had gone abroad after 1 May
1793.[36] Many bourgeois and even some nobles or priests appear to
have taken advantage of these exemptions, with the aid of
complaisant local authorities like those to the west of Toulon and
above all at Marseille. Rumours of these abuses provoked great
consternation at Toulon where attitudes towards the *émigrés*
remained uncompromising. When a shipload of forty-four suspects
landed along the coast at Saint-Tropez, in mid-pluviôse (early February 1795), they were promptly arrested by vigilant Jacobin administrators.[37] The influx continued unabated; a month later thirteen putative *émigrés*, who had come ashore at nearby Hyères, were
similarly seized and despatched to Toulon. As they were led through
the streets to be imprisoned there, on 20 ventôse (10 March), seven
of them were grabbed by demonstrators and beaten to death.

Shades of the massacres of summer 1792 loomed ominously. For two days mobs roamed the town, searching for suspects and threatening the gaols, before invading the Arsenal on the evening of 22 ventôse (12 March) in search of weapons.[38] Thousands of workers broke into the dockyards where they were urged to arm themselves against an attack by 'royalists'. The *représentants* successfully appealed for calm, while the garrison commander imposed a curfew and arrested numerous 'partisans of Robespierre'. Troops were subsequently sent into the surrounding communities to pick up more 'terrorists', but nothing was done to remove the underlying causes of insecurity at Toulon. In retrospect the events of ventse can be seen as a rehearsal for the full-blown insurrection of floréal/prairial (May). Lacking confidence in the authorities, who were failing to prevent anti-Jacobin atrocities elsewhere, the Toulonnais Jacobins decided to take matters into their own hands. Plans for a punitive and pre-emptive strike against Marseille were already taking shape.

Fear of returning *émigrés* only intensified when a general amnesty was granted to all 'federalists' on 22 germinal (11 April 1795). By the end of floréal (mid-May) tales abounded of royalist and *émigré* bands congregating around Solliès, some ten miles to the north of Toulon. A large number of Jacobins from the *port de guerre*, accompanied by colleagues from the hinterland, accordingly set out to deal with them. In the words of municipal officials at Solliès: 'Some 300 armed men left La Valette (on the outskirts of Toulon) for a march on Solliès, with the intention of massacring ... those citizens who had returned to their homes by virtue of the law of 22 germinal.'[39] After engaging in some violent disturbances during the night of 27–28 floréal (16–17 May) these 'Jacobin patriots' haled eleven suspected *émigrés* back to Toulon where they were taken into protective custody. Crowds had gathered to meet the prisoners but dockyard workers, who bulked large among the demonstrators, were persuaded to return to the Arsenal that afternoon. In the evening, however, they reassembled and drew up a petition bearing 500 signatures which sought the punishment of repatriated *émigrés*, the release of all incarcerated Jacobins and the re-creation of a National Guard at Toulon (an institution which had lapsed since the rebellion of 1793).[40]

The following day, 29 floréal (18 May), masses of dockyard workers and sailors thrust aside garrison sentries and helped themselves to weapons from the magazine at the Arsenal. The current military governor, a recent replacement for the general who had acted so firmly in ventôse, was unwilling to resort to force, partly because his men were discontented over poor conditions. Nor was the representative Brunel prepared to resist on this occasion. He acceded to the rebels' demands and then committed suicide, the second *conventionnel* to die in this manner at Toulon in the space of two years.[41] His death, widely believed to have been assassination, only worsened the unrest and two fresh ultimatums were issued: first, for a delay in the departure of the Mediterranean fleet waiting in the roadstead, since its setting sail was reckoned to be the signal for a royalist attack on the town; and second, for an armed expedition against Marseille, 'the *émigrés*' rallying point.'[42] The outlook of the insurrectionaries, who had effectively taken charge of Toulon (though an ineffectual municipal commission was left in being), is best illustrated by their various proclamations, for example: 'The liberty of the people is at risk and we have spontaneously taken up arms in order to protect it . . . *émigrés* are returning from all points of the compass and assassinating patriots with impunity. We have had recourse to force in order to expel this band of brigands from French territory . . . .'[43] This particular address was signed by some 700 'Republican workers from the Arsenal of Toulon'. Their leaders, *soi-disant* 'deputies of the sovereign people', demanded 'the Constitution of 1793' and 'the democratic and indivisible Republic'.

A march on Marseille had already been mooted, but the rebels' major objectives were defensive ones, aimed at maintaining locally the policies and ideals that the Thermidoreans were discarding nationally. The Toulonnais insurgents therefore consolidated their grip upon the town and continued negotiations with the *représentants*. Niou, who had done nothing to curb the disorders, was joined by Chiappe on 1 prairial (20 May) and then by Guérin and Poultier, on mission in the Bouches-du-Rhône, a couple of days later. It was agreed that the fleet, which had been won over to the rebellion, would remain in port while the re-formed National Guard assumed patrol duties around the town. On 4 prairial (23 May), however, this fragile accord was broken and the revolt brought to a climax by rumours of massacres at Marseille. That evening some 3,000 insurgents, armed with handguns and a dozen cannons, stormed out of Toulon to fly to the aid of their beleaguered colleagues in the neighbouring city.[44]

They were to meet with doom less than half-way there but, even so, their ill-fated sortie provoked a general panic in the Midi. The size of the rebel force was grossly exaggerated, like its degree of discipline. In reality, as Fréron later asserted, it comprised a band of 'wretched workers, ill-clad, poorly armed, marching in a disorderly fashion . . . and lacking effective leaders.'[45] The authorities had ample time to prepare resistance; as early as 1 prairial (20 May) Chiappe had slipped out of Toulon to seek assistance from the *armée d'Italie*, only to return with 10,000 troops after the rebels had been defeated. Other *représentants* were busy raising volunteer battalions in adjacent departments. At Aix, for example, the bloodthirsty Isnard encouraged inhabitants to join his crusade against resurgent terrorism with a famous battle cry: 'If you have no weapons, if you have no guns, well then, dig up your fathers' bones and use them to exterminate all these brigands.'[46] Such vigilantes were not required because the rebels were quickly crushed, near Le Beausset, only twelve miles from Toulon. A detachment of regular soldiers from Marseille proved more than adequate to deal with them. The troops suffered only a single fatality, yet the encounter on 5 prairial (24 May) was a fierce one; some forty insurgents were killed and 300 persons arrested.[47] The news of this *débâcle* demoralised those Jacobins who had stayed at Toulon. They were instructed to lay down their weapons – 6,000 guns were deposited with the authorities – and allow the fleet to depart, or face the consequences. Most readily compiled and on 10 prairial (29 May), when the Arsenal was working again and sailors were back on board ship, victorious government forces entered Toulon without firing a shot.[48] The history of 1793 was being repeated, though on this occasion the surrender was conducted peacefully and the subsequent repression was relatively mild.

Many arrests were made in and around Toulon, as Jacobin sympathisers were rounded up, together with putative rebels like the *conventionnel* Charbonnier. Most of these prisoners were later released, or amnestied when the new Constitution of the Year III came into effect in the autumn of 1795. Harsher treatment was generally reserved for leaders of the insurrection and those who had been captured in the fighting at Le Beausset. On 8 prairial (27 May) deputies in the Convention at Paris, where another uprising had just been suppressed, ordered the establishment of a military commission to punish the Toulonnais rebels. This special court was duly constituted in the naval town, but it was proceeding in too indulgent a fashion for the Thermidorean representative Rouyer. On 20 messidor (8 July) he transferred it to Marseille where a harsher approach was adopted, until the commission was dissolved at the end of fructidor (15 September) with 100 prisoners still awaiting trial. By that time, although 152 individuals had been acquitted, fifty-two had been executed, another fifteen sentenced to prison and fourteen sent before regular departmental courts.[49]

Although information relating to those who died on the battlefield is lacking, evidence is available for the 300 or so persons who were indicted by the *commission militaire*.[50] What is immediately striking is the fact that 90 per cent of those charged with rebellion were members of the popular classes and 60 per cent of them were illiterate. Most of the prisoners were dockyard workers, naval gunners and sailors, plus a smaller contingent of artisans and rural labourers. The vast majority originated from outside Toulon; only 9 per cent were natives and over 50 per cent hailed from beyond Provence. Most of them were recent arrivals, drawn in by the 'colonisation' that followed the defeat of the 'federalist' revolt. They were young men in the main (not a single woman was arrested), in their twenties or thirties, though several teenagers were also involved, the youngest of whom was fourteen.

Those sentenced to death were broadly representative in terms of literacy and age, but they did include a lower percentage of non-Provençaux and a slightly higher proportion of bourgeois. Not unnaturally, local militants long involved in Jacobin politics headed or inspired the insurrection. These seasoned campaigners were typified by J. L. Bonhomme, a Toulonnais retailer whose premises were used to plot the upheaval. A leading member of the *Club Saint-Jean* and a municipal office-holder, Bonhomme had been incarcerated by sectionaries in 1793. J. X. Portal, who emanated from Le Beausset where he had been a tax-collector, was also linked to the Jacobin network based on Toulon. He had been active in 1792 and 1793 and, during the uprising of the Year III, he was elected commander of the re-formed National Guard. J. S. Suffren, a rentier and former mayor of Le Castellet, had recently come to the naval port seeking refuge from Thermidorean violence. Like Portal he had been picked up after the disturbances of ventôse and then released, at the insistence of demonstrators, on 29 floréal (18 May).

Stalwarts like these readily confessed to being 'solid Republicans', who wished to rid the region of returning *émigrés* and were anxious to defend Toulon against a royalist offensive. Some of their closest associates in the insurrection, such as the hatter Mouriès who hailed from Marseille, even admitted to aiming at the liberation of the commercial city from reactionary dominion. Yet, in spite of a claim that 'in comparison with the terrorists of 1792' the rebels of the Year III were 'well-informed and politically conscious', the testimony of the rank and file is generally unenlightening.[51] A small minority of those executed for armed rebellion did say they wished to overthrow royalism at Marseille, or prevent the killing of patriots there. But the majority, perhaps confused and politically naïve, claimed to be acting under instructions from the *représentants*, or simply said they were going to visit family and friends.

Since the uprising at Toulon coincided with the *journées* of prairial in the French capital, events in the naval town were inevitably seen as part of 'a plot directed from Paris'.[52] The alleged involvement of Charbonnier, a Varois deputy on sick leave in his native Toulon, seemed to lend substance to the conspiracy thesis. Yet, while they were rhetorically formulated, the political objectives of the Toulonnais rebels were essentially local ones. There were no plans for marching on Paris and the simultaneity of the two spring uprisings constituted spontaneous popular outbursts against economic crisis and the Thermidorean reaction. In the case of Toulon political factors were uppermost as indigenous and refugee Jacobins unleashed their anger against royalists in the region. In the upshot their efforts only succeeded in making matters worse. Some thirty patriots had already been butchered at Aix on 21 floréal (10 May), and volunteers returning from combat with the Toulonnais rebels massacred no less than 100 prisoners in the Fort Saint-Jean at Marseille. From Lyon to Arles, along the Rhône valley, the spate of atrocities continued in an eruption of violence more hideous than the dreadful summer of 1792. No wonder Jacobins in the region wrote fearfully of 'a Provençal Vendée', a counter-terror which cast its shadow over all of them.[53]

Toulon itself was spared these appalling incidents, but the town did witness a degree of reaction that had not been experienced since the sectionary revolt. The municipal commission, like the *agent maritime* at the Arsenal, had made little effort to suppress the disturbances of floréal/prairial. When order was restored the naval agent was duly replaced, while the municipal commissioners were initially suspended and then purged by Guérin and Poultier.[54] This was not enough for the more combative *représentant* Rouyer, who was put in charge of Toulon during the summer of 1795. He undertook a more radical remodelling of the *commission municipale* which, he alleged, was full of 'persons of low intelligence, who hold highly suspect political opinions'. His decree of 3 messidor (21 June) removed all existing personnel and replaced them with professional administrators from outside the town, 'none of whom has any connection with local party-politics'.[55]

According to Edmond Poupé, in his magisterial history of the Var, by the end of the Year III (September 1795), 'at Toulon, like everywhere else in the Var, the Jacobins were reduced to impotence'.[56] Rouyer was successful in stifling any further hints of unrest. He and his colleague, Durand-Maillane, busied themselves by persecuting Jacobins on the one hand, while permitting the repatriation of *émigrés* and the celebration of mass on the other.[57] Yet this period of reaction came to an end when a new system of government was instituted in France in the autumn; Rouyer and his fellow *représentants* were subsequently recalled and the political climate again changed profoundly.

The Constitution of the Year III, which established an executive Directory and a bicameral parliament, was submitted to a referendum at the end of fructidor (early September 1795). The electoral assemblies were accordingly summoned for the first time in two years but at Toulon, as elsewhere, the meetings to discuss and vote upon the new arrangements were poorly attended.[58] In France as a whole roughly 16 per cent of the electorate cast an opinion; at Toulon the turnout was less than 10 per cent, though fleet and garrison were consulted separately. Few refusals were recorded anywhere and all eight Toulonnais sections were unanimously in favour of acceptance, though one garrison soldier apparently voted against. The notorious 'two-thirds' decree accompanying the Constitution, which restricted the voters' choice of two in every three legislators to former *conventionnels*, was either endorsed or ignored at Toulon. Rouyer reported that 'voting was conducted freely and fairly' throughout the town.[59]

There was another undisturbed, if low turnout when the Toulonnais electorate reconvened a few days later to create a new departmental college. The Constitution of the Year III retained a two-tier electoral procedure, but reintroduced property qualifications for participants at the second stage. A minimal tax requirement was also reimposed upon primary voters, although it seems unlikely that it was actually applied at Toulon in 1795 or thereafter. Leading Jacobins were chosen in the naval town and also in some cantons along the littoral, but this was not the general outcome in the Var. Poupé suggests that 'more or less overt royalists' had a clear majority at the electoral college which met at Grasse in vendémiaire IV (October 1795).[60] A smaller assembly than hitherto (one delegate per 200 instead of 100 registered voters) returned Girondin and Thermidorean deputies, including Isnard and Boissy d'Anglas, from the list of *ex-conventionnels*. The 'new' men selected were both royalists: Pastouret, a former marquis and J. Portalis, once a prominent Aixois lawyer. College delegates went on to elect a departmental administration, now reduced to a directory of five without a council, and gave it a strongly conservative complexion.

The departmental headquarters had been removed from Toulon during the rebellion of 1793 and districts were abolished in the new Constitution. The Toulonnais Jacobins were, nonetheless, able to regain control of the lowest level of local government, where the canton supplanted the commune and became an administrative as well as a judicial and electoral division. This new arrangement was intended to liquidate small, rural municipalities by amalgamating them at cantonal level. Not without some confusion the hill-village of Le Revest was briefly integrated into the cantonal municipality based on Toulon. The change was accompanied by a sharp reduction in personnel: a council of only eight members was initially elected, though this number was based upon a misinterpretation of the rules and was subsequently lowered to seven.[61] A president (the office of mayor having been abolished) was chosen annually by the council itself, which was to be partially renewed each year. Municipal elections under this regime were held on 10 brumaire IV (1 November 1795) and the small scrap of evidence that survives suggests another poor turnout. The continuing indifference of the electorate is attested by two *représentants* at Toulon, who bemoaned 'a criminal lack of interest in exercising the most sacred of civic duties'.[62] The absence of popular enthusiasm did no harm to Jacobin notables, who were duly returned to power as councillors and justices of the peace.

The arrival of Fréron in the Midi as a roving commissioner for the Directory, at the end of frimaire IV (late November 1795), helped ensconce the Jacobin elite in its stronghold at Toulon. Although he had repudiated his terrorist past Fréron cracked down hard upon *émigrés* and royalists in Provence. He was determined to enforce the recent law of 20 fructidor (6 September), which excluded afresh from the Republic all those who had fled with the allies in 1793.[63] The many Toulonnais affected by this renewed 'persecution' later complained that some 800 *émigrés* were either arrested or obliged to leave the Var as a result of Fréron's campaign.[64] The municipal council at Toulon, having requested the destruction of all 'the old seeds of royalism and betrayal which are quietly germinating and will continue to do so as long as *chouans* infest our department', was naturally delighted.[65] While most other administrations in the region were heavily purged Toulon was singled out for praise as a 'truly patriotic commune'.

No sooner had Fréron departed than his old enemy Isnard was launching a vitriolic assault upon the town in the *Conseil des Cinq-Cents* at Paris. Isnard's target was a recently created Literary Society at Toulon, which he lambasted in typically unrestrained fashion as 'A hotbed of violent cut-throats . . . a Jacobin club more extreme than ever, whose members desire nothing less than the Constitution of 1793 and the resurrection of the abominable Montagne.'[66] The Society had been founded by Jacobin notables but, in the opinion of the garrison commander who was instructed to close it down, its only activity had been the provision of republican newspapers like *L'ami des lois* or *Le journal des patriotes de 1789*. Soldiers posted at Toulon protested that no political debate had ever occurred and swore that the dreaded Constitution of 1793 had never been mentioned.[67]

Yet the Society may have linked to the reappearance of Gracchus Babeuf's radical journal, *Le tribun du peuple*. No less than twenty-one out of 300 provincial subscribers to *Le tribun* were resident in the Var, eight of them at Toulon. Five of these Toulonnais were members of the Jacobin elite, including J. L. Bonhomme, who had been implicated in the insurrection of the Year III but subsequently amnestied, and Jean Terrin, a rentier and municipal councillor. Two dockyard clerks and a naval engineer were also listed while E. Barry, administrator at the Arsenal and current chairman of the municipal council, corresponded with the paper on the subject of 'social happiness'.[68] These individuals were doubtless trying to keep abreast of republican thought rather than plotting a revolutionary coup with the paper's editor. Nevertheless, with Jacobins like them in charge, Toulon was one of few places in the Var where the Republican calendar was still being scrupulously observed. A 'considerable number of citizens' were even given permission to celebrate the cult of Theophilanthropy at the town's Temple of Reason, while requests to reopen churches were flatly refused.[69]

The inauguration of the Directory marked a recovery in the fortunes of Jacobinism at Toulon, but not of the economic situation, which continued to deteriorate. The total collapse of the *assignat* was chiefly to blame; by nivôse IV (the end of 1795) it was virtually worthless. Rouyer had complained in the summer that laundering a shirt was costing him 10 *livres*. More importantly the price of the bread ration went on rising until, in the spring of 1796, it reached 70 *sols* a pound. Even worse, this civilian ration, 'a mixture of bad grain, straw and soil', shrank in size from ¾ lb. to ½ lb. a day.[70] For the poor, who were eventually deprived of their free bread dole in the autumn of 1796, this was a period of extreme distress. The municipal council was unable to offer much institutional aid and the central government was deaf to pleas for financial support. In vain local administrators sought assistance: 'We are in dire straits here' – they wrote – 'the Arsenal apart, there are no wealthy nor extensive industrial or commercial resources that we can draw upon.'[71]

It was the navy which saved Toulon from complete disaster, not simply by continuing to provision its own employees, but also by loaning stocks of grain to the municipal authorities. However, the dockyard administration itself was in difficulties at the turn of 1796. Najac, newly arrived as naval agent, feared disorder would occur when he realised that 'the warehouses were almost completely devoid of essential foodstuffs'.[72] On 17 pluviôse (6 February 1796) striking workers at the naval bakery decorated their ovens with useless *assignats* in a protest over living standards, but it proved to be an isolated incident.[73] The insertion of a small amount of specie into wages, together with a pay rise a few weeks later, served to pacify the demonstrators. Even so, it was another twelve months before a complete return to hard currency and a more plentiful supply of foodstuffs brought the long crisis of the years III and IV to a close.

Besides grappling with these intractable economic and social problems the Toulonnais Jacobins also had to face a fresh political challenge, when General Moynat d'Auxon arrived in the latter part of 1796. This reactionary *militaire*, a *protégé* of the equally dubious General Willot, described Toulon as a 'stronghold of anarchy', where 'assassins and enemies of the government abound'.[74]

Moynat's appointment coincided with elections in the spring of 1797. His mission was allegedly to assist Provençal royalists who, like their colleagues elsewhere, hoped to win at the polls and then seize control of the Republic by constitutional means.[75] Fearful of this grand design Jacobins at Toulon were soon denouncing Moynat for failing to punish suspected *émigrés*, while imprisoning good republicans; 'military despotism grows daily more odious', as they rhetorically put it.[76]

In the event Moynat's efforts to influence the electoral outcome proved counter-productive. On 7 germinal V (27 March 1797) the municipal administration at Toulon was able to proclaim triumphantly:

The eight primary assemblies in this town met in a most calm, orderly and correct fashion. The polls have never been so well-attended since the Revolution began ... the choice of all the electors has fallen upon honest and committed Republicans ... Neither the dreadful military devices deployed by General Moynat d'Auxon, nor his consistently tyrannical conduct have succeeded in frightening the voters.[77]

The Directory later received a complaint signed by some 400 inhabitants, including many former sectionaries, who protested that they had been prevented from participating. 'Respectable citizens' who had never set foot outside the Republic had been barred from the assemblies. By contrast, 'a horde of obnoxious anarchists ... chased out of other departments in the Midi ... had persuaded compliant municipal officials to give them the certificate of residence' required of voters.[78] Evidently the Toulonnais Jacobins had mounted a vigorous campaign. Permission was secured for workers to leave the dockyard to vote and, undoubtedly, individuals who were not listed on the electoral register were admitted to the poll. The intense competition resulted in a high turnout: roughly 33 per cent to elect Toulon's delegation to the departmental college and 36 per cent to choose local councillors.[79] These figures had only been surpassed once before, during another period of bitter factional strife in 1791.

In the Year V (1797) the individuals who joined the municipal council at Toulon, like those despatched to the electoral assembly at Brignoles, were solid Jacobins drawn from the minor liberal professions, or among shopkeepers and artisans. Yet, while they dominated their own town, these men were heavily outnumbered at the *assemblée départementale*. The Var deputed royalists to Paris, all of whom were ousted six months later when the Directory took drastic measures to protect the régime.[80] In the meantime the Toulonnais Jacobins themselves had been forced on to the defensive. On 7 floréal (26 April) municipal councillors wrote in despair to Barras and his fellow Directors bemoaning a spate of 'arbitrary and illegal arrests' taking place in Toulon. 'The tyranny of general Moynat', they wailed, 'is reducing us to a state of abject servility.'[81] Marseille was vividly described as 'another Vendée', while attention was drawn to the rising tide of political murders in the Var. Some 600 persons were killed over a period of two years, including F. Aubert, a Toulonnais serving on the criminal tribunal, who was assassinated at nearby La Valette. The White Terror seemed to be closing in on Toulon. Indeed, in thermidor V (August 1797) it was widely rumoured that the departmental administration was preparing to suspend the municipal council at Toulon, one of the few remaining Jacobin strongholds in the Midi.[82]

This desperate situation recalled the summer of 1791 when the town had been similarly threatened by hostile departmental officials. In 1797 the Directory's *coup d'état* of 18 fructidor (4 September) saved the day. The Legislative Councils at Paris, local administrations, judicial bodies and military commands were all purged of anti-republican elements. The departmental Directory of the Var was replaced, along with the troublesome government commissioner (*commissaire du Directoire*) attached to the municipal council at Toulon, and Moynat d'Auxon was incarcerated. The Toulonnais Jacobins were delighted with this 'most glorious event'. 'Modern-day Brutuses,' wrote relieved municipal councillors to the Directors, 'once again you have saved the Republic and prevented a free people falling back into the abyss of slavery.'[83] Equally adulatory addresses emanated from other groups in the city: from 500 'Toulonnais republicans'; from no less than 3,600 'Marseillais who had found sanctuary at Toulon'; and, finally, from a newly created Constitutional Circle, a reincarnation of the former *Club Saint-Jean*, which mustered another 300 signatures.[84]

The Circle's address applauded legislation subsequently passed on 19 fructidor (5 September) as 'a real palladium of liberty' which outlawed returning *émigrés*, royalists and non-juring priests. Something of a 'Fructidorean Terror' ensued as columns of National Guards were despatched into the department and a military commission was set up at Toulon to try those who were captured. Over the following two years it sentenced ninety-nine persons to death for various political offences.[85] Of those recorded with a profession roughly half were notables, precisely the social profile of twenty victims with Toulonnais origins. An initial flurry of executions between vendémiaire and frimaire VI (October to December 1797) was followed by intense repression in fructidor VI (August–September 1798), as a result of harsh legislation against enemies of the Republic passed in messidor (July). Sporadic death sentences continued to be delivered until operations ceased in nivôse VIII (December 1799). The final person to be condemned to the guillotine under this 'militarised' judicial procedure was Joseph Galle, a merchant from Toulon who had emigrated after taking part in the revolt of 1793.

The 'colony of patriots' was undoubtedly secured from the threat of royalism by these draconian measures, the effectiveness of which was revealed in the elections of the Year VI (spring 1798). The turnout of a mere 19 per cent at Toulon was much lower than the previous year because this time 'the royalists had not dared to show themselves'.[86] At the departmental college of the Var moderate Jacobins dominated the proceedings. Barras, an existing Director, and two Toulonnais were among the six deputies elected. All of them survived a fresh purge of the Legislative Councils, in floréal (May), which on this occasion was directed against a widespread upsurge of radical Republicanism.

The period between the coup of fructidor in the Year V and renewed crisis in the Year VII was a relatively tranquil and productive one at Toulon. Improvements were made in the provision of both education and poor relief. Public primary schooling was sparse, but a secondary school was opened in germinal VI (April 1798), offering places to sixty pupils.[87] Meanwhile, the almshouse of La Charité had been returned for use by the elderly and infirm.[88] The single administration now dealing with sickness and indigence remained chronically underfunded but, in the year VI, the cost of living at last stabilised. The harvest of 1797 was a good one, supplies from the Mediterranean increased and, for the following two years, the price of a pound of bread was held below 3 *sols*. Paper money was abandoned and, following the switch to metal currency, rationing for naval employees could finally be lifted.

Any threat of disorder was removed by the lowering of activity at the Arsenal, where the number of workers was cut to 7,000 in 1796 and then 3,000 a year later.[89] As thousands of unruly and ill-disciplined conscripts departed the population of Toulon fell to a more manageable total of some 25,000 inhabitants. Demobilisation at the dockyards marked the completion of reconstruction work which had been undertaken since the recapture of the town at the end of 1793. It also reflected the changes made to French naval strategy in the Mediterranean. In ventôse and prairial III (March and June 1795) sizeable fleets of twenty to thirty ships had set out to recover Corsica and break the British stranglehold at sea, but neither sortie had succeeded. These failures highlighted the fragility of the restored Toulonnais fleet and, not least, its lack of operational expertise. Thereafter the Republic fell back on a policy of harrying enemy warships and merchantmen which amounted to little more than privateering. Such operations kept the base at Toulon ticking over, while General Bonaparte's Italian campaigns required the regular transport of troops and munitions along the riviera. It was, in fact, victories on land which eventually dislodged the British fleet from the Mediterranean in 1797 by removing their portage facilities on the littoral.[90]

The defeat of its continental enemies allowed the French Republic to concentrate on the war at sea: 'Britain is the only adversary left to overcome . . . the hopes of the entire nation therefore rest upon the navy . . . Sailors, It is up to you to finish the fight.'[91] The Arsenal at Toulon was the scene of increasing activity from the turn of 1798 onwards, but it was only in spring that the Directory issued secret orders for the famous Egyptian expedition. The assault on the Orient demanded an enormous, if short-lived effort at the Mediterranean naval base. Much was achieved and considerable credit must go to Najac, the *ordonnateur* (as the head of the dockyards was once again entitled), who overcame three huge obstacles: 'Firstly, the shortage of funds; secondly the lack of naval stores, and thirdly the difficulty of recruiting sufficient sailors to man our ships.'[92]

Vice-admiral Brueys arrived in the *port de guerre* on 2 April to take command of a hastily assembled fleet. Thirteen ships of the line, six frigates and over 150 smaller craft departed from Toulon the following month, on 30 floréal (19 May 1798). Bonaparte, who had initially proposed the venture and now led the 18,000 troops on board, memorably exhorted his men to fresh feats of bravery: 'You have successfully fought in the mountains, on the plains and against great cities, now you must do the same at sea.'[93] Acerra and Meyer, authors of a splendid recent survey of the navy in the Revolution, suggest that the expedition was doomed from the outset. Brueys was fortunate to evade the British and reach Egypt in the first place, but his fleet was annihilated at Aboukir Bay on 14 thermidor (1 August). No less than eleven ships of the line and two frigates were lost, not to mention further disasters as the surviving vessels limped home. 'The Battle of the Nile, as the British call it, was the first decisive defeat in naval history. It marked . . . the end of the French navy as a force capable of counter-balancing the might of Britain. This crushing blow could not be overcome and the seeds of Trafalgar were sown at Aboukir.'[94]

The consequences of this catastrophe were not just felt in naval terms, as the Mediterranean reverted to British control, but also in the diplomatic and political spheres. Bonaparte's bold assault on Egypt brought the formation of a second European coalition against France, which suffered reverses all along its frontiers after the revival of the land war in 1799. For the first time since 1793 the Republic was threatened with invasion and defeat inevitably took its toll upon internal stability. Conscription and emergency legislation provoked a recrudescence of desertion, brigandage and terrorism, a potent mixture that was compounded by economic dislocation and food shortages.[95] The Var, despite its exposed location on the Italian frontier, was by no means the worst affected area, but the relative calm of the preceding two years was shattered. The crisis encouraged opponents of the regime to mount a fresh challenge and elections in germinal VII (spring 1799) were bitterly contested as a result.

At Toulon the turnout for both primary and municipal polling was slightly higher than in the Year VI, but experienced Jacobin notables were returned as usual. Elsewhere in the department voting was accompanied by violence; at least seven primary assemblies were rent by secessions on the part of determined minorities. At the electoral college, which met in Draguignan on 20 germinal (9 April 1799), Jacobins outnumbered conservative republicans and royalists by two to one. Delegates from Toulon, Draguignan and Grasse led the Jacobin majority which was strenuously opposed by reactionaries from the western and upper Var. The latter subsequently seceded from the assembly alleging that many of the dominant 'anarchists', numerous Toulonnais among them, had failed to meet the property requirements for college members. According to the government commissioner the Jacobins also employed a good deal of intimidation, 'wearing favours which recalled the dreaded Montagne and singing hymns in honour of Marat'.[96] The Directory nonetheless endorsed the work of the main assembly and ignored the secessionist minority. Toulonnais Jacobins were exultant, proudly proclaiming themselves 'the vanguard of the Revolution'.[97]

Yet military defeat and political uncertainty gradually sapped Jacobin morale and cut short the upsurge of radicalism. Small wonder that Bonaparte's unexpected return from Egypt, on 17 vendémiaire VIII (9 October 1799), was greeted with great relief and rejoicing. At Toulon the town council was convened at 4.00 a.m. the following morning to hear the 'wonderful news' and a celebration was planned for later the same day. A tree of liberty was planted, with an inscription honouring both the 'everlasting Republic' and 'the hero of Italy, the immortal Bonaparte'.[98] The general's presence was reassuring at a moment of grave crisis and, though his *coup d'état* a month later was not greeted with the same enthusiasm, its acceptance was never in doubt. Fabre de l'Aude, a special envoy of the new regime, was swiftly sent to offer reassurance: 'Purchasers of national properties have no need to be fearful, their ownership is sacred . . . as for traitors and *émigrés*, they are forever banished from the *patrie*.'[99] Anxious citizens of Toulon could only trust that this latest upheaval in Paris would succeed in rescuing the beleaguered Republic which they had so energetically sustained for so long.

Toulon had been a bastion of the directorial regime in a way that neighbouring Aix or Marseille were not. The explanation for Jacobin hegemony in the naval town resides, to a large extent, in the emigration of so many members of the old elite in the wake of their abortive rebellion. These bourgeois *émigrés* may have begun to return after 1795, but they were confronted by solidly entrenched Jacobin notables who were in no mood to compromise. Dedication to the Republic also reflected Toulon's role as a naval base, ever reliant upon the flow of government funds and personnel to conduct the war at sea. Moreover, until the advent of the crisis of the Year VII, the town had begun to enjoy a degree of stability that it had rarely experienced since 1789. It remained to be seen whether or not Bonaparte would underwrite the local Jacobin leadership and endorse the firm political line it had unerringly pursued.

Notes

1 AN D1 41, Rouyer, 3 messidor III (21 June 1795).

2 AM L115, Arrêté de Jeanbon Saint-André, 22 vendémiaire III (13 Oct. 1794). His comment was echoed by another *représentant*, Durand-Maillane: 'At most ten bourgeois families of ancient extraction remain in the town.' Aulard (ed.), *Recueil*, t. 28, p. 286; Durand-Maillane, 16 vendémiaire IV (8 Oct. 1795).

3 AN AD XVI 78, Administration municipale, 11 germinal IV (31 Mar. 1796).

4 AP 1A2 81, Agent maritime, 5 nivôse II (25 Dec. 1793); Brun, *Port de Toulon*, t. 2, pp. 250–3 and Hampson, *La marine de l'an II*, pp. 219–21.

5 AN BB3 57, Sous-chef de Toulon, 26 ventôse II (16 Mar. 1794).

6 AP 3A1 9, Conseil, 8 nivôse II (28 Dec. 1793) and 1A2 81, Agent maritime, 8 nivôse II (28 Dec. 1793).

7 AP 1A2 119, Etat de situation des ouvriers, 30 prairial II (18 June 1794) and AM L318, Situation des ouvriers, 21 fructidor II–20 pluviôse III (7 Sept.–8 Feb. 1795).

8 AP 2G1 32, Matricule des ouvriers, an II (1794).

9 AN D1 41, Rouyer, 3 messidor III (21 June 1795).

10 Aulard (ed.), *Recueil*, t. 12, pp. 528–9 and p. 795; Moltedo, 22 germinal and 3 floréal II (11 and 22 Apr. 1794).

11 Aulard (ed.), *Recueil*, t. 14, p. 748; arrêt, 18 messidor II (6 July 1794) and L. Levy-Schneider, *Le conventionnel Jeanbon Saint-André*, 2 vols., Paris, 1901, t. 2, pp. 919–20.

12 AN BB3 62, Jeanbon Saint-André, 9 thermidor II (27 July 1794).

13 AM L68(11), Délibérations, 7 frimaire III (27 Nov. 1794).

14 AP 3A1 9, Conseil, 10 ventôse II (28 Feb. 1794) and Hampson, 'Les ouvriers des arsenaux', pp. 455–62.

15 AN BB3 62, Jeanbon Saint-André, 12 thermidor II (30 July 1794).

16 AM L190, Arrêté, 15 thermidor II (2 Aug. 1794).

17 AM L115, Arrêté, 10 thermidor II (28 July 1794) and L318, Situation des ouvriers, 21 fructidor II (7 Sept. 1794).

18 AM L284, Chef des bureaux civils, 4 vendémiaire III (25 Sept. 1794).

19 AM L284, Commissaire des classes, 2 pluvise III (21 Jan. 1795) and L286, Etat des équipages, 20 nivôse III (9 Jan. 1795).

20 Aulard (ed.), *Recueil*, t. 20, p. 26; Jeanbon Saint-André, 14 pluviôse III (2 Feb. 1795).

21 AM L95 bis(4), Adresse, 20 thermidor II (7 Aug. 1794).

22 AM L68 (8), Délibérations, 10–11 nivôse II (30–31 Dec. 1793).

23 AM L204, Contribution foncière, an III (1794–95).

24 AD Q876–1145, Vente des biens des émigrés de Toulon, an II (1794).

25 Aulard (ed.), *Recueil*, t. 20, p. 401; Letourneur, 1 ventôse III (19 Feb. 1795).

26 AM L68(11), Délibérations, 4 and 24 brumaire and 3 pluviôse III (25 Oct., 14 Nov. 1794 and 22 Jan. 1795) and 3, 24 and 27 germinal III (24 Mar., 13 and 16 Apr. 1795).

27 Aulard (ed.), *Recueil*, t. 23, p. 498; Niou, 5 prairial III (24 May 1795).

28 AM L190, Chef de comptabilité, 20 nivôse III (9 Jan. 1795) and AP 1A2 81, Agent maritime, 24 floréal III (13 May 1795).

29 G. Rudé, *The crowd in the French Revolution*, Oxford, 1959, pp. 143–4. Rudé asserts that in the *journées* of germinal–prairial at Paris, p. 157, 'it was not political agitation but economic hardship that was the primary cause'.

30 AM L314, Décès aux hôpitaux maritimes, an III, in addition to the *Etat civil*. The mortality rate at Rouen was only twice the annual average during the Year III, though it rose higher in the Year IV, when that of Toulon was falling: R. C. Cobb, *Terreur et subsistances*, Paris, 1965, p. 321.

31 Aulard (ed.), *Recueil*, t. 22; Letourneur, 23 germinal III (12 Apr. 1795).

32 AM L567, Rapports sur les maladies, 28 vendémiaire and 22 frimaire III (19 Oct. and 12 Dec. 1794) and Marquis, *Considérations médico-chirurgicales*, pp. 10–11.

33 Cited in Levy-Schneider, *Le conventionnel Jeanbon Saint-André*, t. 2, p. 961.

34 AM L68(11), Délibérations, 1–8 pluviôse III (20–27 Jan. 1795) and Aulard (ed.), *Recueil*, t. 19, p. 794; Jeanbon Saint-André *et al.*, 12 pluviôse III (31 Jan. 1795).

35 Aulard (ed.), *Recueil*, t. 20, pp. 768–9; Mariette and Chambon, 19 ventôse III (9 Mar. 1795).

36 Greer, *The incidence of the Emigration*, pp. 96–9 and Honoré, *L'émigration*, pp. 73–82.

37 AM L68(11), Délibérations, 17 pluviôse III (5 Feb. 1795) and Poupé, *Le département du Var*, p. 375.

38 AM L68(11), Délibérations, 20–22 ventôse III (10–12 Mar. 1795); L369 and 370, Troubles, ventôse III (Feb.–Mar. 1795); AP 1A2 81, Agent maritime, 23 ventôse III (13 Mar. 1795) and Aulard (ed.), *Recueil*, t. 21, pp. 146–51; Mariette *et al.*, 27 ventôse III (17 Mar. 1795).

39 AM L372, Extrait des délibérations de la commune de Solliès, 28 floréal III (17 May 1795).

40 AN D1 10, Brunel, 28 floréal III (17 May 1795); AM L68(11), Délibérations, 28 floréal III (17 May 1795) and AP 1A2 81, Agent maritime, 29 floréal III (18 May 1795).

41 AM L68(11), Délibérations, 29–30 floréal III (18–19 May 1795); AP 1A2 81, Agent maritime, 30 floréal and 1 prairial III (19–20 May 1795) and F. Masson, *La révolte de Toulon en prairial an III*, Paris, 1875, pp. 32–9.

42 AN F7 3693 Var 1, Républicains ouvriers de l'arsenal de Toulon, 30 floréal III (19 May 1795).

43 AN AD XVI 78, Républicains ouvriers, 30 floréal III (19 May 1795).

44 AM L68(11), Délibérations, 1–4 prairial III (20–3 May 1795) and Masson, *La révolte de Toulon*, pp. 50–3. See also M. Crook, 'La dernière insurrection jacobine du Midi: la révolte de Toulon en floréal/prairial an III', *Actes du 113ᵉ Con. Nat.*, 1988.

45 S. Fréron, *Mémoire historique sur la réaction royale et sur les*

massacres du Midi, Paris, an IV, p. 16; R. C. Cobb, *The police and the people. French popular protest, 1789–1820*, Oxford, 1970, p. 143 and Aulard (ed.), *Recueil*, t. 23, pp. 544–6; Chambon *et al.*, 6 and prairial III (25 May 1795).

46   Cited in Poupé, *Le département du Var*, p. 387.

47   Aulard (ed.), *Recueil*, t. 23, pp. 768–70; Chambon *et al.*, 12 prairial III (31 May 1795).

48   AM L68(11), Délibérations, 6–9 prairial III (25–28 May 1795); AP 1A2 81, Agent maritime, 8 prairial III (27 May 1795) and Masson, *La révolte de Toulon*, pp. 68–73.

49   E. Poupé, 'La répression de la révolte terroriste de Toulon, fin floréal an III', *VHG*, 1924, pp. 283–7.

50   *Ibid.* and AD 2L 291, Supplément 14, Commission militaire, prairial-fructidor III (June–Sept. 1795).

51   Agulhon (ed.), *Histoire de Toulon*, p. 195.

52   Aulard (ed.), *Recueil*, t. 23, p. 696; Cadroy, 10 prairial III (29 May 1795).

53   Baratier (ed.), *Histoire de la Provence*, p. 433 and C. Lucas, 'Themes in southern violence after 9 Thermidor' in G. Lewis and C. Lucas (eds.), *Beyond the Terror. Essays in French regional and social history*, Cambridge, 1983, pp. 152–61.

54   AM L68(12), Délibérations, 23 prairial III (11 June 1795).

55   Aulard (ed.), Recueil, t. 24, pp. 602–3; Rouyer, 3 messidor III (21 June 1795).

56   Poupé, *Le département du Var*, p. 397.

57   AD 1L1735, Délibérations du district de Toulon, 23 and 25 messidor III (11 and 13 July 1795) and Aulard (ed.), *Recueil*, t. 24, p. 694; Rouyer, 6 messidor III (24 June 1795).

58   AN BII 64, Plébiscite, 27 fructidor III (13 Sept. 1795) and A. Lajusan, 'Le plébiscite de l'an III', *La Révolution française*, LX, 1911.

59   AN D1 41, Rouyer, 28 fructidor III (14 Sept. 1795).

60   Poupé, *Le département du Var*, pp. 413–14.

61   AN F1 BII Var 1, Registre des délibérations du Directoire, 28 brumaire VI (10 Nov. 1797) and AN XVI 78, Rapport de Renault, 5 prairial VI (24 May 1798).

62   AM L593, Procès-verbal, 10 brumaire IV (1 Nov. 1795) and L115, Arrêté de Niou et de Servière, 15 brumaire IV (6 Nov. 1795).

63   Fréron, *Mémoire historique*, pp. 10–11; Greer, *The incidence of the Emigration*, pp. 102–3 and Honoré, *L'émigration*, pp. 83–5.

64   AN F1 CIII Var 1, Au général Moynat, 17 ventôse V (7 Mar. 1797).

65   AM L95 bis(5), Correspondance, 2 frimaire IV (23 Nov. 1795).

66   M. Isnard, *Discours sur la situation du Midi*, Paris, an IV, p. 2.

67   AN AD XVI 78, Pièces à décharge, germinal IV (Mar.–Apr. 1796).

68   AN F7 4278, Liste des abonnés, an IV; M. A. Iafelice, 'Le babouvisme en province. Les abonnés méridionaux au Tribun du Peuple', *Cahiers d'histoire de l'Institut de recherches marxistes*, 1984, pp. 94–5; A. Saitta, *Le tribun du peuple, textes choisis*, Paris, 1969, p. 276 and R. B. Rose, *Gracchus Babeuf. The first revolutionary communist*, London, 1978, pp.

219–20.
  69 AM L68(12) and (13), Délibérations, 14 ventôse IV (4 Mar. 1796) and 29 prairial V (17 June 1797).
  70 AM L68(12), Délibérations, 19 frimaire, 18 nivôse and 2 germinal IV (10 Dec. 1795, 8 Jan. and 22 Mar. 1796) and Aulard (ed.), *Recueil*, t. 24, pp. 693–5; Rouyer, 6 messidor III (24 June 1795).
  71 AM L95 bis(5), Correspondance, 29 germinal IV (18 Apr. 1796) and L68(13), Délibérations, 6 brumaire V (27 Oct. 1796).
  72 AP 1A2 82, Agent maritime, 8 nivôse IV (29 Dec. 1795).
  73 AP 1A2 82, Agent maritime, 17 pluviôse IV (6 Feb. 1796).
  74 P. Pouhaer, 'Un vieux soldat dans la tourmente: le général Moynat d'Auxon à Toulon, 1796–1797'. *Bull. T.*, 1937, pp. 176–7 and, on Willot, J. Devlin, 'A problem of royalism: General Amédée Willot and the French Directory', *Renaissance and Modern Studies*, XXXIII, 1989, pp. 125–43; G. Lewis, 'Political brigandage and popular disaffection in the south east of France, 1795–1804', in Lewis and Lucas (eds.), *Beyond the Terror*, pp. 206–8 and Poupé, *Le département du Var*, pp. 428–9.
  76 AM L68(13), Délibérations, 22 frimaire and 26 nivôse V (12 Dec. 1796 and 15 Jan. 1797). Willot was also accused of interfering with judicial matters: AN BB18 875, Municipalité de Toulon au ministre, 25 fructidor IV (11 Sept. 1797).
  77 AM L95 bis(6), Correspondance, 7 germinal V (27 Mar. 1797).
  78 AN F1 CIII Var 1, Protestation des habitants, 2 germinal V (22 Mar. 1797).
  79 AD 1L233, Procès-verbaux, 1–2 germinal V (21–2 Mar. 1797) and AM L586, Procès-verbaux, 6 germinal V (26 Mar. 1797).
  80 Poupé, *Le département du Var*, pp. 432–8.
  81 AM L95 bis(6), Correspondance, 7 floréal V (26 Apr. 1797).
  82 Poupé, *Le département du Var*, pp. 440–2.
  83 AM L95 bis(6), Correspondance, 29 fructidor V (15 Sept. 1797).
  84 AN AF III 265, Adresses, 29 fructidor and 1er jour complémentaire V and 12 vendémiaire VI (15 and 17 Sept. and 3 Oct. 1797) and F1 BII Var 1, Adresse des républicains de Marseille, 29 fructidor V (15 Sept. 1797). Only one document relating to the *Cercle constitutionnel* at Toulon has survived. For similar bodies elsewhere, see I. Woloch, *Jacobin legacy. The democratic movement under the Directory*, Princeton, 1970, p. 83 *et seq.*
  85 Mongin, *Toulon ancien*, t. 2, pp. 117–23 and C. Doyle, 'Internal counter-revolution: the judicial reaction in Southern France, 1794–1800', *Renaissance and Modern Studies*, XXXIII, 1989, pp. 106–24.
  86 AN AF III 265, Commissaire du directoire, 6 germinal and 2 floréal VI (26 Mar. and 21 Apr. 1798); AM L586, Procès-verbaux, 5 germinal VI (25 Mar. 1798) and Poupé, *Le département du Var*, pp. 458–61.
  87 AM L744, Ecole centrale, 12 germinal VI (1 Apr. 1798); L. Bourilly, 'Historique du Collège de Toulon, depuis sa fondation jusqu'à son érection en lycée', *Bull. Var*, 1901, p. 45 *et seq.* and R. R. Palmer, *The improvement of humanity: education and the French Revolution*, Princeton, 1985, pp. 248-9.
  88 AM L68(13), Délibérations, 13 vendémiaire V (4 Oct. 1796); Corda,

Les hospices civiles, p. 25 and A. Forrest, *The French Revolution and the poor*, Oxford, 1981, pp. 56–62.

89   AP 1A2 81, Agent maritime, 29 fructidor III (15 Sept. 1795) and Brun, *Port de Toulon*, t. 2, p. 304.

90   Acerra and Meyer, *Marines et Révolution*, p. 198.

91   AP 1A2 45, Dépêches ministérielles, 24 frimaire VI (14 Dec. 1797).

92   AP 1A2 84, Ordonnateur, 7 nivôse VI (27 Dec. 1797).

93   AP 1A2 84, Ordonnateur, 30 floréal VI (19 May 1798) and Tulard, *Napoléon*, pp. 93–9. See also Crook, *Journées révolutionnaires*, pp. 110–18.

94   Acerra and Meyer, *Marines et Révolution*, p. 215.

95   Poupé, *Le département du Var*, pp. 474–9 and M. Lyons, *France under the Directory*, Cambridge, 1975, pp. 224–9.

96   AN AF III 265, Commissaire, 25 germinal VII (14 Apr. 1799) and AD 1L233, Procès-verbaux, 20–8 germinal VII (9–17 Apr. 1799).

97   AN C584–162, L'administration municipale de Toulon aux Corps législatifs, 20 messidor VII (8 July 1799).

98   AM L68(15), Délibérations, 18 vendémiaire VIII (10 Oct. 1799).

99   AM L68(15), Délibérations, 30 frimaire VIII (21 Dec. 1799).

8

Return to order:
Consulate to Empire

'Long may you continue to consolidate the regime which has saved France.
You dominate the continent of Europe and you even compelled the tyrants
of the seas to quit a port they had so treacherously occupied . . .'

These fulsome phrases addressed in 1806 to the Emperor, or rather
'Napoléon le grand', reveal much of the basis for a pronounced
Bonapartism at Toulon. They indicate the historical connection
which bound Napoléon to the Toulonnais people: the little known
artillery officer had made his reputation by bringing the 'federalist'
revolt to heel in 1793 and, as General Bonaparte, he had looked to
the *port de guerre* to sustain his Italian campaigns and provide a fleet
for the ill-starred Egyptian expedition. The proclamation also
reveals the importance of the patriotic mantle in which Napoleon
had draped himself. Despite their profound misgivings where his
political ambitions were concerned, Jacobin notables at Toulon, like
the military elites, were captivated by French victories in Europe.
Success proved elusive at sea, but the maritime wars of the Empire
continued to demand a high level of activity at the Mediterranean
Arsenal. Personal association and national pride were underpinned
by solid material benefits. After 1800 Bonapartist Toulon remained
as much at odds with the rest of Provence as it had been under the
Republic.

Nevertheless, few Toulonnais initially welcomed the new regime
and the inauguration of the Consulate in the Year VIII was received
with resignation rather than rejoicing.[1] When news of Bonaparte's
coup had arrived on 26 brumaire (17 November 1799) the
ordonnateur de la marine took the precaution of visiting each
workshop in the Arsenal to deter his employees from engaging in any
disruptive 'political activity'.[2] Civilian and military leaders stepped
up security measures and issued a joint communiqué urging calm.
They stressed that the new government was firmly committed to the
Republic and the combat against royalism. Above all, workers were

assured that 'it would concern itself with improving their lot'.[3] No
signs of any overt opposition were recorded, but the 'tired acceptance' reported by the departing *commissaire du directoire* was far
removed from the congratulations which had greeted the Directory's
coup of fructidor in the Year V, for example. The *commissaire*
ventured to suggest that the lack of enthusiasm stemmed from mistrust among 'those suffering from the effects of the Thermidorean
reaction', and that only 'partisans of the monarchy hoped for anything', while most citizens remained indifferent.[4]

Still, the name of Napoleon inspired confidence and a constitution, that of the Year VIII, was quickly introduced to allay fears
of dictatorship. It nominated Bonaparte as the first of three Consuls,
who were empowered to act in an executive capacity and make
provision for fresh elections. Following established practice these
new arrangements were submitted to a plebiscite. Turnout was
disappointing and the published figures were grossly inflated. The
Constitution of the Year VIII generally attracted more support than
that of 1795, but rather less than the Constitution of 1793, though
few negative opinions were recorded. The Var conformed to this
national pattern, as did Toulon, where 830 voted in favour with just
one against (a Jacobin shoemaker).[5] A higher proportion of the
electorate in the town took part than in the Year III, roughly 17 as
opposed to 10 per cent, but a comparison with the earlier
referendum can be misleading because in the Year VIII votes were
not cast in assemblies. Instead they were individually autographed in
registers opened for a week at fourteen locations around the town,
which included the *hôtel de ville* and various government offices.
Similar facilities were also available to inhabitants at the dockyards,
where 2,000 officials and sailors, but few workers, gave their
unanimous approval.[6]

The whole procedure was hastily organised and the absence of
overwhelming enthusiasm – the special case of the Arsenal apart –
was hardly surprising given the adverse circumstances in which
Bonaparte's advent to power occurred. A subsistence crisis had been
impending since the poor harvest a year before and, during the early
summer of 1799, a pound of bread at Toulon passed through the 3
sols mark for the first time in two years. It kept rising, reaching 3 *sols*
8 *deniers* by the end of the year and peaking at 5 *sols* 3 *deniers* in the
spring of 1800, doubling in price in the space of just twelve months.[7]
Local shortages were exacerbated by the loss of Italian resources and

the blockade of Mediterranean supply routes, as the tide of war turned against the French.

As always it was the poor who fared worst. The crisis of the Year VIII (1799–1800) threatened to overwhelm what survived of the system of poor relief at Toulon: 'The hospitals have run out of materials and funds, but they are overflowing with sick people and abandoned children', wrote a government envoy.[8] Inmates at the infirmary of Saint-Esprit, who were receiving less than a pound of bread a day, had few sheets on their beds and no straw in their mattresses. The newly appointed prefect of the Var recoiled in horror at 'a hideous and disgusting situation . . . in which several sick people are thrown together in the same bed . . . These poor souls come for treatment but end up in a coffin.'[9] The central government was unable to provide any assistance, so existing facilities were effectively catering for fewer and fewer persons. In the Year IX (1800–01), for example, outdoor relief was being afforded to just sixty-six families, as opposed to almost 200 in 1789. The Saint-Esprit hospital was running a deficit of 50,000 *livres*, the almshouse of La Charité some 36,000; only a gift of foodstuffs from naval warehouses allowed both institutions to see out the year.[10]

The dockyard authorities also came to the rescue by restoring payment in kind to employees on 9 brumaire VIII (31 October 1799). According to the *ordonnateur* 'almost all the inhabitants of Toulon' were being nourished by the Arsenal, because the ration was intended for families as well as the workers themselves.[11] As a result of fraud naval bread also found its way into civilian homes. However, in pluviôse (February 1800), even these resources were disappearing and the ration was reduced to just half a pound a day per person. The *ordonnateur* warned that he would soon have to discontinue assistance altogether, though his workers' plight was already so desperate that 'they were begging in the streets'.[12] As he added a week later, 'discontent arose when rations were distributed' while, in the town, 'distress and anger are apparent on people's faces. Tempers are wearing thin, the embers of unrest are ready to ignite; it will only take a spark to set them ablaze.'[13] Fearing a recrudescence of insurrection wealthier inhabitants opened a subscription to help the poor survive until, in ventôse (early March 1800), some long awaited grain shipments finally began to arrive.[14] The worst was over, though not until 1802 were supplies adequate and prices once more stable.

The naval administration helped the citizens of Toulon weather the crisis, but financial difficulties at the Arsenal had been partly responsible for its severity. In the autumn of 1799 the *ordonnateur* deplored the demoralisation of his unpaid workers, who 'cannot obtain anything on credit in a town where the inhabitants only have the dockyards as a source of income'.[15] Craftsmen were three months in arrears at the end of the year and five months behind in February 1800; administrative staff were owed no less than nine months' salary; and contractors were refusing to supply any more materials since the promissory notes issued to them had become worthless.[16] Only in the early summer of 1800 did matters begin to improve though, like bread prices, pay remained irregular for the next two years.

Problems also stemmed from a much reduced level of activity at the Arsenal. There were one or two expeditions to re-provision the army which Napoleon had left in Egypt, besides some abortive efforts in 1800 to retain control of Malta, but the Mediterranean fleet had virtually been destroyed at the battle of Aboukir. The port of Toulon was devoid of warships and the funds to finance a reconstruction programme were lacking until Napoleon decided to anticipate fresh hostilities with Britain and ordered a number of new vessels in 1802. In the meantime there were substantial lay-offs at the Arsenal, where the labour force – already reduced to some 3,500 workers following the departure of the fleet for Egypt – contracted still further. By the beginning of the Year IX (autumn 1800) only 1,965 shipwrights remained on the books, and relatively few sailors were left on the payroll, while administrative personnel and seagoing officers were less than 700 strong.[17]

The naval 'colony' thus shrank to something like its eighteenth-century, peacetime strength with familiar consequences for the locality. In 1800 and 1801, for example, the number of marriages celebrated in the town fell below the 250 mark for the first time in a decade. In the Year VIII an attested, if undocumented census put the population at just 22,000.[18] Despite appearances to the contrary this was not an artificially 'rounded' figure, but it was less than the total recorded at the beginning of the Revolution. Census-takers indicated that the number of inhabitants had dropped sharply of late, because 'the lack of activity at the dockyards has dispersed some 3,000 workers among neighbouring departments'.

The depths of this recession, in the early spring of 1800, also coincided with an invasion scare. The Italian peninsula had been evacuated by the French under pressure from the Second Coalition and only Genoa resisted.[19] The resurgent Austrians were, in fact, preparing to cross the river Var in April, with the intention of arriving at Toulon at the same time as a British naval force from the island of Minorca. The Toulonnais authorities braced themselves for another siege, equally fearful 'that certain ill-intentioned persons will exploit these momentary difficulties to foment unrest'.[20] The municipal council was accordingly convened in permanent session from 19 floréal to 2 prairial VIII (9–22 May), to lay contingency plans in conjunction with the authorities at garrison and Arsenal. In the event Bonaparte pulled off another great victory and the Toulonnais had fresh cause to thank him. Having crossed the snow-covered Alps the French army was able to hit the Austrians in the rear and narrowly defeat them at Marengo. This was the prelude to the reconquest of Italy, the downfall of the enemy alliance and a general armistice in 1802.

With the peace Bonaparte sealed his reputation as the saviour of France, but the internal changes which accompanied the con-solidation of his regime were not always well received at Toulon. Reform of the navy generated particular resentment. A decree of 7 floréal VIII (27 April 1800) resolved the perennial problem of divided authority within the naval dockyards by coming down in favour of a single, all-powerful head.[21] A naval prefect (*préfet maritime*) was placed in charge of both military and civilian affairs within the Arsenal. The traditional bifurcation of responsibilities was thus terminated and, although it was not spelled out in the legislation, it was obviously intended that naval prefects should be drawn from the military branch of the service. When the first crop of naval prefects was named a couple of months later Vice-admiral J. G. Vence, who had risen through the ranks during the Revolution, was appointed at Toulon. Tirol, the last *ordonnateur*, was offered a post as *commissaire*, but he preferred to resign and scarcely concealed his displeasure with the new arrangements.[22] His departure, like that of several seagoing officers who were pensioned off at the same time, produced a good deal of disaffection in the Mediterranean port.[23] Some naval personnel blamed Napoleon for the Egyptian *débâcle* and it was feared that the service would receive short shrift with an army general in control of the government.

By contrast, the law of 28 pluviôse VIII (17 February 1800), which placed civilian prefects (*préfets*) at the head of the departments, produced few reverberations in the Var.[24] Despite some lobbying from the Toulonnais aimed at recovering the status of *chef-lieu* for their town, the first incumbent took office at Draguignan on 17 germinal (17 April). Joseph Fauchet, a northern barrister who had served as a central administrator during the Revolution, proved to be a popular choice as prefect.[25] He sought to heal divisions in the department and brought his organisational talents to bear in restoring its fortunes. Even after his transfer to the Gironde in 1806 Fauchet was remembered with great affection and later, during Napoleon's Hundred Days, he was elected as a deputy for the Var to the short-lived Legislative Chamber.

Similarly honoured in 1815 was Jean-Baptiste Senès, who was named in 1800 as first sub-prefect (*sous-préfet*) for the newly-created *arrondissement* of Toulon.[26] There were four of these departmental subdivisions in the Var (Draguignan, Brignoles and Grasse were the others) and, like his sub-prefectoral colleagues, Senès exercised a legal profession. As a Toulonnais with sound revolutionary credentials he appeared a solid guarantee of Bonaparte's political intentions. A leading member of the town's Jacobin Club, he had been incarcerated as a *patriote opprimé* during the rebellion of 1793. Thereafter he had taken little active part in municipal politics, preferring to establish himself as a notary, an occupation he continued to practise after his installation as sub-prefect on 14 prairial VIII (3 June 1800). The government was pressing him to relinquish this competing career when he resigned his post in 1806 in order to serve in the Napoleonic parliament, his local reputation undimmed.

The appointment of a mayor for Toulon, on the other hand, proved extremely contentious. Local Jacobins were doubtless dismayed by the new system of municipal government as a whole. In future urban executive power was to be vested in a mayor, assisted by three deputies or *adjoints*. Provision was also made for a town council, to comprise thirty individuals at Toulon, but its role was to be essentially consultative. Like the councils simultaneously created for department and *arrondissement* no more than a single, annual meeting was required, though extraordinary sessions could be convened with the permission of the prefect. Moreover, in large towns like Toulon, in keeping with the Napoleonic principle of nomination, mayors and their deputies were to be chosen by the central government, rather than elected locally.

As if to add insult to injury the first individual to be named mayor of Toulon was Martelly-Chautard, a former nobleman and military officer.[27] Since he numbered several *émigrés* among his close relatives it was naturally believed that, as mayor, he would favour the return of remaining Toulonnais exiles. As a consequence the deputies listed to serve under him, on 6 floréal VIII (26 April 1800), all refused to do so and their protest threw the municipality into disarray. Prefect Fauchet, who was wrestling with a similar problem at Draguignan, could only warn the government that replacements would be hard to find: 'You will discover few men renowned for their love of liberty who wish to work with Martelly-Chautard.'[28] The existing municipal council was allowed to choose a caretaker body until the matter was resolved, an expedient approved by the sub-prefect on the anachronistic grounds that 'the nomination of personnel rightly belongs to members of the municipal council'! Paul Courtès, chairman of the defunct directorial council, accordingly became mayor for the interim.[29]

Martelly-Chautard was eventually invested on 26 messidor (15 July 1800) but, as a sop to local sentiment, Courtès and two other Jacobin notables were retained in office as *adjoints*. Vallavieille, who had also refused to work with Martelly-Chautard, later accepted an appointment as president of the *Tribunal de Première Instance* established at Toulon as part of the consular judiciary. Then, when the prefect of the Var nominated a municipal council on 15 frimaire IX (16 December 1800), one of the men who had originally declined to serve as deputy took a post as councillor.[30] The list of Toulonnais councillors revealed considerable continuity with the late 1790s: one-third comprised well-heeled Jacobin notables, another third was recruited from the ranks of retailers and members of the lesser liberal professions, who were well versed in local politics; and only the final segment was drawn from merchants and *rentiers* who had not previously fulfilled any administrative function. Initial hesitations were thus gradually overcome and collaboration with the new regime became the rule as Bonaparte firmly ensconced himself in power. At the beginning of 1800 it had been said of the Toulonnais Jacobins that 'they still believe they will succeed in overthrowing the régime', but by the close of the year they were resigning themselves to the Consulate, *faute de mieux*.[31]

Republicans like Escudier, Hernandez and Terrin may have been denounced as natural enemies of the new order but J. Gal, a leading naval doctor, assured the Minister of the Interior that he had not come across any evidence of alleged plots 'against the First Consul or in favour of Sieyès'. The citizens said to be involved in conspiracies were, he argued, attached to the regime by 'their political opinions, the offices they hold and their acquisition of *émigré* property'.[32] The government's emissary to the Midi, François de Nantes, confirmed this impression when he wrote *à propos* Toulon: 'Extremists are still thick on the ground, but those with a modicum of intelligence have all rallied to the government ... Party allegiances have greatly diminished.'[33] Even those ardent Jacobins who found no niche in the Bonapartist system were politically dormant. Marquésy, for example, who had been a parliamentary deputy under the Directory, was once more a 'simple ironmonger' and 'concerned himself solely with his business, which he should never have abandoned in the first place'. Even hardened republicans, François de Nantes concluded, were not immune to the allures of patriotism and even waxed enthusiastic about the Consulate, 'when you mention our military victories, the treaties signed, or the heroic stature of our government'. At the close of 1800 the prefect was able to report with some satisfaction that cries of 'Vive Napoléon' were frequently heard on the streets of Toulon, as initial misgivings were gradually overcome.[34]

However, the plebiscite of the Year X (1802), on Bonaparte's Life Consulate, revealed little improvement on the low Toulonnais turnout of 1800. In France as a whole some 50 per cent of the electorate voted, mostly in the affirmative. Figures for the Var reached the 30 per cent mark, but in Toulon itself a mere 18 per cent cast their opinions (864 individuals were in favour of the new constitution, as opposed to 830 a couple of years earlier). Support was once again strong at the Arsenal, where 2,000 positive votes were recorded including those of some dockyard workers and sailors, but in the town an overwhelming degree of indifference persisted.[35]

This absence of commitment, which can be interpreted as a sign of deep-rooted republican sentiment, was echoed in local electoral behaviour in the Year IX (1801). Polling was required under Sieyès' plan to create lists of 'notables', at *arrondissement*, departmental and national levels, from which the government would select suitable candidates for office.[36] Universal suffrage was retained at base and 4,833 voters were registered at Toulon. Those chosen at the first stage were to elect notables for the departmental list, who would

Table 8 *Notables elected at Toulon in the Year IX (1801)*

Occupational category	Communal notables		Departmental notables	
	No.	%	No.	%
Military officers	3	1.0	1	1.9
Retired officers & officials	4	1.3	1	1.9
Leading administrators	17	5.6	6	11.5
Rentiers	20	6.6	8	15.4
Legal professions	8	2.7	5	9.6
Medical professions	17	5.6	7	13.5
Merchants	16	5.3	5	9.6
Retailers	21	7.0	8	15.4
Clerks	65	21.6	9	17.3
Artisans & shopkeepers	85	28.2	2	3.8
Dockyard workers	19	6.3	–	–
Sailors & fishermen	2	0.7	–	–
Rural occupations	10	3.3	–	–
Unskilled workers	10	3.3	–	–
No profession indicated	4	1.3	–	–
Total	301		52	

Source: AD 2M2–1, Liste des notables communaux, départementaux et nationaux de l'arrondissement de Toulon, an IX (1801).

in turn compile a national list. It was a deliberately complex mechanism, designed to cloak the authoritarianism of the Consulate in a semblance of democracy.

It was a device that earned the approval of the prefect of the Var. He maintained that by so regulating the exercise of the franchise the new system endowed the people with a 'real political choice'.[37] Regarding the electoral assemblies of the revolutionary period as a mistake Fauchet also commended the introduction of an individual ballot. Citizens were invited to vote, at public and private addresses during the course of a given week, by listing up to one-tenth of their number as *arrondissement* notables. No precise figures are available for the turnout at Toulon in this first stage of the proceedings, but it was apparently rather low. The sub-prefect bemoaned the lack of interest, complaining that voters had excused themselves on the flimsiest of pretexts; 'there is little interest in politics these days', he concluded.[38]

This particular system was employed only once, but its results are nonetheless informative.[39] At Toulon, 329 individuals were elected as arrondissement (or 'communal') notables and almost one-fifth of them were drawn from the popular classes. Continuity with the elections of the directorial period was equally apparent in the selection of most of the Jacobin elite. Significantly enough, the name of Martelly-Chautard was only appended to the list *ex-officio* and it was omitted when these *arrondissement* notables voted a few weeks later, once again on an individual basis, for 10 per cent of their number to constitute a departmental list. No more than a handful of 'popular' candidates were maintained at this second stage but leading Jacobins, like the former *conventionnels* Escudier and Charbonnier or the directorial deputy Marquésy, were selected again. As 'departmental notables' they then participated in balloting for the choice of 61 'national notables' from the Var. Among this third, and final category appeared eight residents of Toulon. They comprised the sub-prefect Senès, the former municipal chairman Courtès, Vallavieille, who had refused the post of mayoral deputy under Martelly-Chautard, *ex-conventionnel* Escudier, a retired naval clerk and three non-native officials. Their selection was indicative of the political sway which the old Jacobin elite continued to exert in Toulon.

It was a familiar contention that men such as these, who had supplanted the old-regime oligarchy during the revolutionary decade, lacked any deep roots in Toulon. In 1800, for example, the wealthy, retired naval officer, N. Chaubry protested to Bonaparte that the town was controlled by mere 'colonists', whose arrival dated from the suppression of the 'federalist' revolt.[40] Yet few of the individuals who had administered Toulon under the Directory were recent arrivals. Indeed, the list of 550 'most highly taxed inhabitants' (*plus imposés*) that was drawn up for electoral purposes in the Var in the year XI (1803), after further modifications to the political system, suggests that the wealthiest property-holders in the town during the Consulate were mostly of local provenance.[41]

In the Var as a whole 85 per cent of the individuals who appeared on the list of *plus imposés* were well-established residents, while twenty-four out of thirty-three Toulonnais entries had been inhabitants of the naval town in 1789. Many leading families of the late *ancien régime*, who had been so heavily compromised by their involvement in counter-revolution, retained a representative on this list. There were some significant absentees: members of the aristocratic Missiessy family, who served in the armed forces, or merchants like Laurent Caire, who had emigrated in 1793. Yet in occupational terms the Toulonnais *plus imposés* of the Year XI bore a great resemblance to their equivalents a decade earlier, listed on a document drawn up for the purpose of levying a property tax in 1791.

Just three individuals had arrived at Toulon in the wake of the 'federalist' rebellion and made substantial fortunes as a result: one of these was a watchmaker from Besançon, who became a merchant, while the other two were military contractors, who had been soldier and comb-manufacturer respectively in 1789. Native purchasers of large quantities of *émigré* property, like the former *conventionnels* Charbonnier and Escudier, were to be found among the post-revolutionary *plus imposés*. Yet they might have expected their wealth to increase as their careers advanced, even without the unexpected opportunities which the revolutionary upheaval presented to them. There was just one newcomer, the native grain merchant Boisselin, among the four Toulonnais who were listed separately in 1803 as members of the thirty *plus imposés du Var*. The others, Chaubry, Martelly-Chautard (both ex-nobles) and Granet, had already been assessed as three of the five biggest property-holders in Toulon at the end of the *ancien régime*.

The real basis for complaints by well-heeled, long-established notables like Chaubry was not that an influx of outsiders had become substantial property owners at Toulon. Rather they were aggrieved that, even after Napoleon had seized power, native Jacobins of modest means were continuing to exercise local political authority. This was soon to change; under Bonaparte's Life Consulate more affluent and conservatively-inclined individuals gradually returned to the helm. Property-holding and control of the municipality, which had been disassociated to a considerable degree during the Revolution, once again began to coalesce.

The regressive electoral decree of 16 thermidor X (4 August 1802) of which the list of *plus imposés* was part, hastened this reaction.[42] It removed less wealthy individuals from office by reintroducing a fiscal criterion for many positions of responsibility. This legislation, which supplanted the brief experiment with a 'pyramid' of elections and individual balloting, was even more complex than its predecessor. Universal suffrage was retained, but electoral assemblies were reintroduced for the purpose of selecting municipal personnel and members of electoral colleges at both *arrondissement* and departmental level. However, the voters' choice was now restricted to the 100 *plus imposés*, for municipal councils in the larger towns and to the 600 *plus imposés* for the departmental electoral assembly, which was to nominate candidates as national deputies. It was the government which made the final selection of personnel at all levels, from the names duly submitted to it.

This hybrid system did not become fully operative at Toulon until 1810. There were cantonal elections during the Year XII (towards the end of 1803), but these assembled men elected in the Year IX, under Sieyès scheme, not the democratic base instituted by the recent decree.[43] This cavalier attitude towards elections on the part of the government ironically gave the Toulonnais Jacobins a final opportunity to dominate the local assemblies. They were, however, obliged to select candidates from among their more affluent associates to serve on the departmental college or the municipal council; hence the popular classes disappeared from both bodies.[44] A few did survive in the *arrondissement* college (where there were no restrictions on membership), but otherwise the political role that artisans and shopkeepers had enjoyed during the Revolution came to an end.

When, on 5 frimaire XIII (26 November 1804), an imperial decree named sixteen municipal councillors at Toulon, all drawn from the list of candidates elected a year earlier, merchants and the liberal professions predominated.[45] Only the inclusion of a wealthy baker was exceptional in an occupational profile which resembled that of the oligarchic municipality of the old regime. Inevitably this development carried political as well as social consequences. As the pool of individuals from which council members was chosen contracted, so men with a Jacobin past were omitted in favour of those with a counter-revolutionary background. In 1808, for instance, the first *émigrés* began returning to office, when the leading sectionaries Laberthonie, Fauchier and Saurin were appointed to fill vacancies in the Toulonnais municipality.[46]

This reaction at Toulon mirrored similar changes at higher levels of the Bonapartist administration. The departmental college now comprised wealthy *rentiers*, government officials and merchants, similar to the social elite which had controlled the Var at the beginning of the Revolution. When prefect Fauchet was transferred in 1806 his replacement emanated from a more traditional *milieu*. The new incumbent, the baron d'Azémar, was a former nobleman and retired military officer.[47] Likewise, when sub-prefect Senès became a member of parliament, his successor at Toulon was a former barrister from the Parlement of Provence who had been politically tarnished by his 'federalist' activities in 1793.[48]

A major shift also occurred at the heart of the regime when, in 1804, Napoleon crowned himself Emperor. Although support seems to have remained firm in naval circles, where official pressure was easily exerted, the subsequent plebiscite revealed considerable reservations among the civilian population of Toulon.[49] Only 434 votes were registered in the town itself, a turnout of just under 9 per cent, if the outdated electoral register of the Year IX is taken as a basis. The creation of the Empire appears to have been a greater source of disappointment to the Toulonnais than to most other Frenchmen. Many Jacobins in Toulon had swallowed their initial objections to Bonapartism, but the wholesale return of *émigrés* under the Consulate, the restriction of office to the wealthy and the increasing degree of administrative centralisation clearly dismayed them. Hence their cold response to the referendum on the First Empire.

Former republicans at Toulon were also extremely disturbed by another restoration, that of the Church. Elsewhere in Provence the re-establishment of Catholicism was a major aspect of the Bonapartist *ralliement*, but this was less true in the naval town. No public worship was taking place in Toulon at the turn of the century and there is little evidence of any private masses either.[50] Indeed, on 19 pluviôse X (8 February 1802), some six months after Bonaparte had concluded his Concordat with the Papacy – a matter of which they could hardly be unaware – municipal councillors at Toulon unsuccessfully attempted to convert the redundant parish church of Saint-Louis into a theatre.[51] Boisselin, then mayor, was vehemently opposed to the revival of organised religion and he dragged his feet over reopening the old cathedral church of Sainte-Marie. The prefect was obliged to put pressure upon the recalcitrant municipality and it was with evident relief that he eventually reported a resumption of worship on 18 fructidor X (5 September 1802). The service of rededication at the cathedral passed off without incident. It was conducted by Archbishop Champion de Cicé of Aix, who controlled a huge, sprawling diocese which now included the Var.[52]

It was likewise prefectoral intervention which expedited the reconsecration of Saint-Louis as a parish church and that of Saint-François (once used by the Jacobin Club), as additional places of worship the following year. In 1805, when the available premises proved insufficient, it was decided to re-purchase the church of Saint-Pierre (where the Jacobins' rivals had once met), though this proved difficult because the building was in private hands. Its owner, municipal councillor Dussap, was extremely reluctant to sell and it was 1808 before the church opened its doors to worshippers again.[53] The town council was equally loath to finance repairs to church buildings or provide accommodation for priests. Once again prefect and sub-prefect were obliged to remind local administrators of their duties in this regard but, as late as 1810, Toulonnais councillors were still refusing to hand over 50,000 francs earmarked for the refurbishment of presbyteries and church interiors.[54]

Opposition to the Church was not simply a matter of ingrained anti-clericalism, it also reflected political differences with ecclesiastical personnel. In the Year VI (towards the end of 1797) no less than fifty-eight constitutional clergy were resident at Toulon, doubtless because they found the naval town more congenial than many of the surrounding communities.[55] Yet only one of these ecclesiastics was given a minor role in the re-established Church because the clerical authorities deliberately favoured non-juring and *émigré* priests. Any truck with the Civil Constitution of the Clergy was usually regarded as a disqualification for reappointment. Of twenty parish priests who were active at Toulon in 1804, six had previously held posts in the town, but four of them had refused the oath in 1790, while the other two had subsequently retracted.[56] Ecclesiastical personnel paid lip-service to the Bonapartist regime but Vigne, a former archdeacon from Marseille who became *curé* at Sainte-Marie in 1803, was a notorious royalist who revelled in political controversy.

The concordatory church at Toulon was even less well endowed than its relatively poor, pre-revolutionary predecessor; its clergy were elderly and fewer in number than those of the *ancien régime*. Yet in spite of its depleted resources, both human and material, Catholicism was woven back into the texture of public life and attracted a considerable following. The church was, of course, prominently involved in fêting Napoleon's victories and offered frequent *te deums* to its benefactor, but the old, popular Fête-Dieu and Saint-Jean celebrations were revived too. The prefect of the Var remarked with some surprise in 1806 that 'a good number of people go to mass', while archbishop Champion de Cicé asserted that 'Toulon today is a town which gives a great deal of comfort to all

Christians.'[57] Many people volunteered to clean up the old cathedral in 1802, in readiness for its rededication. There was also a rush to baptise children who had been born since 1793 and lacked a clerical blessing. Divorces, which averaged 10 per cent of the annual total of marriages in the 1790s and rose to 18 per cent in 1802, were reduced to less than 2 per cent after 1804. A change in legislation was primarily responsible, but the tradition of postponing wedding ceremonies until after Advent and Lent was resumed, presumably because couples were again marrying in Church rather than simply registering with the civil authorities.

Those recalled to municipal office under the Empire exhibited a conspicuous piety which had often been forged out of adversity. Reignery, for example, the retired military officer who was nominated mayor in 1808, was an active Christian. He patronised a charitable association created to assist with hospital work and another which concerned itself with prison visitations.[58] There was also a renaissance of traditional devotion represented by the penitent fraternities. Although it was only during the Bourbon Restoration that *pénitents gris* and *pénitents blancs* were formally reconstituted, the *bleus* had begun to meet again as early as 1807.[59] To judge by the comments of the local chronicler *père* Letuaire, all of them inclined to royalism, but each recruited from a different social *milieu*: the *pénitents gris* were upper class; the *blancs* bourgeois; and the *bleus* emanated from the artisan and shopkeeper strata.[60] Equally redolent of the *ancien régime* were the misgivings these organisations aroused in the clerical hierarchy, which once more struggled to regulate their activities.

There was no shortage of threats to the church from outside forces. In 1805, for instance, the garrison commander was asked to position guards outside the sanctuaries so as to prevent interruptions to worship.[61] It was said that *curé* Brun was so fearful of assault that he kept a loaded pistol under his altar napkin. Opposition from military elements in the armed forces, which tended to act as schools for dechristianisation, in a town of shifting population and often loose morals, was perhaps inevitable. Nor was the situation at Toulon helped by a massive resurgence of freemasonry, which was under way even before Napoleon signed his Concordat with the Pope. During the Bonapartist era, according to Letuaire: 'Freemasonry was practised with an enthusiasm that cannot be over-emphasised; everyone was a mason, from greatest to least.'[62]

Letuaire was exaggerating somewhat but, between 1800 and 1815, well over 1,000 Toulonnais adherents were recorded at lodges registered with the Grand Orient in Paris.[63] Many of those who joined were only fleeting residents and an extreme example is constituted by half-a-dozen Russian naval officers who visited Toulon in 1808 when Napoleon was in alliance with the Tsar. There were also a good many passive members who rarely participated in gatherings, if at all, and whose names only appear on the lists once. Nonetheless, the overall total surpassed the pre-revolutionary peak of the 1780s. In 1811, the year which marked the apogee of Toulonnais masonry, there were no less than eight lodges in existence.

Freemasons at Toulon had ceased to meet during the Revolution. As a former member of the Elèves de Minerve lodge put it, he and his colleagues had 'more pressing and important matters on their minds than masonry'.[64] Only in 1800 was any reference to masonic gatherings made when the *commissaire du directoire*, still in office pending the arrival of a prefect, informed the government that he was taking steps to disband a 'society of freemasons'.[65] He was evidently unsuccessful because two lodges, *La Paix* and *La Parfaite Union*, continued to meet regularly from that point onwards. There were joined in 1801 by the *Double Union* and the following year the *Vrais Amis Réunis d'Egypte* was established. The latter had been set up in Alexandria and was transplanted to Toulon by returning naval personnel.[66] During the next three years two other lodges were re-founded – *Les Elèves de Mars et de Neptune* and *Les Elèves de Minerve* – together with a new creation, *Les Vrais Amis Constants*. A final pair of lodges received constitutions in 1811, before the difficulties which clouded the closing years of the Empire put paid to most organisations, masonry included.

Official policy towards freemasonry quickly became one of toleration. On 28 brumaire XI (20 November 1802) the prefect of the Var informed his sub-prefect at Toulon that masonic activity was to be permitted, subject to surveillance. Since it was 'composed of government officials and good bourgeois' it could be exempted from the severe regulations which governed public assemblies.[67] As the prefect's remarks indicate, servants of the Napoleonic state were intimately involved in masonry, at Toulon as elsewhere. Indeed, Bonaparte's brother Jérôme was initiated at the town's *La Paix* lodge in 1801, while General Masséna was an honorary member of *Les Elèves de Minerve* to which he had been affiliated prior to 1789.

Table 9 *The occupational structure of freemasonry at Toulon, 1800–1815*

Occupation	No.	%	% pre-1789
Military officers	178	21.9	33.3
Leading administrators	43	5.3	4.3
Retired officers, officials & civilian nobles	15	1.8	0.6
Rentiers	40	4.9	2.7
Legal professions	17	2.1	0.6
Medical professions	73	9.0	5.1
Merchants	61	7.5	11.7
Retailers	40	4.9	8.2
Clerks	140	17.2	9.0
Artisans & shopkeepers	165	20.3	15.3
Soldiers & sailors	25	3.1	8.2
Clergy	0	0.0	0.6
No profession indicated	15	1.8	0.0
Total	812		Numerical total 489

Source: BN FM2, Loges maçonniques de Toulon.

More than half the recorded adherents at Toulon during the Napoleonic era were in government service as army or navy officers, medical staff attached to the armed forces, leading officials and dockyard clerks.

The presence of these servants of the state had been similarly marked at the end of the *ancien régime*; then they had comprised 59 per cent of the total, now they furnished 56 per cent. However, military officers had declined in importance (22 instead of 34 per cent), while clerks had become rather more conspicuous (17 as opposed to 9 per cent). The 'civilian' side of masonry still embraced mercantile elements, though these had diminished somewhat, to be replaced by a larger proportion of *rentiers* and a rise in the ranks of artisans and shopkeepers, from 15 to 20 per cent. The social profile of masonry had, therefore, tilted decisively away from domination by aristocratic military officers – the *militaires* now involved were mostly commoners by origin anyway – towards the bourgeoisie and popular classes. At Toulouse, where government servants also comprised the biggest group of adherents, Michel Taillefer has likewise uncovered a strong artisan and shopkeeper presence. As he comments, masonry 'adapted extremely well to the new order'.[68]

Accompanying this degree of 'democratisation', already evident at

Toulon before 1789, was a softening of the sharp social contours which had separated one lodge from another under the *ancien régime*. The exclusive military lodges of old were not reconstituted during the Napoleonic era. Even at *La Paix et la Parfaite Union*, which inscribed leading government servants like Emeriau, the naval prefect and Caillemer, the chief of police, there was a relatively high degree of social interaction. Surgeons and clerks rubbed shoulders with naval officers and administrators, while over 10 per cent of members were self- rather than state-employed. The *Elèves de Minerve*, formerly dominated by army subalterns, was also rather more broadly-based after its re-emergence.

The various lodges did tend to draw upon some sectors of society much more strongly than others. As before, so after 1801, *La Double Union* had an especially 'popular' composition. Indeed, this lodge experienced disorder and expulsions in 1805, just as it had in 1788. Leaders of the *Double Union* also ironically reiterated some derogatory comments about the appearance of 'workers' in the movement. These remarks were directed at the newly formed *Vrais Amis Constants*, which was mainly composed of artisans and shopkeepers, though one or two military officers and government officials were also affiliated. Fears that too many lodges were competing for the allegiance of too few masons clearly lay at the back of complaints that masonic membership was being dispensed too freely. Yet, in 1801, the founding document for *La Paix* had boldly declared: 'In our midst all social differences disappear . . . members cast off the vain titles and distinctions which the world confers upon them, in order to associate and identify one with another, in a more intimate fashion.'[69]

Masonry continued to serve as a geographical as well as a social melting-pot at Toulon. The proportion of non-natives ranged from almost 90 per cent at *La Paix et la Parfaite Union* to just under 40 per cent at *La Parfaite Alliance*, a late foundation in 1811. The great majority of masons were non-Toulonnais and a good many of them were only temporary residents. Thus the *Vrais Amis Réunis d'Egypte* ascribed its lack of contact with the Grand Orient to 'the absence of several brethren that the state has called to serve elsewhere'.[70] The excuse was regularly repeated after 1808 until, between 1812 and 1816, activities at this lodge, like all the others, ground to a complete halt. As a correspondent at the *Parfaite Alliance* put it, masonry was a casualty of 'the great events which have succeeded each other with such rapidity'.[71] Yet several lodges did survive, despite the economic stagnation of Toulon under the Bourbon Restoration. Part of the masons' success in surmounting the crisis which accompanied the collapse of the Empire lay in its ability to attract a new generation of adherents. Older, experienced hands founded and re-founded lodges after 1800, but they soon recruited plenty of young men who had grown up in the lean years of the Revolution.

Masonry continued to offer recreation and mutual aid to members, but its pre-revolutionary cultural role was now overshadowed by the emergence of an academy at Toulon. A prefectoral inquiry of 1811, conducted into masonic activities in the town, actually listed an *Académie des Sciences, Belles Lettres et Arts*, which was catering for more elevated pursuits.[72] Founded in 1800 as *La Réunion Littéraire*, this society had originally served a political purpose. It brought together Jacobins who 'knew no other name than citizen' and represented a successor to the clubs and circles of the 1790s.[73] Its president in 1811, the naval surgeon Hernandez, was once a leading republican. Yet, by then, the Academy had become eminently respectable, with a membership drawn from the elites of both military and civilian society. Current affairs were no longer on the agenda.

Independent intellectual activity was more closely associated with the reading rooms (*cabinets de lecture*) attached to booksellers' premises in the town. The most notable of these belonged to Auguste Aurel, a liberal Bonapartist, who began publishing the first Toulonnais newssheet, the weekly *Affiches*, in 1811.[74] Cultural facilities at Toulon were also strengthened by the foundation of a Public Library which was stocked with former monastic collections and *émigré* property. On account of its origins the collection was heavily biased towards ecclesiastical and commercial subjects, but there was a sprinkling of enlightened works like the *Encyclopédie*.[75] In 1806 a librarian was placed in charge of the 3,600 volumes, which were most frequently consulted by naval cadets, trainee surgeons and schoolchildren.[76]

The low level of 'lay' interest was evidently disappointing, but at least the library was assisting the restoration of public education at Toulon. Some remedial steps had been taken under the Directory but Fauchet, prefect of the Var, was in no doubt that overall educational provision had declined drastically in comparison with 1789.[77] At the turn of the nineteenth century the municipality was employing only seventeen primary-school teachers, all of whom were obliged to charge a substantial fee. Nor was the town's *Ecole centrale*, a secondary institution designed to serve the department as a whole, enjoying much success. It was operating in a dilapidated building and had enrolled a mere sixty pupils, few of whom were taking courses in mathematics and science which the government wished to encourage.[78] For non-Toulonnais the *Ecole centrale* was unfortunately located in a turbulent city, while 'the youth of Toulon' showed little interest in attending.[79]

It would be grossly misleading to posit any sort of relationship between the fate of schooling at Toulon, on the one hand, and local levels of literacy on the other, especially in a town with so unstable a population. Nevertheless, the figures derived from marriage registers do show a downward turn in the number of men and women able to sign their names during the first decade of the nineteenth century. This would correspond with the reduced educational opportunities of the revolutionary period. By contrast, though the situation was ameliorated by the return of demographic stability (the number of natives who could sign being consistently higher than the proportion of non-natives), registers for the years 1816 and 1821 yield percentages of 69 and 75 for male signatures and 34 and 35 for women. These represent a net gain when compared to the closing years of the *ancien régime* and it is tempting to conclude that the Bonapartist educational system had exerted some influence upon them.[80]

The principle of free primary schooling was finally re-established when, in 1806, both Christian Brothers and Sisters were recalled to their tasks of teaching the poor at Toulon.[81] When the *Ecole centrale* was suppressed in 1802 the way was also clear for a revival of the Oratorians' College, if not in name. Only with the Bourbon Restoration was religion restored to the curriculum and a cleric reappointed as principal, but the old building was back in use after 1803, along with several ex-teachers.[82] The *Collège de Toulon*, as it was called, quickly attracted 100 pupils and, since fees remained relatively low, numbers rose to almost 200 at the end of the Empire. The college was fully accredited by the government, but the municipal council at Toulon was irked by the refusal to upgrade it to a *lycée*. Requests for a change of status were finally accepted in 1812, a decision which remained without effect until after the return of the Bourbons.[83]

Bonaparte could justifiably claim, in this respect as in many others, to have reconstituted a good deal of the institutional fabric that had

been destoyed by the Revolution. The return to order under the
Consulate and Empire was, moreover, a matter of circuses as well as
bread. The theatre at Toulon, for example, was flourishing as never
before, despite the regime's heavy-handed supervision. There was
general agreement that theatregoing was a beneficial form of enter-
tainment since it attracted 'a host of persons who might otherwise be
attracted to mischief'. Outbreaks of violence between drunken
soldiers and sailors, or between military personnel and local citizens,
were frequent in this teeming naval town. Harmless diversions were
essential and the government supplied its own particular antidote to
boredom in the endless series of official *fêtes* or firework displays
marking this or that anniversary. Conditions at Toulon remained
relatively harsh and insecure, despite the return of many familiar
landmarks. Yet there were compensations in the pomp and ceremony of the Bonapartist era, what might be termed *la fête impériale*.
It was a period fondly recalled by *père* Letuaire, who concluded in his
memoirs that 'under the Consulate and during the Empire there was
a good deal of dancing at Toulon'.[84]

Notes

1 Only F. A. Aulard (ed.), *L'état de la France en l'an VIII et l'an IX*,
Paris, 1897, p. 75, suggests otherwise.
2 AP 1A2 86, Ordonnateur, 28 brumaire VIII (19 Nov. 1799).
3 AP 1A2 86, Ordonnateur, 1 frimaire VIII (22 Nov. 1799).
4 AN FI CIII Var 6, Commissaire, 30 brumaire VIII (21 Nov. 1799).
5 AN BII 440, Plébiscite de l'an VIII, arrondissement de Toulon and C.
Langlois, 'Le plébiscite de l'an VIII, ou le coup d'état du 18 pluviôse an VIII',
AHRF, 207–9, 1972.
6 AN BII, 466, Port de Toulon.
7 AM L68(15), Délibérations, 19 prairial VII–1 germinal VIII (7 June
1799–22 Mar. 1800).
8 F. Rocquain (ed.), *L'état de la France au 18 brumaire*, Paris, 1874, p.
31.
9 AD 4M6, Compte rendu, 1 germinal X (22 Mar. 1802).
10 AM L726, Situation des hospices, 22 nivôse IX (12 Jan. 1801).
11 AP 1A2 86, Ordonnateur, 29 pluviôse VIII (18 Feb. 1800).
12 AP 1A2 86, Ordonnateur, 20 pluviôse VIII (9 Feb. 1800).
13 AP 1A2 86, Ordonnateur, 29 pluviôse VIII (18 Feb. 1800).
14 AM L68(15), Délibérations, 4 and 5 ventôse (23 and 24 Feb. 1800).
15 AP 1A2 86, Ordonnateur, 6 vendémaire VIII (29 Sept. 1799).
16 AP 1A2 86, Ordonnateur, 21 nivôse and 29 pluviôse VIII (11 Jan.
and 18 Feb. 1800).
17 AP 2A1 39, Préfet maritime, 23 brumaire IX (14 Nov. 1800) and

Brun, *Port de Toulon*, t. 2, pp. 346–59.

18 AN F20 399, Dénombrement, an VIII–IX (1800) and AM L456, Relevé de la population, 9 pluviôse VIII (29 Jan. 1800), a confirmatory fragment of the door-to-door census on which the figures were based.

19 J. Lovie and A. Palluel-Guillard, *L'épisode napoléonien. Aspects extérieurs, 1799–1815* (Paris, 1972), pp. 18–19.

20 AM L68(15), Délibérations, 19 floréal VIII (9 May 1800).

21 Wyott, 'De l'ordonnateur au préfet', p. 19.

22 AP 1A2 86, Préfet, 7 fructidor VIII (25 Aug. 1800) and Brun, *Port de Toulon*, t. 2, pp. 354–6.

23 AD 3M1–1, Préfet, 18 fructidor VIII (5 Sept. 1800).

24 Godechot, *Les institutions*, pp. 586–92 and Poupé, *Le département du Var*, pp. 500–1.

25 C. Alleaume, 'Joseph Fauchet, premier préfet du Var', *Bull. Drag.*, 1940–41.

26 AD 1M5–3/1, Sous-préfets de Toulon and *ibid.*, Renseignements sur les fonctionnaires publics.

27 AD 1M5–3/1, Décret, 6 floréal VIII (26 Apr. 1800).

28 AD 3M1–1, Préfet, 16 prairial VIII (5 June 1800) and Poupé, *Le département du Var*, p. 506.

29 AM L68(15), Délibérations, 18 prairial VIII (7 June 1800).

30 AM L587, Conseil municipal, 15 frimaire IX (6 Dec. 1800).

31 AN FI CIII Var 11, Anon. au sous-préfet, 18 pluviôse VIII (7 Feb. 1800).

32 AN F7 3693 Var 2, Gal au Ministre de l'Intérieur, 2e jour complémentaire (19 Sept. 1800).

33 Rocquain (ed.), *L'état de la France*, p. 12 and p. 24.

34 AN FI CIII Var 6, Préfet, 21 brumaire IX (12 Nov. 1800).

35 AN BII 629B, Plébiscite de l'an X, arrondissement de Toulon; AD 2M1–1, Dépouillement général, 20 prairial X (30 May 1802) and F. Bluche, *Le plébiscite des Cent-Jours*, Geneva, 1974, p. 39. For voting at the Arsenal, see AN BII 669F, 6e arrondissement maritime. This time there is a clear indication that dockyard workers voted at the Arsenal. The sub-prefect of Toulon stated on 12 prairial X (22 May 1802) that the opening of registers at the Arsenal had inevitably diminished the votes recorded on the civilian registers; AD 2M1–1.

36 AM L68(16), Délibérations, 1 prairial IX (21 May 1801) and J.-Y. Coppolani, *Les élections en France à l'époque napoléonienne*, Paris, 1980, pp. 41–8.

37 AN DXL 78, Discours prononcé par le préfet, 1 vendémiaire X (23 Sept. 1801).

38 AN FI CIII Var 6, Sous-préfet, 10 fructidor IX (28 Aug. 1801) and Coppolani, *Les élections*, pp. 213–5.

39 AD 2M2–1, Listes de notables communaux, départementaux et nationaux de l'arrondissement de Toulon, an X (1801–02).

40 AN FI CIII Var 6, Chaubry au citoyen Bonaparte, 4 pluviôse VIII (24 Jan. 1800).

41 AD 2M2–5, Les 550 plus imposés parmi les 600 imposés du Var, 28

ventse and 26 floréal XI (19 Mar. and 16 May 1803) and M. Agulhon, 'Les notables du Var sous ie Consulat', *RHMC*, XVII, 1970, pp. 720–5. (The article mistakenly refers to the lists of the year IX rather than the year XI.) See also L. Bergeron and G. Chaussinand-Nogaret, *Les 'masses de granit'. Cent mille notables du Premier Empire*, Paris, 1979 and F. d'Agay, *Grands notables du Premier Empire*, t. 18, *Var*, Paris, 1988.

42 Coppolani, *Les élections*, p. 60 *et seq.* provides a splendid guide through the complexities of this legislation which have baffled many historians.

43 AD 2M2–2, Procès-verbaux, 4–15 frimaire XII (26 Nov.–7 Dec. 1803).

44 AD 2M2–2, Liste des notables, an XII (1804).

45 AM L587, Décret impérial, 5 frimaire XIII (26 Nov. 1804).

46 AM L587, Décrets, 1808; AN FI BII Var 3, Décrets impériaux, 1806–13 and FI BII Var 25, Personnel de Toulon, an X–1812. For similar developments at Nîmes, see A.–M. Duport, 'Le personnel municipal de Nîmes de l'ancien régime à l'Empire: étude sociale et politique', *Bulletin de la Société languedocienne de géographie*, 1982, pp. 211–21.

47 AD 1M14–1, Renseignements sur les fonctionnaires publics and P. Pouhaer, 'Le baron d'Azémar, second préfet du Var', *Bull. Drag.*, 1912–13.

48 AD 1M5–3/1, Sous-préfets de Toulon and J. Salvarelli, *Les administrateurs du département du Var, 1790–1897*, Draguignan, 1897, p. 310.

49 AN BII 842D, Plébiscite de l'an XII, arrondissement de Toulon; BII 852, L'armée navale; AD 2M1–1, Plébiscite de l'an XII and Bluche, *Le plébiscite*, pp. 39–47, for comparisons with other parts of France.

50 Rocquain (ed.), *L'état de la France*, p. 22.

51 AM L68(16), Délibérations, 19 pluviôse X (8 Feb. 1802).

52 AM FI CIII Var 6, Préfet, 30 fructidor X (17 Sept. 1802); AM L720, Réouverture de l'église Sainte-Marie, fructidor X (Aug.–Sept. 1802) and Tortel, *Notice historique*, p. 146.

53 AM L68(17), Délibérations, 24 vendémiaire XIV (16 Oct. 1805) and AD 3Z26–1, Minutes de la secrétairie d'état, 12 July 1808.

54 AD 4V1, Etat de la situation des églises, 31 Dec. 1810.

55 AM L613, Prétres assermentés, 27 vendémiaire VI (18 Oct. 1797) and AD 1V1, Etat des pensionnaires ecclésiastiques, an VIII (1799–1800).

56 Tortel, *Notice historique*, pp. 147–50 and 348–9.

57 AN FI CIII Var 11, Préfet, 9 July 1806 and L. Levy-Schneider, *L'application du Concordat par un prélat d'ancien régime: Mgr. Champion de Cicé, archévêque d'Aix et d'Arles*, Paris, 1921, p. 457.

58 Tortel, *Notice historique*, pp. 175–6.

59 AD 6V1–1, Tableaux des communautés religieuses, 27 May 1819.

60 L. Henseling (ed.), *Les cahiers de P. Letuaire*, 2 vols., Toulon, 1910–14, t. 2, pp. 70–1.

61 AM L97(17), Correspondance dite particulière, 13 ventôse XIII (4 Mar. 1805).

62 Henseling (ed.), *Les cahiers*, t. 1, p. 21.

63 BN FM2, Fonds maçonniques, Loges de Toulon, 1800–15 and D.

Ligou (ed.), *Histoire des francs-maçons en France*, Toulouse, 1981, pp. 168–76.

64 BN FM2 436, *Les Elèves de Minerve*, correspondance, 29 Mar. 1792.

65 AD 1L196, Commissaire, 1 and 11 ventôse VIII (20 Feb. and 2 Mar. 1800).

66 AD JIV Cote 85 (Fonds Castinel), *Vrais Amis réunis d'Alexandrie*, 1800–01.

67 AD 3M1–4, Préfet, 28 brumaire XI (30 Nov. 1802).

68 M. Taillefer, 'La franc-maçonnerie toulousaine et la Révolution française', *AHRF*, 239, 1980, p. 90. See also G. Gayot, *La franc-maçonnerie française. Textes et pratiques (XVIIIᵉ–XIXᵉ siècles)*, Paris, 1980, pp. 32–8.

69 BN FM2 436, *La Paix*, discours, 5 messidor IX (24 June 1801).

70 BN FM2 442, *Vrais Amis réunis d'Egypte*, correspondance, 28 Nov. 1806.

71 BN FM2 438, *La Parfaite Alliance*, correspondance, 11 May 1816.

72 AN F7 8779, Préfet du Var, 15 Oct. 1811.

73 AD 11T1–1, Règlement de la Société d'Emulation, 18 pluviôse VIII (7 Feb. 1800) and Agulhon, *Pénitents*, p. 314.

74 Parès, *L'aurore du journalisme*, pp. 7–16.

75 AD 8T1–1, Bibliothèque de Toulon, 17 floréal XI (7 May 1803).

76 AD 8T1–1, Sous-préfet de Toulon, 24 Apr. 1813.

77 Fauchet, *Statistique*, p. 180.

78 AN F17 1344, Ecole centrale du Var, an 7 (1789–90).

79 AD 2T2, Projet d'amélioration de l'Ecole centrale, no date.

80 Furet and Ozouf, *Reading and writing*, pp. 197–210.

81 AM L68(17) Délibérations, 8 May 1806; L750, Ecole de filles, 16 Oct. 1807 and AD 5T8–1, Frères des Ecoles chrétiennes, 10 Apr. 1818.

82 Bourilly, *Historique du Collège*, pp. 70–81.

83 AD 2T2, Etats du Collège de Toulon, 1807–20 and AM L746, Comptabilité du Collège, 1811–15.

84 Henseling (ed.), *Les cahiers*, t. 2, p. 4.

9

The Imperial decade and the Hundred Days

'Under the Empire Marseille wept, while Toulon smiled; Marseille was ruined, but Toulon prospered.'

The intense level of military activity during the Empire explains the contrast between political attitudes in Toulon and those elsewhere in Provence. The commerce of Marseille, like that of the great ports in general, was ruined by incessant warfare whereas, at Toulon, mobilisation generated many opportunities for employment and enrichment. Under Napoleon the French navy experienced a long series of disasters. The Mediterranean fleet lurched from one defeat to another, from Aboukir to Trafalgar, to the less famous engagement off the Greek peninsula at Lissa in 1811. Yet these unremitting failures, which have understandably been avoided by most French historians, should not obscure the heroic efforts made to reverse the grim succession of catastrophes.[1] The British were well aware of the resources which Bonaparte was amassing in the port of Toulon, especially after 1807 when he made 'a great drive to win command of the seas'.[2] It was this sustained, albeit tardy and abortive attempt to turn the tide of maritime fortune which laid the basis for Toulon's buoyancy until the very end of the Empire. The Bourbon Restoration, which brought peace, was greeted unenthusiastically as a result. The following year, a final spasm of upheaval revealed strong support for Napoleon's return during the Hundred Days.

When Bonaparte abdicated for the second time, in 1815, no less than twenty-four ships of the line (*vaisseaux*), eleven frigates, three corvettes and a host of smaller craft had been assembled at Toulon.[3] Indeed, a further three *vaisseaux* and a frigate were under construction, a statistic which reflects the importance attached to the Toulonnais base throughout the Empire. Only Antwerp constructed more ships, without experiencing the same level of operations and expeditions as Toulon. Naval rebuilding had recommenced a couple of years after the Aboukir débâcle and, by the time hostilities restarted in 1804, the Toulonnais dockyards already housed a fleet of twelve *vaisseaux*. The following year most of these ships were lost at Trafalgar, but another renaissance was soon under way. When Admiral Ganteaume arrived with reinforcements from Rochefort in 1808 he was able to muster a total of fourteen *vaisseaux*, not to mention support from allies like the Russians, who made a celebrated visit to Toulon in that year.[4]

Over the period as a whole some 160 million *francs* were expended at the Mediterranean Arsenal. Twenty *vaisseaux* and seven frigates were built in the course of a sustained effort, unequalled either during the Revolution or the American War of the 1780s. Activity reached a peak in 1811, when sixteen vessels of all types were completed.[5] Only towards the end of 1813 did defeat on land take a serious toll on this maritime campaign, as resources were diverted to the army and shipyard supplies, especially of wood, became impossible to obtain. Toulon was thus a veritable hive of industry for most of the imperial decade.

This high level of activity was translated into the total of workers employed at the Arsenal, in numbers which rarely fell below 2,000 and were often far greater. Naturally there were periodic fluctuations in the dockyard labour force. A reduction in the total of directly employed men to just over 800, following the departure of a Trafalgar-bound fleet in 1805, is a good case in point.[6] Yet a reliable census taken in January 1806 recorded an overall urban population of 32,954 shortly afterwards.[7] When 'floating' elements, such as soldiers and convicts on the prison hulks, are removed the remaining total of 28,170 fixed, intra- and extra-mural inhabitants represents an increase of 28 per cent over the survey made in the Year IX (1800). In 1811, with a newly constructed fleet ready to sail, but penned into the harbour by the British blockade, the sub-prefect put the civilian population at 36,000. If ships' crews were to be added he reckoned the figure would reach as high as 50,000 persons.[8]

These statistics are quite consistent with demographic movement recorded in the *Etat civil*. The annual number of marriages was dented by the departure of the fleet in 1805, but it rose beyond the 250 mark during the final years of the Empire and, in 1814, the total of live births at Toulon hit an all-time peak of almost 1,600. As a result of continual mobilisation the demographic recovery of Toulon from the ravages of the Revolution was thus rather more rapid than at neighbouring, but stagnant Marseille, or many other cities.[9] On the other hand, 'hothouse' growth of this sort was not destined to last. With the return of peace under the Restoration the Toulonnais population stabilised, at a level not dissimilar to the late *ancien régime*.

Even when burials at hospital and almshouse are taken into consideration (though not those at the military infirmiaries, where many Toulonnais were treated and died) there was a small surplus of births over deaths during the First Empire. This appears to have resulted from an exceptionally high ratio of legitimate births to marriages. At 4.52 the figure was greater than calculations for the years between 1776 and 1785; it also reversed a slight fall registered over the intervening period. Moreover, this elevated ratio does not include illegitimate and abandoned children whose numbers were running at 16 per cent of all live births throughout the imperial decade. The total of '*enfants trouvés*', which was growing at the end of the *ancien régime*, always rose dramatically in time of war, but such a large percentage had never been recorded before.

Nonetheless, it is clear that the recovery and rise of the Toulonnais population during the Empire was primarily due to immigration. In 1808 and 1809, for example, one in every four male marriage partners had originated beyond the boundaries of Provence. Newcomers were making rather less dramatic inroads than in the Year III when, in the wake of the 'federalist' rebellion, one in every two bridegrooms was of distant provenance. Yet, at the outset of the Revolution, the contribution of strangers to the province had been less than one in six. Brides were also drawn from further afield than in the past. In 1808 and 1809 17 per cent of them hailed from outside Provence, compared to 13 per cent in the pre-revolutionary decade and only 7 per cent before that. Finally, an analysis of burial records at the civilian hospital of Saint-Esprit, where many poorer inhabitants were obliged to seek treatment, shows that 50 per cent of deceased adults originated beyond the region as opposed to only 30 per cent in the 1780s.

The impression conveyed by these 'moving pictures' is one of a population which was still extremely fluid, though rather less so than a decade earlier in the middle of the revolutionary upheaval. As fortune has it a 'photograph' can be taken for the geographical origins of the adult male population in 1810. It is not clear why this

Table 10 *Geographical origins of the adult male population of Toulon in 1810*

Category	Toulon		Var		Provence		Elsewhere		Total
	No.	%	No.	%	No.	%	No.	%	
Military officers	65	34.9	19	10.2	21	11.3	81	43.5	186
Leading administrators	16	25.8	4	6.5	20	32.3	22	35.5	62
Retired officers & officials	19	59.4	2	6.2	5	15.6	6	18.7	32
Rentiers	87	72.5	15	12.5	9	7.5	9	7.5	120
Legal professions	11	44.0	6	24.0	5	20.0	3	12.0	25
Medical professions	47	52.8	17	19.1	8	9.0	3	3.4	89
Merchants	37	56.9	14	15.7	7	10.8	7	10.8	65
Retailers	45	70.3	10	15.6	2	3.1	7	10.9	64
Clerks	142	47.2	38	12.6	35	11.6	86	28.6	301
Fab. & sale of food	110	31.3	84	23.9	68	19.4	89	25.4	351
Fab. & sale of clothing	104	32.4	63	19.6	37	11.5	117	36.4	321
Construction	105	51.5	31	15.2	22	10.8	46	22.5	204
Metal working	38	43.2	10	11.4	9	10.2	31	35.2	88
Fab. & sale of instruments	25	23.6	26	24.5	21	19.8	34	32.1	106
Retail & transport	41	29.9	26	19.0	32	23.4	38	27.7	137
Dockyard workers	384	54.2	86	12.1	151	21.3	87	12.3	708
Soldiers & sailors	338	42.2	108	13.5	95	11.9	259	32.4	800
Rural professions	23	31.1	15	20.3	16	21.7	20	27.0	74
Unskilled workers	227	40.1	100	17.7	105	18.6	134	23.7	566
Priests	9	56.2	4	25.0	2	12.5	1	6.2	16
No profession indicated	275	49.8	86	15.6	80	14.5	111	20.1	552
Total	2,148	44.1	764	15.7	750	15.4	1,205	24.8	4,867

Source: AM L132, Registre des habitants, 1810.

register was compiled but, when the necessary adjustments are made, a comparison is possible with the list of those liable for National Guard service drawn up in 1791.[10] Not surprisingly global analysis reveals a fall in the native-born component of the male population, from 62 per cent in 1791 to 47.5 per cent in 1810. Overall, in 1810, 19 per cent of these men emanated from outside Provence, as opposed to 13 per cent in 1791. Even so, the impact of the intervening decades upon the fixed, civilian population of Toulon is less dramatic than other data suggest.

In 1810, as in 1791, government officials and military officers were drawn from further afield than all other socio-professional categories. By contrast notables remained predominantly native in origin, though their indigenous component had fallen from roughly 70 to 60 per cent between 1791 and 1810. Dockyard workers were mostly of local provenance in 1810 too, confirming another feature of the analysis for 1791. The penetration of immigrants remained greatest among the various categories of artisans, excluding those associated with shipbuilding. In 1810 a mere 35 per cent of them were indigenous. Only rural workers (31 per cent), leading administrators (26 per cent) and military officers (36 per cent) included fewer, native-born individuals. The occupational contours of geographical recruitment discernible in 1791 were thus repeated in 1810, though with lower levels of natives in each case.

It should be stressed that the survey of 1810 was not taken in a stable context, for war and the naval draft remained in full swing. The demographic attraction of activity at the dockyards was still being exerted and continued to animate the entire urban economy. The Arsenal was not only nourishing workers and sailors, but a great deal of commerce besides. In their capacity as dockyard suppliers Toulonnais merchants naturally looked to the voracious Arsenal for lucrative contracts. No less than seven of the fourteen merchants from Toulon, who appeared on a departmental list of 'distinguished entrepreneurs' in 1810, were purveyors of naval supplies.[11] Nearly all of them were wealthier than their Toulonnais counterparts who relied solely on civilian trade. Since the British fleet controlled the Mediterranean all seaborne commerce was a hazardous business, but the rewards were much greater where naval contracts were concerned.

While workers pillaged the Arsenal by abusing their right to take home offcuts for firewood (the *droit de copeaux*) merchants enjoyed extremely generous profit margins in their dealings with the dockyards. Of course, overcharging had occurred under the *ancien régime* and its perpetrators were occasionally prosecuted; as the memoirist Letuaire put it: 'from time immemorial the navy has been a milch-cow at Toulon'.[12] Yet Caillemer, the imperial police commissioner, was correct to assert that abuses had escalated since the Revolution, because the current generation of dockyard administrators lacked the experience to control them. To his mind excessive tendering had become commonplace and one merchant in particular, a certain Gérard who was an unsuccessful candidate as mayor in 1812, had made huge profits.[13]

Most naval contractors were also engaged in the provision of foodstuffs, satisfying the enormous civilian and military demands of Toulon and its hinterland. The region remained as deficient as ever in cereals and the coastal supply circuits from Languedoc to Italy, though subject to enemy disruption, were vital to survival. Statistics available for 1810 and 1813 would suggest that roughly 14,000 tons of grain arrived by sea during each of those years.[14] The civilian population in the town consumed just over half of it, while the remainder was absorbed by Arsenal and garrison, or by the locality which Toulon continued to serve as an entrepôt.[15] Almost half of the ships which entered the port in 1810, 1812 and 1813 were bearing grain. The others carried naval stores, various foodstuffs like fruit and pasta, or leather and pottery. The enduring disequilibrium of seaborne trade at Toulon is graphically illustrated by the fact that over 70 per cent of these same vessels left unladen. Only small quantities of wine, brandy, cloth, salt and capers were going for export.[16]

The *savant* Millin, a visitor a few years before, noted the one-way nature of traffic at Toulon and added: 'Trade is limited to coastal routes, along the shores of France and Italy.'[17] In so far as goods were exchanged further afield it was in the bottoms of Marseillais or Genoese vessels, for only rarely did the unladen weight of boats arriving at Toulon exceed 100 tons and their ports of call were usually confined to the littoral. The Toulonnais commercial network had certainly contracted in comparison to the pre-revolutionary decades. As late as 1793 a direct trade with northern Europe had survived, but war against the British and Dutch curtailed it.[18] Hopes that these links would be resumed after the Peace of Amiens had been concluded in 1802 were dashed when maritime conflict recommenced less than two years later.

Municipal councillors were well aware of the need to create additional economic opportunities at Toulon. They were especially eager to reopen trade with India: 'This development offers our unfortunate town a certain means of escaping from its lamentable situation . . . by establishing a new branch of commerce.'[19] Yet this fresh attempt, like its forerunner, foundered for lack of facilities. The naval prefect refused to assist in the provision of warehousing, adding ominously that he was utterly opposed to 'the combination of commercial and military enterprises' in which local councillors were seeking salvation. Despite this setback a proposal to revive bonnet-making was put forward in 1802. While the prefect of the Var agreed that it was essential 'to reactivate the manufacture of bonnets, which was so important in the past', he was opposed to the use of child-labour.[20] The resumption of war effectively put paid to the plan.

Statistics for manufacturing in the Year IX (1801) tell a sorry tale: a total of thirty-eight pre-revolutionary establishments had shrunk to just nineteen a decade later.[21] Sugar-refining, silk-weaving and textile-fulling had disappeared entirely, while soap-boiling and cloth-making had suffered considerable losses. Even this depressing situation represented some progress, for most manufacturing enterprises had been destroyed as a consequence of the revolt of 1793.[22] Business confidence began to return under the Directory and the gradual reprise of activity continued after Napoleon seized power. At the end of 1808 it was reported that thirty-five manufactories were back in operation.[23]

The visitor Millin was wrong to state so categorically that 'all industry at Toulon depends upon the imperial navy'.[24] A good deal of manufacturing, like weaving, nail-making, glass-blowing and paper-making, was heavily dependent upon naval contracts, but there were other activities like soap-boiling, tanning, brewing, brandy-distilling and dyeing which relied upon a local, civilian market. To be sure, most of this manufacturing was conducted on a very modest scale; a survey of 1808 attributed a mere 200 employees to this sector of the urban economy.[25] In 1811, when recession had reduced the figure to 140, only a newly-established silk-mill with forty workers, two tanneries and a glass-blowing enterprise had more than a couple of employees on the books.[26] Just one of the thirty-one manufacturers listed for the town in 1810, the distiller C. Féraud, could match local merchants in terms of income and, significantly enough, he was also involved in trading himself.[27] As the prefect of the Var concluded in 1811, 'Toulon has never been renowned for its manufacturing output.'[28]

The year 1808 marked the apogee of independent economic activity in post-revolutionary Toulon. Thereafter a fall in industrial output occurred.[29] The continental blockade and the vagaries of war were taking their toll, but so too was the weather.[30] During the winters of 1809–10 and 1810–11 temperatures fell well below zero, damaging vines and olives and thereby eroding the supply of raw materials for brandy-distilling, soap and candle-making. The economic crisis of the years 1809–12 was further exacerbated by poor grain harvests, which raised the price of bread and reduced the market for manufactured products. As the prefect commented, at Toulon 'foodstuffs are plentiful, but they are extremely dear'.[31] The cost of a better quality loaf in the town increased from 37 *centimes* a kilo (the new universal unit of measurement that was finally adopted under the Empire) in January 1810 to 65 *centimes* by the end of the year. In 1811 the price fell back to 55 *centimes* per kilo, but hit a peak of 70 *centimes* in the spring of 1812. The cost of meat rose by over 20 per cent, while wine and oil prices more than doubled.[32]

This was a welcome development for producers, who had suffered from surpluses during the preceding years, but it spelled disaster for the poor. The pauper residue of some 1,000 elderly, infirm or sick persons was constantly swollen by the casualties of war and the families of those who had been killed in action or taken prisoner. Yet the provision of relief at Toulon gradually improved under the Napoleonic regime. The means of redress, in essence a return to sources of income exploited under the *ancien régime*, included contributions from local indirect taxes and the encouragement of charitable donations.[33] On the last day of 1802 the prefect of the Var had assured the Minister of the Interior that such remedies were in hand. Above all, the reimposition of local tolls (*l'octroi*), would enable the municipal council to meet annual expenditure of roughly 100,000 *livres* on various types of assistance.[34]

It would be difficult to agree with a suggestion that 'the situation improved beyond all recognition' but, by 1805, numbers treated at the hospital, maintained at the almshouse, or given outdoor relief were once more approaching pre-revolutionary levels.[35] The one area which continued to cause particular concern was the care of abandoned children (*enfants trouvés*). The central government retained financial responsibility for them, but too often defaulted on its obligations. In 1810, for example, the prefect was obliged to protest about the late arrival of funds.[36] Unpaid wet-nurses in the surrounding countryside were threatening to return infants to the hospital at Toulon, thus exposing them to 'certain death'.

From 1810 onwards, as the subsistence crisis took its toll, the system of relief once more began to crack. The annual level of admissions to the hospital of Saint-Esprit doubled and, after an outbreak of influenza occurred in 1811, the wards were overflowing with sick people.[37] The yearly total of civilian burials also increased sharply, from a plateau of some 800 in 1808 to over 1,000 between 1810 and 1812. In 1812 the authorities noted that 2,000 Rumford soups, a recently discovered 'recipe for the poor', were being distributed each day in the town.[38] Yet, as long as the Arsenal remained at full-stretch, the people of Toulon were cushioned from the worst effects of rising food prices. The historian Brun claims that dockyard workers refused Rumford soups while they remained in employment.[39] Such optimism may be unfounded, because in 1812 naval employees' pay was well in arrears. The prefect of the Var was obviously relieved to report that the Toulonnais people were calm despite their suffering and the chief of police concurred: 'There is a good deal of poverty', he wrote, 'but Lent has ended without any disorder.'[40]

The authorities at Toulon had good reason to be on the alert. As the prefect recognised, 'one of the causes of the frequency of insurrection in this town resides in the tardy payment of dockyard workers'.[41] In 1806, when the labour-force had been significantly reduced and considerable arrears of pay had accumulated, a seditious placard duly appeared at the dockyards. The naval prefect, Emeriau, had been threatened with death if wages were not paid promptly and he had badgered the naval ministry into producing some additional funds.[42] In 1812, with their coffers again empty, administrators at the Arsenal feared the worst. Yet a revolutionary plot aroused little popular enthusiasm, despite its authors' expectations to the contrary. The naval prefect was quick to settle arrears the moment rumours of the conspiracy reached him.[43] His expeditious response doubtless explains why the little known affair of 1812–13 was so easily nipped in the bud.

Nevertheless, this plot affords some rare insight into the undercurrents of opposition which persisted in one or two milieux at

Toulon and elsewhere. The prefect of the Var, for example, wrote to his counterpart in the Bouches-du-Rhône: 'Anarchist projects do not surprise me, especially at Toulon. After all, Barras, Fréron and their henchmen filled the town full of Jacobins.'[44] The conspiracy actually originated in 1809, at Marseille, among royalist notables who hoped to exploit the deep unpopularity of the Empire among inhabitants of the commercial city. Links were forged with monarchist elements in Languedoc, but the Marseillais conspirators were prepared to involve republicans in their machinations as well. Their initial contact in Toulon, the old militant Marquésy, refused to become embroiled (he was subsequently indicted for failing to inform the authorities that he had been approached). Thomas Blancard, a master shoemaker with a Jacobin past, responded more enthusiastically and, in the course of 1812, he recruited a number of his political acquaintances. Ex-Jacobins from the Toulonnais hinterland, who had participated in the uprising of the Year III, were also drawn in.

It was eventually decided to take Fort Lamalgue just outside the walls of Toulon, rouse the garrison and then rally general support for the overthrow of Napoleon. However, at the end of March 1813, as meetings were held near Le Beausset to finalise arrangements, the police moved in. The plot had been thoroughly penetrated and all its leading lights were arrested, together with a good many suspects. Ringleaders from Marseille were rounded up and judged by a military commission, which sat at Toulon; twelve of them were quickly sentenced to death. The Toulonnais detainees were sent to Nîmes, where they were still awaiting trial when the Empire collapsed in 1814.[45]

The nineteen Toulonnais accused of direct involvement in the conspiracy originated from the popular classes.[46] The majority, including Blancard himself, were artisans: six were stonemasons, three shoemakers, two tailors, one a clockmaker and another a painter. They were accompanied by a smaller number of persons connected with the Arsenal: three gunners, a caulker, a dockyard fireman and an unemployed clerk. Half-a-dozen *rentiers* and eight rural workers from the countryside surrounding Toulon had also been taken into custody. As Pelet de la Lozère, the councillor of state called in to conduct the proceedings, commented:

At Toulon, as in villages of the hinterland, there remains a nucleus of 'anarchists' created by the Revolution . . . in rather greater numbers than elsewhere . . . Many local artisans – stonemasons, tailors, blacksmiths, wigmakers, etc. – joined clubs and held office in them . . . these individuals lost the will to work, having acquired instead a taste for bar-rooms, meetings and speech-making. In the absence of regular employment they have fallen upon hard times. However, those who appear in the list of 'anarchists' we have arrested are all aged between thirty-eight and fifty years old . . . In time this type of person will disappear because they are growing old and have no successors.

Several of these Toulonnais '*enragés*' were out of work. As Pelet put it, they were 'distrusted by all the landowners and businessmen in the area, who refused to employ them'.

The conspirators were naturally counting upon the inhabitants of Toulon for support:

On dockyard workers who had not been paid for several months; on sailors, marines and gunners who were treated like slaves on board ship; on convicts imprisoned as a result of false evidence or hearsay, who were to be released; and, finally, on all those workers in the town who had been made redundant since reorganisation of the Arsenal put naval contracts into the hands of a few, big employers.

The police commissioner at Toulon confirmed Pelet's last point; sailors suspected that contractors providing their food and clothing were profiteering, while smaller artisans in the town were robbed of customers. Popular support was also anticipated by the plotters on account of their determination to abolish hated indirect taxes, the so-called '*droits réunis*'. Above all, as an anonymous memorandum discovered at Le Beausset put it, 'we have been living in slavery for too long. We must re-establish freedom and crush the tyrant Bonaparte.' Yet neither sailors, nor dockyard workers, nor the artisans of Toulon showed much interest. Former Jacobins who joined the conspiracy thus lacked any purchase upon their old constituency and won no support among former republican notables either. The political situation in the town was becalmed; apathy was the order of the day.

This attitude was reflected in an abysmal turnout for elections which took place during the final years of the Empire. In September 1810 primary elections were held for the first time under the imperial regime.[47] All adult males at Toulon were entitled to vote in the eight urban sections, specifically resurrected for this purpose. They were to choose candidates for the municipal council, as justices of the peace and members of the department and *arrondissement* colleges, but only 6 per cent of the electorate bothered to participate. The next round of polls at Toulon, in August 1813, elicited even less interest.[48] On this occasion only 5 per cent of voters attended the electoral assemblies and turnout for the department as a whole was equally low. An analysis of the Toulonnais proceedings shows that few members of the popular classes took part. In the former section of Saint-Jean (now entitled Arcola: all the sections were re-named after Napoleon's victories) there were just eight voters. All of them were notables, save for a municipal clerk. Not a single dockyard worker or sailor was in evidence, here or elsewhere.

Even so, the acting sub-prefect of Toulon exaggerated when he suggested that

The electoral assemblies are very different today from what they were during the Revolution. At that time the people saw voting as a tremendously important activity and flocked to the polls. As a result it was possible to discern the nature of the interests and opinions of the various classes of citizens, often in the most intimate detail. Today, however, the people have come to realise that the government alone should be entrusted with making the right choice, on account of its expertise in measuring and weighing up the candidates. Indeed, no one would mind if we revoked the articles in our Constitution which retain the practice of democratic elections.[49]

An anonymous correspondent correctly observed that the lack of contemporary interest was hardly surprising since voters were only nominating candidates and not actually electing to office. From the government's point of view the process had become self-defeating; so low turnout made it impossible to gauge opinion among the population.

A more reliable test of popular allegiance resides in the local response to military conscription. Reluctance to join the navy, like desertion from the fleet, seems to have remained commonplace, but the Toulonnais were willing contributors of army recruits. In 1813, at a time when enthusiasm was waning elsewhere, 1,140 conscripts came forward at Toulon when only 680 were required.[50] Artisans and dockyard workers were equally assiduous in their performance of National Guard duties, though their preponderance in the militia disturbed Admiral Ganteaume, who returned to the town in 1814 as a special government envoy. He reported that many bourgeois were finding substitutes in order to avoid serving themselves.[51]

This obervation led Duhamel, sub-prefect at Toulon from 1812 to 1813, to conclude that 'there were few citizens of any standing' at

Toulon who would defend the Empire to the death.[52] Le Roy, prefect of the Var between 1811 and 1814, concurred. According to him many individuals holding public office 'supported the government out of self-interest, but had no real love for it'.[53] The chief of police also agreed that most notables would abandon the regime if matters continued to deteriorate. Members of the elite had congratulated him for uncovering the conspiracy of 1813 but, had the plot succeeded, he felt they would have endorsed it.[54]

Unlike the inhabitants of Marseille the citizens of Toulon did not publicly rejoice in Napoleon's downfall in 1814. The provisional government formed in Paris was reluctantly recognised in an anodyne address from the municipal council on 19 April. In June an inquorate meeting declined to send an official deputation to render homage to the newly installed Louis XVIII, despite the sub-prefect's plea that it do so.[55] At the Arsenal attitudes were much the same. News of the Emperor's abdication had been received 'with sadness' and adoption of the white Bourbon flag was delayed until 20 April.[56] In May 1,000 individuals did sign a fulsome address to the king, while 300 'good and true Toulonnais' sectionaries who had survived the rebellion of 1793 reminded him of their sacrifices.[57] Only the visit of the Comte d'Artois in October 1814 produced more widespread demonstrations of royalist sentiment.

The new regime proceeded cautiously and made few immediate changes in administrative personnel at Toulon. The integration of nobles, sectionary *émigrés* and royalists into the imperial machinery supplied a solid basis for continuity in 1814. The sub-prefect, de la Tourette, who had been in post since 1813, was retained by the Bourbons. The existing municipal council was also kept in office until Mayor Trullet resigned in August 1814. Trullet, a retired naval officer who had risen rapidly from the lower deck during the Revolution, protested about 'the despotism of nobles and priests', which he felt the Restoration was encouraging.[58] Yet Trullet's replacement as mayor, an aristocratic former *émigré*, the Comte de Grimaldy, had already been chosen as a deputy mayor by Bonaparte in 1813. When the restored monarchy, in keeping with Napoleonic practice, renewed half the Toulonnais municipal councillors in the autumn of 1814 only five out of fifteen nominees had not previously appeared on lists compiled during the Empire.[59]

According to the new prefect of the Var, de Bouthillier, the absence of change at Toulon stemmed from a lack of suitable

Table 11 Municipal councillors appointed at Toulon, 1800–1816

Occupational category	1800		1812		First Restoration		Hundred Days		Second Restoration	
	No.	%	No.	%	No.	%	No.	%	No.	%
Military officers	1	3.3	–	–	–	–	–	–	–	–
Leading administrators	1	3.3	1	3.3	3	10.0	3	10.0	4	13.3
Retired officers & officials	–	–	–	–	1	3.3	–	–	3	10.0
Rentiers	4	13.3	3	10.0	7	23.3	4	13.3	5	16.7
Legal profession	2	6.7	2	6.7	–	–	4	13.3	1	3.3
Medical profession	2	6.7	5	16.7	–	–	3	10.0	2	6.7
Merchants	8	26.7	12	40.0	16	53.3	12	40.0	11	36.7
Retailers	3	10.0	2	6.7	1	3.3	2	6.7	1	3.3
Clerks	1	3.3	–	–	–	–	1	3.3	1	3.3
Artisans & shopkeepers	8	26.7	5	16.7	2	6.7	1	3.3	2	6.7
Total	30	–	30	–	30	–	30	–	30	–

Source: AM L587, Municipalité, an IX (1800)–1810 and AN FI BII Var 2, 3, 4 and 25, Personnel de Toulon, an IX (1800)–1816.

candidates rather than deliberate policy. He reckoned that too few individuals in the town were sufficiently devoted to the monarchy. It was a situation which he, like many others, blamed on the destruction of the bourgeoisie in 1793.[60] The prefect was certainly dismayed to discover that, as late as January 1815, the two justices of the peace at Toulon were men who had espoused Jacobin ideas in the past, while the local criminal court was in the hands of 'extreme revolutionaries'.[61] De Bouthillier noted that the Toulonnais notables still clung to some radical ideas at variance with their vested interests and he also highlighted local fears of a revival of noble privileges. There was naturally alarm at Toulon when proposals were made to indemnify those *émigrés* who had forfeited estates during the Revolution. Holders of *émigré* property, so numerous in the naval town, urgently required reassurance. On the very eve of Napoleon's return, in the famous Hundred Days, the prefect of the Var was again writing to Paris about the need to consolidate support at Toulon, for nobles and priests alone were too few and too impoverished to provide a reliable basis for the Restoration. 'There are still a large number of determined opponents of the government here', he warned.[62]

The difficulties confronting the restored monarchy at Toulon were exacerbated by the situation at the Arsenal. The Bourbon regime was associated with the enemies of France and the return of peace brought redundancies at the dockyards. Above all, the continuity of personnel in the municipality contrasted with considerable turnover in the navy, where the general composition of the officer corps was dramatically transformed. The new naval prefect was the unexceptionable Hermitte, an imperial vice-admiral who had risen through the ranks during the Revolution. The higher command in the Mediterranean *port de guerre* was, however, entrusted to former *émigrés* like Rafélis de Brovès, an officer imprisoned at Toulon in 1789 with the notorious Albert de Rions. The names of leading captains appointed at the end of 1814 represented a roll-call of men who had last appeared on the lists as aristocratic naval cadets in the late 1780s.

No less than half the men holding the grade of captain when the Empire collapsed were pensioned off and large numbers of lieutenants were also forced into premature retirement.[63] The wholesale reintegration of royalist personnel meant that imperial officers left in post could entertain few prospects of promotion in future. Their loyalty to the monarchy was obviously not to be counted upon, while those who had been dismissed became bitter opponents of the new regime. The prefect of the Var correctly identified them as subversive elements, to be kept under close surveillance.[64] Former naval officers were popularly known at Toulon as 'Napoleonists', or even 'republicans', and they duly welcomed Bonaparte's return from Elba in April 1815.

Dockyard workers and sailors, like the Toulonnais populace in general, had remained unmoved when Napoleon fell from power. This was hardly surprising since the payment of their wages had become extremely irregular. Towards the end of April 1814 the naval prefect indicated that workers were only just being paid for January, while sailors were owed four months' money and several contractors had bills outstanding form the preceding year.[65] It had become impossible to obtain credit in the town and employees were once more receiving bread from the bakery at the Arsenal. Agents of the Restoration were well aware that unless they could improve this situation there was little hope of winning popular support for the monarchy.[66] Yet funds were slow to arrive and a reduction in armaments had to be made as a condition of the European peace settlement. A few frigates and a dozen brigs were to be kept in commission at Toulon, but three ships of the line were transferred to Brest and the remainder, along with surplus frigates, were mothballed. Only the completion of two vessels already on the stocks and some minor repair work was planned for 1815. All this entailed a diminution in the work-force to just 1,500 men.[67]

Bonaparte's return to power, in April 1815, was thus particularly welcome for it brought a resumption of war and with it renewed activity at the Arsenal. As Joliclerc, a police commissioner, realised: 'Toulon contains a huge number of sailors who were involved in the war at sea and workers for whom the termination of activity at the dockyards spelled disaster. Thus those miraculous events, which returned Napoleon to the helm and reopened hostilities, have been received here with rapture.'[68] Orders were immediately given to recommission part of the Mediterranean fleet and extra workers were taken on to prepare five ships of the line and three frigates for combat. Admiral Duperré, who was named naval prefect by Napoleon, reported with satisfaction that tricolours were flying from every window in the town, while Joliclerc described demonstrations against royalists and dancing in the streets.[69] Yet, as Letuaire later recalled, popular enthusiasm for the restored Empire was rather short-lived.[70] Expectations of renewed affluence were dashed by the absence of any substantial funds to finance the war effort. Dockyard workers received no remuneration and the newly installed *préfet maritime* appealed in vain for assistance. He could only issue promissory notes which traders in the town were understandably loath to accept.[71]

Yet there was no hostility to Bonaparte's return like that which erupted at Marseille, or in the countryside to the west of Toulon.[72] Roederer, the parliamentarian sent as a special commissioner to the Midi, was relieved to arrive in the naval town. 'It's good to be in Toulon, especially after arriving from Marseille', he wrote, adding that in his opinion some four-fifths of the inhabitants were behind the new regime.[73] The favourable response of military personnel and leading civilians to Napoleon's reappearance had obliged royalist elements at Toulon to withdraw. When Rivière and Angoulême tried to rally support for the Bourbons at the end of March they were given a hostile reception by garrison soldiers and popular classes. Sympathetic officers and administrative staff at the Arsenal had subsequently sent an address to the Emperor on 14 April, which emphasised 'our great joy upon hearing the wonderful news of your return'.[74]

Many of the navy and army officers who had recently gone into retirement now re-enlisted, while the *émigrés* and royalists reintegrated into the forces were dismissed.[75] A similar turnover of personnel took place in the civilian administration. The prefect of the Var, Bouthillier, was arrested on 11 April and replaced by Defermon, a former lawyer with prefectoral experience under the Empire.[76] J. B. Senès, the first sub-prefect to be appointed at Toulon, resumed his old post. On the municipal council recently installed Restoration officials gave way to tried and tested imperial personnel. P. Courtès, naval doctor and holder of the *légion d'honneur*, re-emerged as mayor, assisted by three deputies with a wealth of previous experience in the office. The Toulonnais municipality during the Hundred Days remained dominated by the bourgeoisie, but the reappearance of former Jacobins like the surgeon Hernandez marked a significant political shift.[77]

These changes hardly amounted to a 'return of the anarchists', as a prefectoral report claimed after the Second Bourbon Restoration later in the year.[78] The Hundred Days were not so much a return to the Revolution as a reversion to Bonaparte's Consulate. Many

notables were dismayed by reactionary developments under
Bourbons who had allegedly 'learned nothing and forgotten
nothing'. Their misgivings were trenchantly expressed by the
returning sub-prefect, Senès, who claimed that 'Feudalism has burst
its fetters and is about to enslave us again ... the most odious
privileges have been restored, everywhere.'[79] A resurgence of anti-
clericalism was also evident: at Sainte-Marie demonstrators taunted
the ultra-royalist *curé* Vigne, chanting that he was 'a man to hang'
and the cathedral 'a church for sale'.[80] More to the point the re-
establishment of the Empire offered considerable comfort to those
Toulonnais who were holders of *émigré* property. The final
Bonapartist fling also drew upon deep wells of patriotism. As prefect
Defermon stated: 'the name of Napoleon is inseparable from that of
the *patrie*'.[81]

Municipal councillors at Toulon were certainly quick to evoke
'the great days of the Empire', although their reference to the
Emperor's 'liberal ideas' was, to say the least, debatable.[82] In 1815
Bonaparte felt obliged to match the half-hearted liberalism of the
Bourbons' Constitutional Charter. His rapidly produced Additional
Act was remarkably similar, though it provided for an expanded
electorate. Unlike the Bourbon charter, however, Napoleon's new
scheme was put to a democratic vote. This plebiscite was hurriedly
organised, held in difficult circumstances and poorly supported. The
new Act generally received the same number of favourable votes as
had actually been cast in the Year VIII, but turnout was rather lower
than in the Years X and XII.[83] At Toulon the 458 affirmative votes
(opposed by one negative opinion, from a civilian doctor) surpassed
the total for the foundation of the Empire in 1804 and reflected the
existence of enduring republican sentiment.[84] Yet the great majority
of the Toulonnais participants were officials or notables. It was, in
truth, a disappointing response, but one which contrasted with the
indifference apparent in western parts of Var and outright hostility
to Napoleon in the Bouches-du-Rhône.

During the Hundred Days there were also elections in the departmental and *arrondissement* colleges to find deputies for a new Legislative Chamber in Paris. In May 1815 college members who had
been elected in 1810 were invited to reassemble. While the level of
attendance was generally low in the Var, it was relatively high at
Toulon.[85] In the *arrondissement* 107 members participated out of a
possible total of 161, with 58 Toulonnais present. This should be

compared to a turnout of only 36 at Brignoles and 52 at Draguignan. At the departmental college a mere 37 individuals appeared out of 226, but nine of them came from Toulon. This college nominated Fauchet, the former prefect and Senès, once more sub-prefect at Toulon, as its representatives. The choice of the *arrondissement* college likewise fell upon another old Jacobin, the naval surgeon Hernandez. Toulonnais inhabitants inevitably formed the overwhelming majority (no less than sixteen out of nineteen members) of a Varois delegation to the *Champ de Mai* celebrations in Paris which officially marked the reconstitution of the Napoleonic regime. The *ex-conventionnel* Escudier was among these envoys, together with former mayors of Toulon under the Empire.[86]

The town was naturally a centre for Bonapartist propaganda, with the local printer Aurel playing an especially active role.[87] However, as on numerous occasions in the recent past, the political stance of Toulon generated little support elsewhere in the region. Eastern Provence did remain predominantly Bonapartist in sentiment but, to the north and west, royalism was deeply entrenched. When news of Waterloo arrived in Provence towards the end of June 1815 there was a great upsurge of popular monarchism at Marseille, Aix and Avignon. Imperial troops and Napoleonic sympathisers were obliged to flee to Toulon where they fruitlessly demanded reprisals against their adversaries. Shades of the Year III were succeeded by echoes of 1793, as royalist sentiment gradually gained ground. The naval prefect was rightly alarmed and wrote on 5 July: 'Royalism is making inroads all around us. We are cut off and deprived of foodstuffs. Less then a month's supply remains.'[88]

Not only was there a subsistence crisis to contend with but, as in 1793, Toulon was threatened by allied forces. A British fleet was back in the Mediterranean and the Austrians were advancing overland. The town itself was drained of troops, who were despatched to protect the frontier. Only 1,700 soldiers were left at the garrison, but many citizens were persuaded to re-enlist in the National Guard and co-operate in strengthening the town's defences. The patriotic will to resist remained strong, despite an increasingly hopeless situation; the monarchists' liaison with foreign enemies only stiffened the Toulonnais' resolve. Napoleon's commander in the region, General Brune, was equally determined that Toulon should not surrender, either to the allies or to the royalist committee at Marseille. On 11 July, leaving a garrison at Antibes, Brune brought the rest of his troops to the naval town where he could still rely on the bulk of the population.[89] A bloody confrontation with the advancing allied forces seemed likely, but both sides yielded to compromise. On 20 July the naval prefect at Toulon decided to resign and so did Defermon, prefect of the Var.[90] Brune himself was prepared to recognise the authority of the royal commissioner, the Marquis de la Rivière, provided he was given a promise of no reprisals against those who had supported the Bonapartist cause. Once this guarantee had been granted Brune recommended adoption of the white Bourbon flag as a symbol of the town's submission. Dockyard and garrison personnel were especially reluctant to give way and only on 24 July, six weeks after Waterloo, was the *drapeau blanc* belatedly raised at Toulon.[91] Unlike 1793 the royalist embrace of 1815 was designed to end rebellion rather than reinforce it. Brune duly handed over control to Rivière and left the town. *En route* to Paris, where he was to answer for his recent conduct, the Bonapartist general was assassinated by an Avignonnais porter.[92] He was the last victim of more than two decades of upheaval at Toulon. The collapse of the Hundred Days finally brought a long period of war and revolution to an end.

Notes

1   The best naval histories for this period are those of A. T. Mahan, *The influence of seapower upon the French Revolution and Empire, 1793–1812*, 2 vols., London, 1892 and P. Mackesy, *The war in the Mediterranean, 1803–1810*, London, 1957. Some perceptive comments are also to be found in Acerra and Meyer, *Marines et Révolution*, pp. 242–4.

2   R. Glover, 'The French fleet, 1807–1814: Britain's problem and Madison's opportunity', *JMH*, 39, 1967, p. 233.

3   Brun, *Port de Toulon*, t. 2, pp. 614–17.

4   *Ibid.*, p. 386 and pp. 462–3.

5   F. Poncioni, 'Administration et production d'un port militaire sous le Consulat et le Premier Empire, Toulon 1800–1815', *Prov. hist.*, 39, 1989, pp. 538–41.

6   AP 3A1 13, Conseil, 22 nivôse XIII (12 Jan. 1805).

7   AD 11M1–4, Recensement, Jan. 1806.

8   AN F1 CIII Var 7, Sous-préfet, 1 July 1811. The 'national' census of that year (AN F20 411) contains no figures for the Var.

9   Dupâquier, *La population française*, pp. 91–2.

10   AM L132, Registre des habitants, 1810 and for the earlier survey, L391, Registre pour le service, 1791.

11   AD 16M1–2, Liste des négociants et commerçants, 1810 and AM L138, Etat des banquiers et négociants, 6 Dec. 1810.

12 Henseling (ed.), *Les cahiers*, t. 1, p. 34.

13 AD 2M7–3–5, Rapport de la police, 9 Aug. 1812.

14 AM L185 bis, Etat des navires chargés de blé, 1810 and 1813.

15 AM L161, Produit des récoltes, 1809 and 1812 and Fauchet, *Statistique*, p. 283.

16 AM L185 bis, Etat des mouvements and AN F12 1691 and 1712, Port de Toulon, mouvements, 1810 and 1812.

17 Millin, *Voyage*, t. 2, p. 430.

18 AM L295, Procès-verbal de l'embargo, 5 Feb. 1793.

19 AM L68(16), Délibérations, 26 brumaire XI (17 Nov. 1802).

20 AD 4M6, Préfet, an X (July 1802).

21 AM L142, Manufactures et fabriques existantes avant 1789 et en l'an IX.

22 AM L146, L'état des fabriques à savon, 7 germinal II (28 Mar. 1794) reveals that soap-boiling, for example, had ceased altogether.

23 AM L142, Etat du nombre des individus occupés dans les fabriques, 29 Aug. 1808.

24 Millin, *Voyage*, t. 2, p. 430.

25 AM L142, Etat du nombre des individus.

26 AD 16M1–1 and 2, Statistique industrielle et manufacturière, 1811–12 and 16M4–1, L'industrie textile, 1811–14.

27 AD 16M1–2, Etat détaillé des manufacturiers, 28 Sept. 1810.

28 AD 16M1–2, Sous-préfet, 21 June 1811.

29 AD 16M1–1 and 2, Statistique industrielle.

30 J. Vidalenc, 'La vie économique des départements méditerranéens pendant l'Empire', *RHMC*, III, 1954, pp. 193–4.

31 AD 4M7, Préfet, 16 Jan. 1813.

32 AM L68 (18 and 19), Délibérations, 1809–13 *passim* and M. Fournel, *Les problèmes de ravitaillement et le mouvement des prix au XIXe siècle (d'après les archives hospitalières de Toulon)*, Aix, 1969, *passim*.

33 Rocquain (ed.), *L'état de la France*, pp. 31–2 and Jones, *Charity and bienfaisance*, p. 201 *et seq.*

34 AN F15 1220, Préfet, 10 nivôse XI (31 Dec. 1802) and AD 4M6, Préfet, 1 germinal X (22 Mar. 1802).

35 AN F1 CV Var 1, Délibérations du conseil général du Var, an XIII (1805).

36 AN F15 2524, Situation des enfants trouvés, 7 Dec. 1810 and S. Pieuchet, 'Les enfants trouvés et abandonnés à Toulon au XIXe siècle', mémoire pour la maîtrise, University of Aix, 1970, p. 65 *et seq.*

37 AM L730, Rapport sur la situation des hôpitaux, 25 Feb. 1815.

38 AM L740, Secours extraordinaires, 1812.

39 Brun, *Port de Toulon*, t. 2, pp. 582–3.

40 AN F7 3693 Var 3, Préfet, 20 Apr. 1812 and Commissaire de la police, 13 Feb. 1812. Both contradict the comment in Agulhon (ed.), *Histoire de Toulon*, p. 207 that the crisis provoked 'disaffection and unrest'.

41 AD 4M6, Compte rendu, an X (1802–03).

42 AM L318, Préfet maritime au maire, 10 Feb. 1806; AP 2A 146, Préfet maritime, 4 and 5 Feb. 1806 and Brun, *Port de Toulon*, t. 2, pp. 451–2.

43   AN BB3 397, Préfet maritime au ministre, 1 Apr. and 3 May 1813.
44   A. C. Thibaudeau, *Mémoires 1799–1815*, Paris, 1913, p. 337. For
general histories of the conspiracy see P. Gaffarel, 'Les complots de Marseille
et de Toulon (1812–1813)', *Annales de la Société d'Etudes provençales*,
1907, and, for a more récent view, M. Agulhon, 'Le rôle politique des
artisans dans le département du Var de la Révolution à la Deuxiéme
République', in *Colloque d'histoire sur l'artisanat et l'apprentissage*, Aix,
1965.
45   AN F7 6591, Complot de Toulon, 1812–13, is the main source for
the analysis that follows.
46   AN BB3 397, Préfet maritime, 5 Apr. 1813.
47   AN F1 CIII Var 3, Liste des membres du collège, 10 Nov. 1810 and
see Coppolani, *Les élections*, pp. 226–33.
48   AD 2M7–3–3, Procès-verbaux des élections, Aug. 1813.
49   AD 2M2–1, Sous-préfet, par intérim, 17 Sept. 1813 and E. Poupé,
'Une enquête ministérielle sur l'esprit public dans le Var en août 1813',
VHG, 1930, pp. 186–96.
50   Lardier, *Histoire populaire*, p. 78 and AN F7 7022, Commissaire
extraordinaire au ministre, 1 Apr. 1814. See also I. Woloch, 'Napoleonic
conscription: state power and civil society', *Past and Present*, 111, 1986, pp.
122–7.
51   Cited in L. Benaerts (ed.), *Les commissaires extraordinaires de
Napoléon 1er en 1814, d'après leur correspondance inédite*, Paris, 1915, p.
37.
52   AD 4M7, Etat de situation, 16 Jan. 1813.
53   AN F1 CIII Var 7, Préfet, 7 Oct. 1813.
54   AN F7 6591, Commissaire de police, 10 Apr. 1813.
55   AM L68(19), Délibérations, 19 Apr. and 8 June 1814 and AD 4M7.
Préfet, 8 June 1814.
56   AP 2A 163, Préfet maritime, 17 April. 1814 and Brun, *Port de
Toulon*, t. 2, p. 613.
57   AN F1 CIII Var 9, Adresses, 6 and 12 May 1814.
58   AN F1 CIII Var 7, Trullet au ministre, 16 May 1815.
59   AN F1 BII Var 3, 4 and 25, Personnel: municipalité de Toulon, an X
(1802–03)–1822 and AD 2M7–5, Liste des candidats, Aug. 1814.
60   AD 4M7, Préfet, 7 Nov. 1814 and, for similar remarks from a
visiting *commissaire du Roi*, AN F7 7028, Commissaire au ministre, 27 May
1814.
61   AN F1 CIII Var 12, Préfet, 19 Jan. 1815.
62   AN F1 CIII Var 12, Préfet, 6 Mar. 1815 and E. Poupé, 'Le
département du Var à la veille des Cent-Jours', *VHG*, 1928, pp. 373–9.
63   AP 2E4 119 and 123, Revues et soldes, 1813 and 1815.
64   AN F1 CIII Var 7, Préfet, 6 Mar. 1815.
65   AP 2A 163, Préfet maritime, 27 and 29 Apr. 1814.
66   AN F7 7028, Commissaire, 27 May 1814.
67   Brun, *Port de Toulon*, t. 2, pp. 625–7.
68   AN F7 9237, Lieutenant de police, 14 May 1815.
69   AP 2A 235, Préfet maritime, 20 Apr. 1815.

70 Henseling (ed.), *Les cahiers*, t. 1, p. 56.
71 AP 2A 165, Préfet maritime, 29 June 1815.
72 Baratier (ed.), *Histoire de la Provence*, pp. 443–4 and Brun, *Port de Toulon*, t. 2, p. 655.
73 AN F1A 554, Roederer au ministre, 5 May 1815.
74 AP 2A 165, Préfet maritime, 14 Apr. 1815 and C. Alleaume, 'Les Cent-Jours dans le Var', *Bull. Drag.*, 1938, pp. 43–4.
75 Brun, *Port de Toulon*, t. 2, p. 652.
76 Alleaume, 'Les Cent-Jours', pp. 59–67.
77 AN F1 BII Var 4, Municipalité de Toulon, 4 May 1815.
78 AN F7 9707, Préfet, no date.
79 AM L68(19), Délibérations, 8 May 1815 and AD 4M8, Pacte fédératif, 22 May 1815.
80 AD F7 9237, Préfet, 2 May 1815.
81 AN F7 9707, Préfet, 10 May 1815.
82 AM L68(19), Délibérations, 15 Apr. 1815.
83 Bluche, *Le plébiscite*, pp. 36–7.
84 AN BII 951B, Relevé des votes, 15 May 1815.
85 AD 2M3–1, Procès-verbaux, May 1815 and L. Honoré, 'Les élections des députés du Var à la Chambre des représentants des Cent-Jours, mai 1815', *VHG*, 1925, pp. 31–4.
86 AN F1 CIII Var 3, Electeurs, May 1815.
87 Alleaume, 'Les Cent-Jours', pp. 108–9.
88 AP 2A 235, Préfet maritime, 5 July 1815.
89 E. Coulet, 'La situation politique et militaire de Toulon en 1815', *Actes du 88e Con. Nat.*, 1963, pp. 35–7.
90 Alleaume, 'Les Cent-Jours', p. 59.
91 AP 2A 166, Préfet maritime, 25 July 1815 and Brun, *Port de Toulon*, t. 2, p. 663.
92 Coulet, 'La situation politique', pp. 55–6.

Conclusion:
The Restoration at Toulon

'Having searched so long for fulfilment, in places where it could not be found, it was only natural that France should turn back to its established traditions . . . to the old ways which guided our forefathers so surely in the past.'

The Second Restoration marked the end of a protracted period of upheaval at Toulon. But was the principal at the College of Toulon, whose words are quoted above, correct in his assertion that it represented a return to the tried and tested principles and practices of the *ancien régime*? The Revolution was over, yet the changes it had wrought in the great naval town were not entirely obliterated. This conclusion will attempt to draw up a more precise balance sheet, by posing that familiar question: how much did the Restoration actually restore?

The aftermath of the Hundred Days brought a much harsher reaction than the First Restoration in 1814. There were immediate scores to be settled, often in violent fashion. At Toulon the royalist mayor and his deputies resumed office, but those former imperial councillors who had acquiesced in Napoleon's return were summarily dismissed. On 21 September 1815 a set of monarchical nominees replaced them. These new councillors were all conservative notables, men who had not only emigrated at the end of 1793, but who had refused to compromise with Bonaparte's regime. They were barristers and *rentiers* rather than merchants or manufacturers.[1] The monarchist police commissioner was not the only person to consider their appointment a mistake. The departing 'Bonapartists' were wealthy and well-known individuals while their successors, by contrast, were 'obscure figures of modest means'.[2]

The sub-prefect of Toulon was soon sacked by the new regime too. De la Tourette was guilty of serving under Napoleon and he was also accused of protecting Toulonnais Bonapartists, like the printer Aurel, from royalist reprisals. He was publicly insulted and his property was vandalised, outrages which he readily blamed upon 'monarchist fanatics' in the town.[3] His resolute attempts to stem the rising tide of reaction led to his replacement in November 1815, when an *émigré* member of the local Aguillon family was provisionally awarded the post.

De la Tourette was the victim of an unofficial, royalist gang, the so-called *comité de recherches*, which was rooting out leading 'Napoleonists' at Toulon. This committee comprised prominent *émigrés* like J. B. Roux, who had been instrumental in the 'federalist' revolt of 1793, and it made some forty arrests in the latter part of 1815.[4] The individuals who were taken into custody received heavy sentences from the local criminal court, which condemned one unfortunate person to four years' incarceration simply for shouting 'Vive Napoléon'. This campaign of intimidation, which included threats of death against leading ex-Jacobins like the former parliamentarian and regicide Escudier, prompted up to 1,000 'revolutionary sympathisers' to leave the town, at least for a while.[5] Yet the reaction at Toulon was relatively mild, especially in comparison to the bloody White Terror raging elsewhere in the Midi. Toulonnais royalists simply lacked the weight and numbers to carry their vengeance as far as they would have liked.

The weeding-out of suspect civilian officials was accompanied by a thoroughgoing purge of military personnel. Any officer who had shown the slightest sympathy for Napoleon during the Hundred Days was deemed guilty of 'treason and rebellion' and immediately dismissed.[6] Earlier in 1815 *émigré* officers had supplemented their imperial counterparts; now they comprehensively supplanted them. At Toulon over 100 naval officers were sacked. Only four out of the thirty captains enlisted in 1816 had served under Bonaparte in 1813. Nearly all of the newcomers were elderly aristocrats, who had been members of the 'grand corps' at the end of the *ancien régime*.[7] The nobility thus recovered a commanding place in the navy, which was administratively reorganised by bringing back *intendants* in the dockyards, instead of Napoleonic prefects. Many of the officers who were dismissed continued to reside in Toulon, their bitterness 'all the greater as they watched their successors arrive and take their places'.[8] It was precisely among these disaffected, unemployed ex-officers that the Carbonarist Armand Vallé sought support for an abortive conspiracy at Toulon in 1822.[9]

Redundancies at the dockyards, both in the officer corps and among administrative personnel, were a product of post-war

economies as well as royalist *revanche*. The navy now received a
much smaller share of government expenditure and, as a consequence, just two frigates were retained in commission at Toulon. The
port's naval council had no alternative but to cut the direct labour
force to a mere 1,341 men and institute a four-day week.[10] Even so,
funds were failing to materialise and in August 1815, with
shopkeepers in the town refusing further credit, the municipal
council raised a loan of 50,000 *francs* to provide some transitional
relief.[11] Such misery conjured up shades of the late 1780s, especially
since in 1816 the crisis at the Arsenal was accompanied by a poor
harvest and a rise of 50 per cent in bread prices.[12] On this occasion,
however, Toulon remained calm.

Such an adverse situation, arriving in the wake of two decades of
almost uninterrupted naval activity, only served to emphasise the
dependence of the community upon the dockyards. As a 'company
town' Toulon had relatively few autonomous enterprises to lose;
nonetheless, the revolutionary turmoil had destroyed a good many
independent economic activities. In the short run naval mobilisation
compensated for the damage inflicted upon local manufacturing and
commerce, but the port was left dreadfully exposed when peace
eventually returned. During the second half of 1816, for example,
there were less than fifty sailings a month in and out of Toulon,
compared to well over 100 a few years earlier.[13] The places of origin
or destinations of these visiting ships were all located on the
Mediterranean littoral, with the exception of one or two sorties to
the Channel ports and a solitary expedition to the Levant. Although
the ending of hostilities permitted free passage to the North Sea,
neither Dutch nor Baltic trade revived. The growing reliance of
long-haul commerce upon intermediaries at Marseille was consequently confirmed.

Few naval stores were needed at the Arsenal, so remaining trade
was concentrated upon the import of foodstuffs, with little to export
in return. More than two-thirds of the vessels which entered Toulon
left unladen. Those which did depart with freight were carrying
familiar items – wine, brandy, olive oil and capers – but in smaller
quantities than ever before. Apart from brandy none of these items
could be considered part of the manufacturing base at Toulon, which
continued to suffer severe reductions. Tanning, which provided
employment for forty workers during the heyday of the Empire,
occupied a mere sixteen men after 1815.[14] Soap-boiling, the premier

activity at the end of the *ancien régime*, supported only four workers as output declined sharply between 1816 and 1819. Denied orders from the dockyards paper-making had once again disappeared. Finally, woollen production was in the hands of just two masters and six artisans in 1818; its stagnation was blamed upon the high cost of raw materials and poor sales.

This depressing situation was mirrored in the movement of population at Toulon. After 1815, for the first time in forty years, the annual number of births registered in the town fell below the 1,000 mark. The total of marriages, which had been running at over 300 per annum between 1811 and 1815, was likewise reduced, to an average of 240 in the following quinquennium. Immigration into the port rapidly diminished too. In 1816, for example, 42 per cent of bridegrooms were Toulonnais by birth, as opposed to 36 per cent in 1809, and two years later the native contingent had risen to almost half. In 1816 the proportion of male partners drawn from beyond the boundaries of Provence remained at an elevated 27 per cent, similar to 1785; by 1818, however, the share of these 'foreigners' had fallen to 18 per cent, a level close to that of the 1760s. Michel Vovelle, in a similar demographic survey of Chartres, also discovered that by 1820 'few traces of the revolutionary upheaval remained; its consequences seem to have been relatively short-lived'.[15]

The level of population at Toulon was, in fact, much the same under the Restoration as it had been on the eve of the Revolution. A reliable census, carried out in 1821, recorded 29,912 fixed, civilian inhabitants for the town and its adjacent territory.[16] The intra-mural total of 25,525 persons represents an increase of just 2,390 over the comparable figure for 1791, an almost negligible advance over a period of thirty years. Toulon fared rather better than neighbouring Marseille and other commercial cities, which experienced overall decline during the same decades.[17] Yet demographic fluctuation as a result of mobilisation was a familiar wartime experience in the naval town. None of the huge increases which occurred at Toulon under the Revolution or the Empire proved lasting and the threshold of 30,000 peacetime inhabitants remained to be crossed.

Relatively few profound changes appear to have taken place in the social profile of Toulon either. To judge by the survey of adult males undertaken in 1810, the pre-revolutionary, socio-professional structure had altered only slightly.[18] The service element of military officers and administrators, at Arsenal and garrison, contributed almost 10 per cent of the heads of household and the urban bourgeoisie a similar proportion, both before and after the Revolution. The popular classes were a little more numerous in 1810 than in either 1765 or 1791, but not significantly so. After the tremendous upheaval of the intervening years a rather more pronounced structural shift might have been expected. Instead, the essential contours reveal a remarkable durability over a period of almost half a century.

Broad comparisons of this sort, conducted solely on the basis of occupational data, can be supplemented by a more refined analysis of the upper echelons of Toulonnais society. In 1812, among the thirty biggest taxpayers (*plus imposés*) resident at Toulon, there were no less than ten government officials and two naval officers, as opposed to just seven in a similar sample for 1791.[19] At the later date two of the doctors on the list were employed by the navy, while the notary Senès had been sub-prefect. This close identification of propertied wealth with service to the state was also reflected in registers for a forced loan, which was raised by General Brune during the Hundred Days.[20] Of twenty-eight males upon whom this emergency tax was levied at the highest rate, eight were professional administrators and three were active naval officers, not to mention Senès, recently reinstated as sub-prefect.

However, the increased weight of officialdom was, for the most part, a transitory product of the war effort. The electoral census of 1819, which was based on a very narrow franchise according to fiscal criteria, included only four administrators and a single military officer among the twenty-six *plus imposés* at Toulon.[21] Merchants had raised their share in the taxpaying elite from one third of the places, in 1812, to almost half in 1819. This represented a continuation of the progress they had made since 1791 when they formed only a quarter of the *plus imposés*. The prominence that mercantile elements had achieved during the Revolution, rising from the ranks of retailers by purchasing former ecclesiastical and *émigré* properties, was amply confirmed under the Restoration. The promotion of merchants in the social hierarchy at Toulon was a major, lasting feature of the period between 1750 and 1820.

In this respect, at least, there was a 'bourgeois revolution' in the naval town. The former 'privileged orders' at Toulon had lost what segments of the middle classes gained. The Church fared especially badly, having been entirely expropriated during the upheaval.

Bishop and chapter disappeared for good, while only the teaching orders returned in the nineteenth century as representatives of the once important monastic communities. Nor were nobles prominent in civilian society after the Restoration. Admittedly the indigenous Toulonnais nobility was a small one, but there were four noblemen among the thirty *plus imposés* of 1791. In 1819 their absence from the electoral register was a reflection of the general decline of aristocratic property-ownership in the town. An imperial survey showed that most scions of the *ancien-régime* nobility had returned to Toulon by 1812, but only the Missiessy, Antrechaux and Chaubry families retained much wealth.[22]

Where office-holding in the municipality was concerned a retreat to pre-revolutionary patterns was more apparent. The days of the popular movement and lower-class involvement in the municipal administration had been relatively short-lived. Artisans and shopkeepers were less prominent under the Directory and they disappeared entirely with the Consulate. The 100 *plus imposés* from whom personnel were selected, under the Restoration as during the Empire, may be compared to the 113 individuals who were eligible for the posts of consul and councillor under the *ancien régime*. Wealth alone, rather than a combination of occupation and wealth, determined eligibility to office in the post-revolutionary period. Yet few affluent retailers were actually appointed by the restored monarchy, which preferred to select *rentiers* and members of the liberal professions to serve on the municipal council. No less than ten of the thirty-five individuals nominated in 1816 had been members of the old oligarchy in 1788. The Bourbons also revived the practice of placing retired military officers or administrators at the head of the municipality, as mayor and *adjoints*. After 1815, as before 1789, the same justification was employed: the need to maintain 'a good understanding between town and Arsenal'.[23]

These Toulonnais notables hoped to recover the local independence which they had enjoyed at the beginning of the revolutionary decade, but their expectations were disappointed. The Revolution ultimately facilitated rather than halted the advance of centralisation in France. The Napoleonic system of nominated municipal officials was perpetuated by the restored monarchy and so was close administrative control of expenditure.[24] Central government supervised policy-making, while it was left to mayor and deputies to conduct day-to-day business. The municipal council was restricted

Table 12 *The occupational structure of the highest taxpayers at Toulon, 1791–1819*

Occupation	1791		An XI (1803)		1812		1815		1819	
	No.	*%*	*No.*	*%*	*No.*	*%*	*No.*	*%*	*No.*	*%*
Military officers	5	15.2	1	3.0	2	6.1	3	10.3	1	3.8
Leading administrators	2	6.1	5	15.2	10	30.3	8	27.6	4	15.4
Rentiers, retired officers & officials	8	24.2	10	30.3	4	12.1	3	10.3	8	30.8
Barristers & notaries	8	24.2	1	3.0	2	6.1	2	6.9	1	3.8
Medical professions	1	3.0	1	3.0	3	9.1	–	–	–	–
Merchants	8	24.2	12	36.4	11	33.3	10	34.5	12	46.2
Retailers	1	3.0	2	6.1	1	3.0	2	6.9	–	–
No profession indicated	–	–	1	3.0	–	–	1	3.4	–	–
Total	33		33		33		29		26	

Sources: AM L202, Matrice foncière, 1791; AD 2M2–5, Les 550 plus imposés parmi les 600 plus imposés du Var, 26 floréal XI (16 May 1803); AN F1 BII Var 25, Les cent plus imposés de Toulon, 23 Apr. 1812; AM L68(19), Emprunt forcé sur les richards, 3 July 1815; and AD 2M2–6, Les membres du collège électoral du département du Var, 13 July 1819.

to a consultative role, timetabled to meet just once a year to review the budget; prefectoral permission was required for any additional assemblies. In 1811, for example, there were only eight meetings, as opposed to an average of 200 per annum during the 1790s. Though greater frequency of assembly returned after 1815 the municipal council failed to regain its former importance. Dissatisfied with their lot as unpaid civil servants, town councillors at Toulon became less assiduous in the exercise of their duties: attendance at meetings rarely rose above 50 per cent.

On the other hand the restoration of order to municipal finances, which had completely broken down in the Revolution, was achieved without taking too much from the notables' pockets. Their wealth was no longer protected from direct taxation to the extent that it had been under the *ancien régime*, but local revenues were derived indirectly via the *octroi*, the Napoleonic successor to the city tolls abolished in 1790. Nor was municipal expenditure excessive. Facilities for education and poor relief were recreated at Toulon but, contrary to the high hopes of the revolutionary era, they were re-established at a modest level which, as in the past, offered no more than minimal provision.

The church continued to play a small part in education but, notwithstanding the clergy's efforts to recover lost ground, Toulonnais society as a whole had become more secularised. Shifts in outlook are notoriously difficult to measure and attitudes towards traditional values of religion or social hierarchy had been evolving even before the Revolution occurred. But the material losses which the church suffered, together with the inroads of freemasonry, must be regarded as significant. At least five masonic lodges survived the turmoil which accompanied the collapse of the Empire and, in 1816, a correspondent from the *Parfaite Alliance* boldly declared: 'Toulon is a powerful and faithful centre of Enlightenment.'[25]

The profound impact of the Revolution upon Toulon is not to be denied, especially where *mentalités* are concerned, for the revolutionary decade represented an historic apprenticeship in democratic politics. Yet in future the struggle for those elusive but essential ideals of liberty, equality and fraternity was engaged in a rather different context. Between 1750 and 1820 areas of continuity can be identified as easily as elements of change, but the middle decades of the nineteenth century witnessed a more radical break with the past.[26] During the 1840s the application of new naval technology began to turn the Age of Sail into the Age of Steam, with enormous consequences for the composition, recruitment and behaviour of the dockyard labour-force. Then, in the 1850s, under the Second Empire, the walled straitjacket around Toulon was finally cast off and the population rose decisively above the pre-industrial ceiling of 30,000 inhabitants. The domination of the mighty Arsenal remained the paramount feature of Toulon, but its pre-eminence was now exercised in a physical and social environment far-removed from the era of War and Revolution at the end of the eighteenth century.

Notes

1   AN F1 BII Var 4, Décret, 26 Aug. 1815 and AM L68(19), Délibérations, 21 Sept. 1815.
2   AM F7 9237, Commissaire de police, 22 Sept. 1815.
3   AM F7 9237, Sous-préfet, 2 Sept. and 9 Oct. 1815.
4   AM F7 9237, Sous-préfet, 22 Aug. and Sept. 1815 and C. Alleaume, 'La terreur blanche dans le Var', *Bull. Drag.*, 1947, pp. 8–13.
5   AN BB18 877, Troubles à Toulon, 18 May 1816 and AM L376 and 377, Désordres politiques, 1815–16.
6   J. Bernardini, *Le port de Toulon et sa marine de 1815 à 1830. La reconstitution de la flotte en Méditerranée*, Toulon, 1970, p. 10.
7   AP 2E4 125, Revues et soldes, 1816. Bernardini, *Le port de Toulon*, p. 111, states that in 1819 over 90 per cent of all *capitaines de vaisseau* in the French navy were nobles.
8   AN F7 9237, Commissaire de police, 9 Feb. 1816.
9   Agulhon (ed.), *Histoire de Toulon*, p. 218.
10   AP 3A1 18, Conseil, 11 and 25 Oct. 1815.
11   AM L68(19), Délibérations, 15 Aug. 1815 and AN BB3 427, Préfet maritime, 18 Aug. 1815.
12   AM L68(20), Délibérations, 6 Dec. 1817 and Fournel, *Les problèmes du ravitaillement*, p. 164.
13   AN F12 1772, Mouvements du port de Toulon, 1816.
14   AD 16M1–3, Statistique industrielle, 1815–24.
15   M. Vovelle, 'Chartres et le pays chartrain: quelques aspects démographiques', *CHESRF, Mémoires et documents*, 14, 1962, p. 154.
16   AD 11M2–1, Recensement, 1821.
17   Dupâquier, *La population française*, pp. 91–2; W. Sewell, *Structure and mobility. The men and women of Marseille, 1820–1870*, Cambridge, 1985, pp. 1–4 and various essays in M. Reinhard (ed.), 'Contributions à l'histoire démographique de la Révolution française', *CHESRF*, Mémoires et documents, 18, 1965.
18   AM L132, Registre des habitants, 1810.
19   AN F1 BII Var 25, Les cent plus imposés de Toulon, 23 Apr. 1812 and AM L202, Foncière, 1791.
20   AM L68(19), Emprunt forcé, 13 July 1815.

21 AD 2M2–6, Liste des électeurs, 17 Nov. 1819.
22 AD 1M14–1, Statistique de l'ancienne noblesse, 1813 and C. Alleaume, 'Napoléon premier et l'ancienne classe nobiliaire', *Bull. Drag.*, 1935, pp. 46–8.
23 AN F1 BII Var 4, Décret, 12 June 1816.
24 F. Ponteil, *Les institutions de la France de 1814 à 1870*, Paris, 1966, pp. 30–2.
25 BN FM2 438, La Parfaite Alliance, correspondance, 11 May 1816.
26 See Agulhon (ed.), *Histoire de Toulon*, p. 211 *et seq*. 'L'essor de la ville contemporaine' and the same author's *Une ville ouvrière*. Sewell, *Structure and mobility*, p. 18, makes a similar comment about the nineteenth-century transformation of Marseille, though in the *port de commerce* 'unprecedented growth' began earlier than at Toulon.

Appendix: The socio-professional classification of adult males in eighteenth-century Toulon

1. Military officers in army and navy
2. Administrators attached to the royal services
3. Civilian nobility, and retired officers and administrators
4. *Rentiers* (bourgeois)
5. Legal professions: barristers, notaries and procurators
6. Medical professions: doctors, surgeons and apothecaries
7. Merchants (*négociants*)
8. Retailers (*marchands notables*): drapers, ironmongers, goldsmiths, grocers, etc.
9. Clerks, including schoolmasters and actors
10. Fabrication and sale of food, and provision of lodgings: butchers, bakers, innkeepers, *restaurateurs*, etc.
11. Fabrication and sale of clothing and textiles: tailors, shoemakers, weavers, wigmakers, etc.
12. Construction and maintenance work: masons, house carpenters, painters, tilers, etc.
13. Metal-working: fabrication, sale and maintenance: locksmiths, tinsmiths, blacksmiths, gunsmiths, etc.
14. Fabrication and sale of instruments and household goods: saddlers, glaziers, potters, toolmakers, etc.
15. Shopkeepers (without other qualification), and those engaged in transportation
16. Dockyard craftsmen (the 'reserved' professions): ships' carpenters, sailmakers, pulley-makers, caulkers, drillers, coopers, sawyers and ropers
17. Fishermen, sailors and gunners
18. Rural occupations (*ménagers* and *paysans*)
19. Unskilled labourers: day labourers, porters and watchmen
20. No profession: invalids, beggars and *sans profession* on lists

Bibliography

ARCHIVAL SOURCES

1. Archives municipales de Toulon

(a) *Ancien régime*   Sadly, O. Teissier, *Inventaire sommaire des archives communales de Toulon antérieures à 1790*, Toulon, 1866–67, offers a misleading guide to extant materials since so much has been lost since his inventory was compiled.

Series AA, Actes constitutifs et politiques de la commune; BB, Administration communale; CC, Impôts et comptabilité; GG, Cultes, instruction et assistance publique; HH, Agriculture, industrie et commerce; II, Documents divers.

(b) *Revolution and Empire*   A. J. Parés, *Inventaire numérique des archives communales de Toulon postérieures à 1789: Révolution et Empire, 1789–1815*, Toulon, 1934.

Series L, Révolution et Empire. This series is numbered consecutively, as in the notes to my text, but there are internal divisions, under letter headings, as follows:

Subseries A3, Etats provinciaux et Etats généraux; B, Actes de l'administration départementale; D1, Délibérations du conseil municipal; D3, Correspondance municipale; D6, Représentants en mission; F1, Population; F2, Industrie et commerce; F3, Agriculture; F4, Subsistances; H1, Affaires militaires; H2, Marine; H3, Evénements politiques; H4, Evénements locaux; H5, Milice bourgeoise – Garde nationale; I2, Police générale; I3, Emigrés et suspects; I4, Clubs et sociétés; K, Elections, personnel et cérémonies municipales; P, Cultes; Q, Assistance et prévoyance;

R, Instruction publique.
Series L2, Période sectionnaire, anti-conventionelle, 1793: a surprisingly rich series, despite the fact that much was destroyed or dispersed when the rebellion collapsed. Records relating to the all-important Comité général des sections are rather sparse, though some registers are to be found in the manuscripts collection of the Cornell University Library. See *French books and manuscripts, 1700–1830,* Ithaca, 1981.

(c) *Etat civil* (including parish registers), 1720–1820.

2. Archives du Port de Toulon
N. Fourcadier, *Guide du fonds des Archives du Port de Toulon. Révolution et Empire, 1789–1815,* Toulon, 1968. The series employed are the same for the *ancien régime.*

Series A, Commandement de la marine: Subseries 1A1, Correspondance; 1A2, Correspondance; 3A1, Conseils de marine; 4A1, Officiers de marine.

Series E, Services administratifs: 2E4, Revues et soldes; 5E, Marchés.

Series G, Personnel: Subseries 2G1, Matricules des ouvriers.

Series L, Contrôle de l'administration de la marine: Subseries 1L, Commissions et brevets.

3. Archives départementales du Var (at Draguignan)
Few useful documents were discovered in the old regime series, for the archives of the *Intendance de Provence* are located at Marseille (see below). By contrast, the revolutionary series L and general administration from 1800 (series M) were especially important. See J. J. Letrait, *Répertoire numérique de la série L, administration et tribunaux de l'époque révolutionnaire, 1789–an VIII,* Draguignan, 1959, and *Répertoire numérique de la série M, administration général, personnel, élections, affaires politiques, an VIII–1940; questions économiques et sociales, an VIII–1951,* Draguignan, no date.

Series L, Administration et tribunaux de l'époque révolutionnaire: Subseries 1L, Administration; 2L, Tribunaux.

Series M, Personnel and administration générale à partir de 1800: Subseries 1M, Personnel; 2M, Elections; 4M, Comptes rendus; 11M, Population; 16M, Industrie.

Series J, Dons et acquisitions.
Series Q, Domaines.
Series T, Enseignement.
Series V, Cultes.
Series X, Etablissements de bienfaisance (though the *archives hospitalières de Toulon*, which have only recently been deposited at AD, are catalogued separately).

4. *Archives départementales des Bouches-du-Rhône*

(a) Aix-en-Provence
Series B, Cours et jurisdictions.

(b) Marseille
Series C, Fonds de l'intendance.
Series L, Révolution.

5. *Archives nationales*
Series AD, Imprimés.
Series AF, Papiers d'état: Subseries AF II, Comité de Salut Public; AFIII, Directoire exécutif; AF IV, Secrétairie d'état impérial.
Series B, Elections et votes: Subseries Ba, Cahiers de doléances, 1789; BII, Plébiscites, 1793–1815; BIII, Procès-verbaux d'élection, 1789.
Series C, Assemblées nationales.
Series D, Missions des représentants en mission et comités des assemblées: Subseries D1, Missions des représentants; DIV, Comité de constitution; DIV bis, Comité de division; DXXIX, Comité des rapports; DXL, Comité des pétitions.
Series F, Versements des ministères et des administrations qui en dépendent: Subseries F1 A, Circulaires du ministre de l'intérieur: items relating to 1815; F1 BII, Personnel administratif; F1 CIII, Esprit public et élections; F7, Police générale; F12, Commerce et industrie; F15, Secours; F20, Statistique.

6. *Archives de la Marine* (at the Archives nationales)
Subseries B3, Correspondance avec le Port de Toulon – ancien régime; Subseries BB3, Correspondance avec le Port de Toulon – postérieure à 1789.

7. *Bibliothèque nationale*
Series F.M. Fonds maçonnique.

8. *Public Record Office, London*
FO 95, Reports from the Mediterranean, 1793.
HO 50, Home Office despatches, 1793.
PC1 124, Materials relating to the occupation of Toulon.

Printed primary sources

M. J. Abeille, *Notes et pièces officielles relatives aux événements de Marseille et de Toulon*, no place, no date.

C. F. Achard, *Dictionnaire de la Provence et du Comté-Venaissin*, 4 vols., Marseille, 1785–87.

G. Antrechaus, *Relation de la peste dont la ville de Toulon fut affligée en MDCCXXI*, Paris, 1756.

Archives parlementaires de 1787 à 1860. Recueil complet des débats législatifs et politiques des chambres françaises (première série, 1787–1799), 92 vols., Paris, 1862–1980.

F. A. Aulard (ed.), *La société des Jacobins*, 6 vols., Paris, 1889–97.

F. A. Aulard (ed.), *Recueil des actes du comité de salut public, avec la correspondance officielle des représentants en mission*, 30 vols., Paris, 1889–1951.

F. A. Aulard (ed.), *L'état de la France en l'an VIII et l'an IX*, Paris, 1897.

P. Barras, *Mémoires*, ed. G. Duruy, 4 vols., Paris, 1895.

L. Benaerts (ed.), *Les commissaires extraordinaires de Napoléon 1er en 1814, d'après leur correspondance inédite*, Paris, 1915.

G. de Brécy, *La révolution royaliste de Toulon en 1793 pour le rétablissement de la monarchie*, Paris, 1814.

R. Busquet, A. J. Parès and L. Roberty (eds.), *Mémoires de Louis Richaud sur la révolte de Toulon et l'émigration*, Marseille, 1930.

G. Elliot, *The life and letters of Sir Gilbert Elliot, first Earl of Minto, from 1751 to 1804*, 3 vols., London, 1874.

J. J. Expilly, *Dictionnaire géographique, historique et politique des Gaules et de la France*, 6 vols., Paris, 1762–70.

J. Fauchet, *Statistique du département du Var*, Paris, an X.

J. Fonvielle, *Mémoires historiques*, 4 vols., Paris, 1824.

S. Fréron, *Mémoire historique sur la réaction royale et sur les massacres du Midi*, Paris, an IV.

E. Garcin, *Dictionnaire historique et topographique de la Provence ancienne et moderne*, 2 vols., Draguignan, 1835.

L. Henseling (ed.), *Les cahiers de P. Letuaire*, 2 vols., Toulon, 1910–14.

V. Hugues, *Acte d'accusation contre les complices de la trahison de Toulon*, Paris, an II.

T. Imbert, *Précis historique sur les événements de Toulon en 1793*, Paris, 1816.

M. Isnard, *Discours sur la situation du Midi*, Paris, an IV.

M. Isnard, *Isnard à Fréron*, Paris, an IV.

M. de Limon, *La vie et le martyre de Louis XVI, suivi d'un exposé des événements de Toulon*, Toulon, 1793.

P. V. Malouet, *Mémoires*, Paris, 2 vols., 1874.

L. G. Marquis, *Considérations médico-chirurgicales sur les maladies qui ont régné pendant et après le siège de Toulon*, Paris, an XII.

J. E. Michel, *Histoire de l'armée départementale des Bouches-du-Rhône, de l'entrée des escadres des puissances coalisées dans Toulon et de leur sortie de cette place*, Paris, an V.

A. L. Millin, *Voyage dans les départements du Midi de la France*, 4 vols., Paris, 1807–11.

Moniteur, Ré-impression de l'ancien Moniteur, mai 1789–novembre 1799, 29 vols., Paris, 1840–45.

A. T. Z. Pons, *Mémoires pour servir à l'histoire de la ville de Toulon en 1793*, Paris, 1825.

E. Poupé (ed.), *Lettres de Barras et Fréron en mission dans le Midi*, Draguignan, 1910.

E. Poupé (ed.), 'Journal d'un ponantais de l'Apollon', *La Révolution française*, LX, 1911.

E. Poupé (ed.), *Observations d'un provençal sur le voyage de M. Millin dans le Var*, Toulon, 1931.

J. M. Puissant, *Toute la France a été trompée sur l'événement de Toulon en 1793. Voici la vérité*, Paris, an V.

Recueil des lois relatives à la marine et aux colonies, Paris, 1789–1815.

F. Rocquain (ed.), *L'état de la France au 18 brumaire*, Paris, 1874.

J. Saint-André, *Rapport sur la trahison de Toulon*, Paris, 1793.

A. C. Thibaudeau, *Mémoires, 1799–1815*, Paris, 1913.

A. Young, *Travels in France and Italy during the years 1787, 1788 and 1789*, ed. C. Maxwell, Cambridge, 1929.

Works of reference

Archives municipales de Toulon, *La décennie révolutionnaire Toulon: inventaire des délibérations du conseil municipal*, Toulon, 1989.

C. Badet, R. Bertrand, B. Cousin and P. Santoni, *Guide des sources régionales pour l'histoire de la Révolution française. Alpes de Haute-Provence, Hautes-Alpes, Alpes-Maritimes, Bouches-du-Rhône, Var, Vaucluse*, Aix, 1987.

E. Baratier, G. Duby and E. Hildesheimer (eds.), *Atlas historique, Provence, Comtat-Venaissin, principauté d'Orange, comté de Nice, principauté de Monaco*, Paris, 1969.

P. Caron, *Manuel pratique pour l'étude de Révolution française*, Paris, 1947.

O. Connelly (ed.), *Historical dictionary of Napoleonic France, 1799–1815*, London, 1985.

M. Fleury and L. Henry, *Nouveau manuel de dépouillement et d'exploitation de l'état civil ancien*, Paris, 1965.

B. Gille, *Les sources statistiques de l'histoire de la France: des enquêtes du XVIIIe siècle à 1870*, Paris, 1964.

J. Godechot, *Les institutions de la France sous la Révolution et L'Empire*, 2nd ed., Paris, 1968.

B. F. Hyslop (ed.), *A guide to the general cahiers of 1789*, 2nd ed., New York, 1967.

M. Marion, *Dictionnaire des institutions de la France aux XVIIe et XVIIIe siècles*, Paris, 1923.

F. Mistral, *Lou trésor dou félibrige, ou dictionnaire provençal–français*, 3rd ed., 2 vols., Aix, 1968.

F. Ponteil, *Les institutions de la France de 1814 à 1870*, Paris, 1966.

M. Reinhard, *Etude de la population pendant la Révolution et l'Empire*, 2 vols., Gap, 1961.

J. Salvarelli, *Les administrateurs du département du Var, 1790–1897*, Draguignan, 1897.

S. F. Scott and B. Rothaus (eds.), *Historical dictionary of the French Revolution, 1789–1799*, 2 vols., London, 1985.

Unpublished secondary sources

M. Corda, 'Les hospices civiles de Toulon', Bibliothèque municipale de Toulon, 1884.

M. Crook, 'A social history of Toulon, 1760–1790', Ph.D.,

University of London, 1977.

C. Ferrucci, 'La vie communale à Toulon de 1750 à 1788', mémoire pour la maîtrise, 2 vols., University of Nice, 1970.

M. Henry, 'Affrontements politiques à Toulon, 1789–1793', mémoire pour la maîtrise, 2 vols., University of Aix-en-Provence, 1969.

C. Morin, 'Le problème des subsistances à Toulon, seconde moitié du XVIIIᵉ siècle', mémoire pour la maîtrise, University of Nice, 1970.

G. Parker, 'The urban geography of Toulon', M.A., University of Wales, Aberystwyth, 1960.

S. Pieuchet, 'Les enfants trouvés et abandonnés Toulon au XIXᵉ siècle', mémoire pour la maîtrise, University of Aix-en-Provence, 1970.

E. Strauss, 'The mentality of counter-revolution at Toulon, July–August 1793', senior dissertation, Princeton University, 1972.

M. Vergé, 'Les officiers du grand corps à Toulon au XVIIIᵉ siècle', mémoire pour la maitrise, University of Nice, 1973.

G. Vitse, 'La contre-révolution à Toulon en 1793', mémoire pour la mâtrise, University of Nice, 1970.

C. Vitse, 'L'émigré toulonnais de la Révolution à la Restauration: essai de caractérisation', mémoire pour la maîtrise, University of Nice, 1972.

Published secondary sources

1. *Works relating to Toulon and Provence*
F. d'Agay, *Grands notables du Premier Empire*, t. 18, *Var*, Paris, 1988.

M. Agulhon, 'Le recrutement du personnel ouvrier de l'arsenal de Toulon de 1800 à 1848', *Prov. hist.*, XII, 1962.

M. Agulhon, 'Le rôle politique des artisans dans le département du Var de la Révolution à la Deuxième République', in *Colloque d'histoire sur l'artisanat et l'apprentissage*, Aix, 1965.

M. Agulhon, *Pénitents et francs-maçons de l'ancienne Provence*, Paris, 1968.

M. Agulhon, *La vie sociale en Provence intérieure au lendemain de la Révolution*, Paris, 1970.

M. Agulhon, *Une ville ouvrière au temps du socialisme utopique.*

Toulon de 1815 à 1851, Paris, 1970.

M. Agulhon, 'Mise au point sur les classes sociales en Provence', *Prov. hist.*, XX, 1970.

M. Agulhon, 'Les notables du Var sous le Consulat', *RHMC*, XVII, 1970.

M. Agulhon (ed.), *Histoire de Toulon*, Toulouse, 1980.

C. Alleaume, 'Napoléon premier et l'ancienne classe nobiliaire', *Bull. Drag.*, 1935.

C. Alleaume, 'Les Cent-Jours dans le Var', *Bull. Drag.*, 1938.

C. Alleaume, 'Joseph Fauchet, premier préfet du Var', *Bull. Drag.*, 1940–41.

C. Alleaume, 'La terreur blanche dans le Var', *Bull. Drag.*, 1947.

E. Baratier, *La démographie provençale du XIIIe au XVIIe siècle (avec chiffres de comparaison pour le XVIIIe siècle)*, Paris, 1961.

E. Baratier (ed.), *Histoire de la Provence*, Toulouse, 1969.

E. Baratier (ed.), *Histoire de Marseille*, Toulouse, 1973.

L. Baudoin, *Histoire générale de la Seyne-sur-mer et de son port*, La Seyne, 1965.

J. Bernardini, *Le port de Toulon et sa marine de 1815 à 1830. La reconstitution de la flotte en Méditerranée*, Toulon, 1970.

M. Bernos *et al.*, *Histoire d'Aix-en-Provence*, Aix, 1977.

M. Bordes, 'L'administration des communautés d'habitants en Provence et dans le comté de Nice à la fin de l'ancien régime: traits communs et diversité', *Ann. Midi*, LXXXIV, 1972.

M. Bordes, 'Le rôle des sub-délégués en Provence au dix-huitième siècle', *Prov. hist.*, XXIII, 1973.

P. Boulanger, 'Salaires et revenus des équipages des navires marchands provençaux durant le XVIIIe siècle', *Prov. hist.*, XXX, 1980.

L. Bourilly, 'Historique du Collège de Toulon, depuis sa fondation jusqu'à son érection en lycée', *Bull. Var*, 1901.

V. F. Brun, *Les guerres maritimes de la France. Port de Toulon, ses armements, son administration depuis son origine jusqu'à nos jours*, 2 vols., Paris, 1861.

C. Carrière, 'Le commerce des eaux de vie à Toulon au XVIIIe siècle', *Prov. hist.*, XII, 1962.

C. Carrière, *Négociants marseillais au XVIIIe siècle. Contribution à l'étude des économies maritimes*, 2 vols., Marseille, 1973.

C. Carrière, M. Courdurié and F. Rebuffat, *Marseille, ville morte: la peste de 1720*, Marseille, 1968.

P. Cottin, *Toulon et les anglais en 1793, d'aprés des documents inédits*, Paris, 1898.

E. Coulet, 'Les fugitifs de Toulon et les anglais dans la Méditerranée après la rébellion de 1793', *Bull. Drag.*, 1929.

E. Coulet, 'Un administrateur hyèrois pendant la Révolution, 1789–1796: François-Thomas Jaume', *VHG*, 1937.

E. Coulet, *Le comité général des sections de Toulon, 13 juillet–17 décembre 1793*, Toulon, 1960.

E. Coulet, 'La situation économique de Toulon pendant la rébellion (juillet–décembre 1793)', *Prov. hist.*, XII, 1962.

E. Coulet, 'La situation politique et militaire de Toulon en 1815', *Actes du 88ᵉ Con. Nat.*, 1963.

E. Coulet, 'Le massacre des administrateurs du Var, juillet 1792', *Actes du 89ᵉ Con. Nat.*, 1964.

M. Crook, 'Federalism and the French Revolution: the revolt of Toulon in 1793', *History*, LXV, 1980.

M. Crook, 'Rouges et blancs à Toulon: l'essor et la chute du jacobinisme populaire dans le port de guerre de 1790 à 1793', *Prov. hist.*, XXXVII, 1987.

M. Crook, *Journées révolutionnaires à Toulon*, Nîmes, 1989.

M. Crook, 'Les élections aux Etats-généraux de 1789 et les origines de la pratique électorale de la Révolution', in R. Chagny (ed.), *Aux origines provinciales de la Révolution*, Grenoble, 1990.

M. Crook, 'Un nouvel espace politique sous la Révolution: les sections de Toulon, 1790–1793', in P. Joutard (ed.), *L'espace et le temps reconstruits. La Révolution française, une révolution des mentalités et des cultures ?*, Aix, 1990.

M. Crook, 'Une absence? Religion et contre-révolution à Toulon en 1793', in *Religion, révolution, contre-révolution dans le Midi*, Nîmes, 1990.

M. Crook, 'The people at the polls: electoral behaviour in revolutionary Toulon, 1789–1799', *French History*, 5, 1991.

M. Cubells, 'La politique d'anoblissement de la monarchie en Provence de 1715 à 1789', *Ann. Midi*, VIC, 1982.

M. Cubells, 'Les mouvements populaires du printemps 1789 en Provence', *Prov. hist.*, XXXVI, 1986.

M. Cubells, *Les horizons de la liberté. Naissance de la Révolution en Provence*, Aix, 1987.

E. Davin, *La prostitution à Toulon*, Toulon, 1940.

M. Derlange, 'En Provence au XVIIIᵉ siècle: la représentation des habitants aux conseils généraux des communautés', *Ann. Midi*, LXXXVI, 1974.

C. Derobert-Ratel, *Institutions et vie municipale à Aix-en-Provence sous la Révolution (1789–an VIII)*, Millau, 1981.

P. Dubois, *Les Capucins dans le Midi: les Capucins varois, Toulon, 1588–1791–1864*, Toulon, 1966.

P. Dubois, *La vie pénible et laborieuse de Jean-Joseph Esmieu, marchand–colporteur en Provence sous la Révolution*, no place, 1967.

J. Egret, 'La pré-révolution en Provence, 1787–1789', *AHRF*, XXVI, 1954.

F. X. Emmanuelli, *Pouvoir royal et vie régionale en Provence au déclin de la monarchie. Psychologie, pratiques administratives, défrancisation de l'intendance d'Aix, 1745–1790*, 2 vols., Lille, 1974.

F. X. Emmanuelli, 'Introduction à l'histoire du XVIIIᵉ siècle communal en Provence', *Ann. Midi*, LXXXVII, 1975.

F. X. Emmanuelli, 'De la conscience politique à la naissance du "provençalisme" dans la généralité d'Aix à la fin du XVIIIᵉ siécle. Prélude à une recherche', in C. Gras and G. Livet (eds.), *Régions et régionalisme en France du XVIIIᵉ siècle à nos jours*, Vendôme, 1977.

C. Fairchilds, *Poverty and charity in Aix-en-Provence, 1640–1789*, Baltimore, 1976.

M. Fournel, *Les problèmes de ravitaillement et le mouvement des prix au XIXᵉ siècle (d'après les archives hospitalières de Toulon)*, Aix, 1969.

P. Fraysse, *Jean-Joseph Rigouard, évêque constitutionnel du Var, 1735–1800*, Marseille, 1928.

P. Gaffarel, 'Les complots de Marseille et de Toulon (1812–1813)', *Annales de la société d'études provençales*, 1907.

J. Gaignebet, 'Les loisirs du chevalier de Sade, lieutenant de vaisseau du roi à Toulon, 1789', *Bull. T.*, 1933.

J. Gaignebet, 'Les limites historiques de la région toulonnaise: étude de géographie historique et politique', *Bull. T.*, 1935.

G. Guibal, *Mirabeau et la Provence en 1789*, Paris, 1887.

G. Guibal, *Le mouvement fédéraliste en Provence en 1793*, Paris, 1908.

O. Havard, *La Révolution dans les ports de guerre*, 2 vols., Paris, 1913.

D. M. J. Henry, *L'histoire de Toulon de 1789 jusqu'au Consulat*, 2 vols., Toulon, 1861.

L. Honoré, *L'émigration dans le Var, 1789–1825*, Draguignan, 1923.

L. Honoré, 'Les élections des députés du Var à la Chambre des représentants des Cent-Jours, mai 1815', *VHG*, 1925.

M. Kennedy, *The Jacobin club of Marseilles*, Ithaca, 1973.

H. Labroue, *Le club jacobin de Toulon, 1790–1796*, Paris, 1907.

G. Lambert, *Histoire de la peste en 1721*, Toulon, 1861.

G. Lambert, *Histoire de Toulon*, 4 vols., Toulon, 1886–92.

A. Lardier, *Histoire populaire de la Révolution en Provence depuis le Consulat jusqu'en 1834*, Marseille, 1840.

F. Laugier, *Le schisme constitutionnel et la persécution du clergé dans le départment du Var*, Draguignan, 1897.

H. Lauvergne, *Le choléra-morbus en Provence*, Toulon, 1836.

H. Lauvergne, *Histoire de la Révolution dans le département du Var depuis 1789 à 1794*, Toulon, 1839.

L. Levy-Schneider, *L'application du Concordat par un prélat d'ancien régime: Mgr. Champion de Cicé, archévêque d'Aix et d'Arles, 1802–1810*, Paris, 1921.

M. Loir, 'La livraison de Toulon aux Anglais, 1793', *Revue maritime et coloniale*, 1897.

C. Lourde, *Histoire de la Révolution à Marseille et en Provence depuis 1789 jusqu'au Consulat*, Marseille, 1838.

F. Masson, *La révolte de Toulon en prairial an III*, Paris, 1875.

L. Mongin, *Toulon ancien et ses rues*, 2 vols., Draguignan, 1901.

C. Morazzani, 'Truguet, amiral toulonnais', *Bull. T.*, 1929.

A. J. Parès, *L'aurore du journalisme à Toulon*, Toulon, 1918.

A. J. Parès, *A propos de pain: conflit entre l'intendance maritime de Toulon et le parlement de Provence, 1782–84*, Toulon, 1919.

A. J. Parès, 'La situation économique de Toulon la veille de la rébellion de 1793', *Bull. Drag.*, 1924.

A. J. Parès, 'Le tribunal populaire martial de Toulon, juillet–décembre 1793', *Bull. hist.*, XI, 1925.

A. J. Parès, 'Le Royal Louis, régiment français à la solde de l'Angleterre', *Bull. Drag.*, 1927.

A. J. Parès, 'Le directoire du département du Var pendant la rébellion de 1793', *Bull. hist.*, XV, 1929.

A. J. Parès, 'Un toulonnais à Alger au XVIIIe siècle. Meifrund, Pierre-Joseph, 1723–1814', *Bull. hist.*, XVI, 1931.

A. J. Parès, 'Une relation inédite de la fusillade du Champ de Mars à Toulon', *Bull. hist.*, XVII, 1932.

A. J. Parès, 'Les prisonniers du Thémistocle, ou patriotes opprimés', *Bull. Var*, 1937.

A. J. Parès, 'Un singulier personnage, Jean-Baptiste Roux dit Louis XVII', *Bull. Drag.*, 1937.

F. Poncioni, 'Administration et production d'un port militaire sous le Consulat et le 1er Empire, Toulon, 1800–1815', *Prov. hist.*, 39, 1989.

P. Pouhaer, 'Le baron d'Azémar, second préfet du Var', *Bull. Drag.*, 1912–13.

P. Pouhaer, 'Un vieux soldat dans la tourmente: le général Moynat d'Auxon à Toulon, 1796–1797', *Bull. T.*, 1937.

E. Poupé, *Les districts du Var*, Draguignan, 1898.

E. Poupé, 'Le 10ᵉ bataillon du Var, 1793-an V', *Bull. Drag.*, 1904.

E. Poupé, 'Les fédérés varois du 10 août', *La Révolution française*, LVIII, 1910.

E. Poupé, 'Le tribunal révolutionnaire du Var', *Bull. Drag.*, 1922.

E. Poupé, 'La répression de la révolte terroriste de Toulon, fin floréal an III', *VHG*, 1924.

E. Poupé, 'Le département du Var à la veille des Cent-Jours', *VHG*, 1928.

E. Poupé, 'Une enquête ministérielle sur l'esprit public dans le Var en août 1813', *VHG*, 1930.

E. Poupé, *Le département du Var, 1790-an VIII*, Cannes, 1933.

G. Rambert, 'Toulon et l'exportation des vins provençaux par Marseille au XVIIIᵉ siècle', *Prov. hist.*, XII, 1962.

J. H. Rose, *Lord Hood and the defence of Toulon*, Cambridge, 1922.

W. Scott, *Terror and repression in revolutionary Marseilles*, London, 1973.

W. Sewell, *Structure and mobility. The men and women of Marseille, 1820–1870*, Cambridge, 1985.

O. Teissier, *Chroniques toulonnais. Histoire de quelques rues*, Toulon, 1872.

O. Teissier, *Histoire des divers agrandissements et des fortifications de la ville de Toulon*, Toulon, 1873.

O. Teissier, *L'armorial de la ville de Toulon*, Toulon, 1900.

M. Tortel, *Notice historique sur l'église Sainte-Marie de Toulon*, Toulon, 1898.

M. Vergé, 'Les officiers de marine au XVIIIe siècle', *Prov. hist.*, XXIX, 1979.

H. Vienne, *Esquisses historiques. Promenades dans Toulon ancien et moderne*, Toulon, 1841.

J. Viguier, *Les débuts de la Révolution en Provence*, Paris, 1895.

J. Viguier, *La convocation des Etats-généraux en Provence*, Paris, 1896.

C. Vitse, 'La contre-révolution Toulon en 1793: les agents royalistes et le faux problème des subsistances', *Prov. hist.*, XX, 1970.

M. Vovelle, 'Les troubles sociaux en Provence, 1750–1792', *Actes du 93e Con. Nat.*, 1968.

M. Vovelle, *Piété baroque et déchristianisation en Provence au XVIIIe siècle: les attitudes devant la mort d'après les clauses des testaments*, Paris, 1973.

M. Vovelle, 'Représentants en mission et mouvement populaire en Provence sous la Révolution française: du nouveau sur Fréron', *Prov. hist.*, XXIII, 1973.

M. Vovelle, 'Y a-t-il eu une révolution culturelle au XVIIIe siècle? A propos de l'éducation populaire en Provence', *RHMC*, XXII, 1975.

J. C. White, 'Un exemple des réformes humanitaires dans la marine française: l'hôpital maritime de Toulon, 1782–1787', *Ann. Midi*, LXXXIII, 1971.

M. Wyott, 'De l'ordonnateur au préfet maritime, ou l'administration du port de Toulon, 1789–1800', *Prov. hist.*, XXI, 1971.

2. General works

Note: As in the preceding section, I have included only those books and articles which were especially useful in the preparation of this study.

M. Acerra and J. Meyer, *Marines et Révolution*, Rennes, 1988.

J. Aman, *Les officiers bleus dans la marine française du XVIIIe siècle*, Geneva, 1976.

P. W. Bamford, *Forests and French seapower, 1660–1789*, Toronto, 1956.

L. Bergeron, *L'épisode napoléonien. Aspects intérieurs, 1799–1815*, Paris, 1972.

L. Bergeron and G. Chaussinand-Nogaret, *Les 'masses de granit'. Cent mille notables du Premier Empire*, Paris, 1979.

D. Bien, 'The army in the French enlightenment: reform, reaction and revolution', *Past and Present*, 85, 1979.

T. C. W. Blanning, *The origins of the French revolutionary wars*, London, 1986.

F. Bluche, *Le plébiscite des Cent-Jours*, Geneva, 1974.

M. Bordes, *La réforme municipale du contrôleur-général Laverdy et son application, 1764–1771*, Toulouse, 1968.

M. Bordes, *L'administration provinciale et municipale en France au XVIIIe siècle*, Paris, 1972.

J. F. Bosher, 'The French crisis of 1770', *History*, LVII, 1972.

J. F. Bosher (ed.), *French government and society, 1500–1850: essays in memory of Alfred Cobban*, London, 1973.

F. Braudel, *L'identité de la France; espace et histoire*, Paris, 1986.

F. Chevalier, *Histoire de la marine française sous le Consulat et l'Empire*, Paris, 1886.

R. C. Cobb, *Terreur et subsistances*, Paris, 1965.

R. C. Cobb, *The police and the people. French popular protest, 1789–1820*, Oxford, 1970.

J. Coppolani, *Les élections en France à l'époque napoléonienne*, Paris, 1980.

F. de Dainville, 'Grandeur et population des villes au XVIIIe siècle', *Population*, 13, 1958.

W. Doyle, 'Was there an aristocratic reaction in pre-revolutionary France?', *Past and Present*, 57, 1972.

J. Dull, *The French navy and American independence. A study of arms and diplomacy 1774–1787*, Princeton, 1975.

J. Dupâquier, *La population française aux XVIIe et XVIIIe siècles*, Paris, 1979.

A.-M. Duport, 'Le personnel municipal de Nîmes de l'ancien régime à l'Empire: étude sociale et politique', *Bulletin de la Société languedocienne de géographie*, 1982.

M. Edelstein, 'Vers une "sociologie électorale" de la Révolution française: la participation des citadins et campagnards, 1789–1793', *RHMC*, XXII, 1975.

W. Edmonds, ' "Federalism" and urban revolt in France in 1793', *JMH*, 55, 1983.

W. Edmonds, *Jacobinism and the Revolt of Lyon, 1789–1793*, Oxford, 1990.

J. Egret, *La pré-révolution française, 1787–1788*, Paris, 1962.

E. Esmonin, 'L'abbé Expilly et ses travaux de statistique', *RHMC*, VI, 1957.

A. Forrest, *Society and politics in revolutionary Bordeaux*, Oxford, 1975.

A. Forrest, *The French Revolution and the poor*, Oxford, 1981.

F. Furet and D. Richet, *La Révolution française*, Fayard ed., Paris, 1973.

M. Garden, *Lyon et les lyonnais au XVIIIe siècle*, Paris, 1970.

M. Garden, 'L'attraction de Lyon à la fin de l'ancien régime', *Annales de démographie historique*, 1970.

G. Gayot, *La franc-maçonnerie française. Textes et pratiques (XVIIIe–XIXe siècles)*, Paris, 1980.

R. Glover, 'The French fleet, 1807–1814: Britain's problem and Madison's opportunity', *JMH*, 39, 1967.

J. Godechot, *La Contre-révolution. Doctrine et action, 1789–1804*, Paris, 1961.

H. Gough, 'Politics and power: the triumph of Jacobinism in Strasbourg, 1791–1793', *HJ*, 23, 1980.

D. Greer, *The incidence of the Terror during the French Revolution*, Harvard, 1935.

D. Greer, *The incidence of the Emigration during the French Revolution*, Harvard, 1951.

J. M. Haas, 'The introduction of task work into the royal dockyards, 1775', *Journal of British Studies*, VIII, 1969.

R. Halévi, *Les loges maçonniques dans la France d'ancien régime aux origines de la sociabilité démocratique*, Paris, 1984.

N. Hampson, 'The "comité de marine" of the Constituent Assembly', *HJ*, 2, 1959.

N. Hampson, *La marine de l'an II*, Paris, 1959.

N. Hampson, 'Les ouvriers des arsenaux de la marine au cours de la Révolution française, 1789–1794', *RHES*, 39, 1961.

N. Hampson, *A social history of the French Revolution*, London, 1963.

P. R. Hanson, *Provincial politics in the French Revolution, Caen and Limoges, 1789–1794*, Baton Rouge, 1989.

O. Hufton, *Bayeux in the late eighteenth century. A social study*, Oxford, 1967.

O. Hufton, *The poor of eighteenth-century France, 1750–1789*, Oxford, 1974.

L. Hunt, 'Committees and communes: local politics and national revolution in 1789', *Comparative Studies in Society and History*, 18, 1976.

L. Hunt, *Revolution and urban politics in provincial France: Troyes and Reims, 1789–1790*, Stanford, 1978.

L. Hunt, *Politics, class and culture in the French Revolution*, Berkeley, 1984.

M. Hutt, *Chouannerie and counter-revolution. Puisaye, the princes and the British government in the 1790s*, 2 vols., Cambridge, 1983.

M. A. Iafelice, 'Le babouvisme en province. Les abonnés méridionaux au Tribun du Peuple', *Cahiers d'histoire de l'Institut de recherches marxistes*, 1984.

E. H. Jenkins, *A history of the French navy*, London, 1973.

H. C. Johnson, *The Midi in Revolution. A study of regional political diversity, 1789–1793*, Princeton, 1986.

C. Jones, *Charity and bienfaisance. The treatment of the poor in the Montpellier region, 1740–1815*, Cambridge, 1982.

S. Kaplan and C. J. Koepp (eds.), *Work in France: representation, meaning, organisation and practice*, Ithaca, 1986.

J. Kaplow, *Elbeuf during the revolutionary period: history and social structure*, Baltimore, 1964.

J. Kaplow, *The names of kings: the Parisian laboring poor in the eighteenth century*, New York, 1972.

M. B. Katz, 'Occupational classification in history', *Journal of Interdisciplinary History*, 3, 1972–73.

M. Kennedy, *The Jacobin clubs in the French Revolution*, 2 vols., Princeton, 1982–88.

G. Lacour-Gayet, *La marine militaire de la France sous le règne de Louis XVI*, Paris, 1905.

G. Lacour-Gayet, *La marine militaire de la France sous le règne de Louis XV*, 2nd. ed, Paris, 1910.

G. Lacour-Gayet, *La marine militaire de la France sous le règne de Louis XIII et de Louis XIV*, Paris, 1911.

A. Lajusan, 'Le plébiscite de l'an III', *La Révolution française*, LX, 1911.

C. Langlois, 'Le plébiscite de l'an VIII, ou le coup d'état du 18 pluviôse an VIII', *AHRF*, 207–9, 1972.

A. Le Bihan, *Loges et chapitres de la Grande Loge et du Grand Orient de la France (deuxième moitié du XVIIIe siècle)*, Paris, 1967.

F. Lebrun and R. Dupuy (eds.), *Les résistances à la Révolution*, Paris, 1987.

M. Leclère, 'Les réformes de Castries, 14 octobre 1780–23 août 1787', *Revue des questions historiques*, 128, 1937.

G. Lefebvre, 'Urban society in the Orléanais in the late eighteenth century', *Past and Present*, 19, 1961.

T. J. A. Le Goff, *Vannes and its region: a study of town and country in eighteenth-century France*, Oxford, 1981.

T. J. A. Le Goff and J. Meyer, 'Les constructions navales en France pendant la seconde moitié du XVIIIe siècle', *Annales ESC*, 26, 1971.

G. Lemarchand, 'Noblesse, élite et notabilité en France: aspects sociaux et politiques', *Etudes sur le XVIIIe siècle*, VII, 1981.

L. Levy-Schneider, *Le conventionnel Jeanbon Saint-André*, 2 vols., Paris, 1901.

G. Lewis and C. Lucas (eds.), *Beyond the Terror. Essays in French regional and social history*, Cambridge, 1983.

D. Ligou, 'A propos de la révolution municipale', *RHES*, 38, 1960.

D. Ligou (ed.), *Histoire des francs-maçons en France*, Toulouse, 1981.

M. Loir, *La marine royale en 1789*, Paris, 1892.

C. Lucas, 'The problem of the Midi in the French Revolution'. *Transactions of the Royal Historical Society*, 28, 1978.

C. Lucas, 'Résistances populaires à la Révolution dans le sud-est', in J. Nicolas (ed.), *Mouvements populaires et conscience sociale*, Paris, 1985.

M. Lyons, *France under the Directory*, Cambridge, 1975.

M. Lyons, *Revolution in Toulouse: an essay on provincial terrorism*, Berne, 1978.

P. Mackesy, *The war in the Mediterranean, 1803–1810*, London, 1957.

J. McManners, *French ecclesiastical society under the* ancien régime: *a study of Angers in the eighteenth century*, Manchester, 1960.

J. McManners, *The French Revolution and the Church*, London, 1969.

A. T. Mahan, *The influence of seapower upon the French Revolution and Empire, 1793–1812*, 2 vols., London, 1892.

J. Meyer and J. Bromley, 'The Second Hundred Years' War (1689–1816)', in D. Johnson, F. Bédarida and F. Crouzet (eds.), *Britain and France. Ten centuries*, Folkestone, 1980.

J. Michelet, *La sorcière*, ed. L. Refort, 2 vols., Paris, 1952–56.

R. Mousnier (ed.), *Problèmes de stratification sociale*, Paris, 1968.

J. Murphy and P. Higonnet, 'Les députés de la noblesse aux Etats-généraux de 1789', _RHMC_, XX, 1973.

R. R. Palmer, _The improvement of humanity: education and the French Revolution_, Princeton, 1985.

J. C. Perrot, 'Conflits administratifs et conflits sociaux au XVIIIe siècle', _Annales de Normandie_, XIII, 1963.

J. C. Perrot, 'Rapports sociaux et villes au XVIIIe siècle', _Annales ESC_, 23, 1968.

J. C. Perrot, _Genèse d'une ville moderne: Caen au XVIIIe siècle_, 2 vols., Paris, 1975.

E. Préclin, _Les jansénistes du XVIIIe siècle et la constitution civile du clergé_, Paris, 1928.

R. Price, _The economic modernisation of France, 1730–1880_, London, 2nd. ed., 1981.

J. Pritchard, _Louis XV's navy, 1784–1762: a study of organisation and administration_, Montreal, 1987.

M. Reinhard (ed.), 'Contributions à l'histoire démographique de la Révolution française', _CHESRF_, Mémoires et documents, 18, 1965.

N. Richardson, _The French prefectoral corps, 1814–1830_, Cambridge, 1966.

J. Rives, 'L'évolution démographique de Toulouse au XVIIIe siècle', _CHESRF Bulletin_, 1968–69.

R. Robin, _La société française en 1789: Semur-en-Auxois_, Paris, 1970.

D. Roche (ed.), _L'histoire sociale. Sources et méthodes_, Paris, 1967.

D. Roche, 'Urban history in France: achievements, tendencies and objectives', _Urban History Yearbook_, 1980.

D. Roche and M. Vovelle, 'Bourgeois, rentiers et propriétaires: éléments pour la définition d'une catégorie sociale à la fin du XVIIIe siècle', _Actes du 84e Con. Nat._, 1959.

R. B. Rose, _Gracchus Babeuf. The first revolutionary communist_, London, 1978.

R. B. Rose, _The making of the sans-culottes. Democratic ideas and institutions in Paris, 1789–1792_, Manchester, 1983.

G. Rudé, _The crowd in the French Revolution_, Oxford, 1959.

S. F. Scott, 'Problems of law and order during 1790, the "peaceful" year of the French Revolution', _AHR_, 80, 1975.

S. F. Scott, _The response of the Royal Army to the French Revolution: the role and development of the line army, 1789–1793_,

Oxford, 1978.

J. Sentou, *Fortunes et groupes sociaux à Toulouse sous la Révolution, 1789–1799. Essai d'histoire statistique*, Toulouse, 1969.

W. Sewell, *Work and revolution in France. The language of labour from the old regime to 1848*, Cambridge, 1980.

A. Soboul, 'Problémes théoriques de l'histoire de la Révolution française', *La Nouvelle Critique*, 1971.

A. Soboul, *La France à la veille de la Révolution: économie et société*, 2nd ed., Paris, 1974.

M. Sonenscher, *Work and wages. Natural law, politics and the eighteenth-century French trades*, Cambridge, 1989.

D. Sutherland, *France 1789–1815. Revolution and counter-revolution*, London, 1985.

M. J. Sydenham, 'The republican revolt of 1793: a plea for less localised local studies', *FHS*, XII, 1981.

T. Tackett, *Religion, revolution and regional culture in eighteenth-century France. The ecclesiastical oath of 1791*, Princeton, 1986.

M. Taillefer, 'La franc-maçonnerie toulousaine et la Révolution française', *AHRF*, 239, 1980.

G. V. Taylor, 'Non-capitalist wealth and the origins of the French Revolution', *AHR*, 72, 1967.

G. V. Taylor, 'Revolutionary and non-revolutionary content in the cahiers of 1789; an interim report', *FHS*, VII, 1972.

N. Temple, 'The control and exploitation of French towns during the ancien régime', *History*, LI, 1966.

O. Troude, *Batailles navales de la France*, 4 vols., Paris, 1867–68.

J. Tulard, *Napoléon, le mythe du sauveur*, Paris, 1981.

M. Vergé, *La Royale au temps de l'amiral d'Estaing*, Paris, 1977.

J. Vidalenc, 'La vie économique des départements méditerranéens pendant l'Empire', *RHMC*, III, 1954.

H. Wallon, *La Révolution du 31 mai et le fédéralisme en 1793*, 2 vols., Paris, 1886.

I. Woloch, *Jacobin legacy. The democratic movement under the Directory*, Princeton, 1970.

Index